Rationality, Psychology and Capitalism

NEW THINKING IN POLITICAL ECONOMY

**Series Editor:** Peter J. Boettke, *George Mason University, USA*

New Thinking in Political Economy aims to encourage scholarship in the intersection of the disciplines of politics, philosophy and economics. It has the ambitious purpose of reinvigorating political economy as a progressive force for understanding social and economic change.

The series is an important forum for the publication of new work analysing the social world from a multidisciplinary perspective. With increased specialization (and professionalization) within universities, interdisciplinary work has become increasingly uncommon. Indeed, during the 20th century, the process of disciplinary specialization reduced the intersection between economics, philosophy and politics and impoverished our understanding of society. Modern economics in particular has become increasingly mathematical and largely ignores the role of institutions and the contribution of moral philosophy and politics.

New Thinking in Political Economy will stimulate new work that combines technical knowledge provided by the 'dismal science' and the wisdom gleaned from the serious study of the 'worldly philosophy'. The series will reinvigorate our understanding of the social world by encouraging a multidisciplinary approach to the challenges confronting society in the new century.

For a full list of Edward Elgar published titles, including the titles in this series, visit our website at www.e-elgar.com.

# Rationality, Psychology and Capitalism

## Defending Economic Theory From Behavioral Imperialism

Arkadiusz Sieroń

*Institute of Economic Sciences, University of Wroclaw, Poland*

NEW THINKING IN POLITICAL ECONOMY

Edward Elgar
PUBLISHING

Cheltenham, UK • Northampton, MA, USA

Published by

Edward Elgar Publishing Limited
The Lypiatts
15 Lansdown Road
Cheltenham
Glos GL50 2JA
UK

Edward Elgar Publishing, Inc.
William Pratt House
9 Dewey Court
Northampton
Massachusetts 01060
USA

Authorised representative in the EU for GPSR queries only: Easy Access System Europe – Mustamäe tee 50, 10621 Tallinn, Estonia, gpsr.requests@easproject.com

A catalogue record for this book is available from the British Library

Library of Congress Control Number: 2026931844

This book is available electronically in the **Elgar**online
Economics subject collection
https://doi.org/10.4337/9781035394012

MIX
Paper | Supporting responsible forestry
FSC® C013604

ISBN 978 1 0353 9400 5 (cased)
ISBN 978 1 0353 9401 2 (eBook)
ISBN 978 1 0353 9402 9 (ePub)

Printed and bound by CPI Group (UK) Ltd, Croydon, CR0 4YY

*To Dad and Mom:*

*The real and the inner ones.*

# Contents

# Acknowledgements

My previous two economic monographs were about inflation and interest rates. This is my first methodological book. Perhaps that is why its publication took longer than I expected. I am all the more grateful to everyone who helped me bring this book to fruition: Philipp Bagus, Walter Block, Peter Boettke, Mateusz Machaj, Alicja Sielska.

My thanks go also to anonymous reviewers and to the entire fantastic editorial team at Edward Elgar.

Last but not least, I would like to thank Ola – for her support and understanding when, during our vacation in Greece, instead of spending time together on the beach, I was writing footnotes (I hate sunbathing anyway).

# Introduction to *Rationality, Psychology and Capitalism*

*Homo economicus* is dead. Economics needs to develop more realistic psychological underpinnings and to become more mindful. This is at least what behavioral economists have declared after the successful emergence of its subdiscipline (e.g., Thaler 2000, 2015, 2016; Camerer 2008). But are they right?

The present volume aims to answer this question. It argues that such reports of *Homo economicus*' death have been greatly exaggerated, as they stem from misunderstanding the nature and purpose of the concept. It is not a psychologically descriptive model of human behavior, but a key methodological device, a foundational principle of economics, which enables us to conduct scientific inquiry about economic phenomena. Indeed, the rationality principle explains the success of economics as a science, because without it economists would not, for example, be able to maintain that individuals react to incentives or, more generally, to understand people with (unobservable) values and beliefs different from their own. Adopting the rationality principle enables economists to preserve the principle of subjectivity of value while fulfilling the requirement of scientific objectivity.

Hence, the book adds to the literature about *Homo economicus*, rationality in economics, and the role of psychology in economics. The problem with the debate about rationality in economics is that its participants conflate different notions of rationality. In particular, behavioral economists[1] oppose the concept of rationality (e.g., Jolls, Sunstein, and Thaler 1998; Mullainathan and Thaler 2000; Rabin 2002; Camerer and Loewenstein 2004; Ariely 2009; Thaler 2000, 2015, 2016), but they refer to rationality as a description of the behavior of individual agents, even though economists generally do not use rationality in this way. They refer either to empirical rationality, dealing with the aggregate effects of individuals' actions within the markets, which most economists focus on in their empirical research and predictions, or to methodological

[1] Behavioral economics have different strands (e.g., Ross 2014, ch. 4). When writing about behavioral economics in this book, I will refer primarily to the "heuristics and biases" program, adopted by such researchers as Kahneman, Tversky, or Thaler (e.g., Kahneman and Tversky 2000).

rationality, which provides an indispensable framework for economics as an scientific inquiry. Thus, this monograph defends the value of traditional economic framework against psychological reductionism.

Another key message of my work is that economics should not be more grounded in psychology, as some researchers seem to believe (e.g., Jolls, Sunstein, and Thaler 1998; Mullainathan and Thaler 2000; Rabin 2002; Camerer and Loewenstein 2004; Ariely 2009; Thaler 2000, 2015, 2016). Psychology is an important field of scientific inquiry, but it is just one science among others, not the basis of all social sciences. The fact that the subject of economics seems to be similar to that of psychology does not mean that economics should adopt a similar research methodology. Economics is not empty without psychology and it is not a mere generalization of psychological tendencies in the context of economizing of scarce resources. Hence, economists should not suppose that, without understanding human nature and psychological motives behind actions, they would not be able to conduct proper research in economics.

In fact, using some of the psychological theories of the business cycle as an example, this book demonstrates that psychological explanations of economic phenomena suffer from several important problems.

The book also shows that psychological factors can be used not only to argue against the free market (because people allegedly suffer from biases which deviate them from full rationality), but also to assert that the anti-market sentiment held by people may be the result of envy and (illusory) perception of control related to the strong role of the government in the economy, or of a tribal bias – i.e., the fact that people could be evolutionary adapted to function in small groups rather than in today's global economy (Hayek 1973, 1988).

Last but not least, the book also engages in the debate about the impact of capitalism on mental health and explores whether societies should take happiness into account when assessing economies. It argues that the fact that some negative psychological and social problems exist in modern capitalist economies does not mean that they are caused by capitalism or are inherent to this economic system. They can result from living within civilizations, hierarchical societies, and/or specific cultures that may not adequately respond to the challenges of human existence. When one analyzes complex systems, such as modern market-based societies, the monocausal explanations are rarely true. It is, of course, important that people can pursue happiness and feel it. However, happiness would be a very problematic social goal. This is because it is not clear what is it, how to achieve it, and how to measure it, if it can be defined, achieved, and measured at all. The aim of the economic system, if it has any aim, is to organize how people produce, exchange, and consume. Capitalism, or the free-market economy, is the impersonal self-ordering process that does not strive for any particular objective, such as happiness or the highest possible pace of GDP growth. It just allows people to reach their own economic goals. And economic growth is the result – the positive externality – of the activities of households and companies in free markets. If anything, this is probably the only thing one should expect from the economic system – the improvement of objective living standards. Even if people are not happier once their living standards have improved, their opportunities are greater (Hayek 1973; Mises 1998 [1949]).

Thus, this publication could be seen as a thorough defense of economics and market-based economies against behavioral imperialism and psychologism – i.e., the idea that psychology should play a greater role either in economic theory or in evaluating economic systems.[2] It is partially a response to the growth in popularity of behavioral economics and resulting misconceptions that this sub-discipline has disproved the orthodox economics and the *Homo economicus* model. From this perspective, the book is a continuation of my article pointing out the problems with behavioral economics (Sieroń 2020).

I am not the first to write about the methodology of economics in the context of 'rationality wars' (Sturm 2012; Rich 2016) and complaints that economics is based on erroneous psychology or is not psychological enough. For example, Brennan (2007), Kirchgässner (2013), and Li (2020) are excellent articles about the rationality principle, while Hudík (2011) brilliantly contrasts psychology, which studies conscious human behavior, with economics, which examines undesigned results of social cooperation.

However, my work overall is not merely an article that focuses on a small part of the debate, but a more comprehensive study of the issues at the intersection of economics and psychology. In this book, I try to thoroughly analyze the different concepts of rationality in economics, and the relationships between psychology and economics, including the question as to whether economics should be more psychological, or whether economic systems should be assessed in terms of their impact on happiness or psychological well-being.

Having said that, the present volume is not a treatise that covers all the important issues related to rationality in economics. In particular, this is not a book about the concept of *Homo economicus*, its history, and problems related to its axiomatic and mathematical form. There are already excellent publications on this topic (e.g., Huerta de Soto 1998; Giocoli 2003). Nor is this book a comprehensive critique of behavioral economics (or even of the heuristics-and-biases research program or the libertarian paternalism). This is because I have already discussed some problems of behavioral economics (Sieroń 2020), and other scholars have done so in a better and more comprehensive way (e.g., Lopes 1991; Gul and Pesendorfer 2008; McKenzie 2010; Saint-Paul

---

[2] On behavioral imperialism, see also the conclusions of Chapter 2.

2011; Levine 2012; White 2013; Abdukadirov 2016; Gigerenzer 2018; Rizzo and Whitman 2020).

Behavioral economics has many strands. I had thought that, to provide an exhaustive assessment of it, I might have to write about each of the main effects or cognitive biases studied by behavioral economics, and such a book would have to be much longer. I decided that I would rather write a more general piece about the rationality and relationship between economics and psychology.

My work is primarily methodological in nature. The book should inspire readers interested in the methodology of economics, rationality in economics, *Homo economicus*, anti-market sentiment, the relationship between psychology and economics, and the discussion of the impact of capitalism on the people's subjective well-being.

The book begins with a chapter on rationality in economics. Whether people behave rationally is one of the most intriguing subjects of controversy in the social sciences in general and economics in particular (Vanberg 2004; Smith 2008; Zouboulakis 2014). The aim of the first chapter is, thus, to contribute to this long-standing debate through detailed examination of different notions of rationality. I distinguish four types of rationality and argue that only two of them (methodological and empirical) are crucial for economics, while individual and metaphysical rationality belong to the realm of psychology and philosophy, respectively. I also claim that disagreement among researchers on rationality in economics stems from focusing on different kinds of rationality. In particular, behavioral economists question the rationality assumption in economics, but they conflate rationality as a description of individual behavior with rationality as a methodological device.

The second chapter deals with the question as to whether economics abstracts too much from psychology, and whether psychology should play a more important role in economics. The claims that economics should be more grounded in (proper) psychology are not new (Lewin 1996; Bondo and Presskorn-Thygesen 2022), but they came back in full force with the development of behavioral economics (e.g., Jolls, Sunstein, and Thaler 1998; Mullainathan and Thaler 2000; Rabin 2002; Camerer and Loewenstein 2004; Ariely 2009; Thaler 2000, 2015, 2016). I argue in this chapter that, although both seem to study human behavior, economics and psychology are distinct domains of social science with different research questions and perspectives, and that they should remain separate fields and respect each other's methodology. While psychology investigate the content of people's actions, economics studies only the formal implications of the fact that people act. Thanks to its formal nature, economics can formulate general theories – i.e., it is more about general equilibrium than situational factors that are interesting for psychology. As economics abstracts from psychological factors, it can explain human actions regardless of the people's motivation. Thus, by making economics more psychological, one would reduce the generality of its theories. Economics is also more interested in studying the (undesigned) effects of human actions rather than their motives, and on aggregate outcomes rather than individual behavior. Hence, economics should not become more psychological, as this would deprive it of its unique character, and could weaken its explanatory power. However, that does not mean psychology has nothing to offer to economics – in this chapter, I point out a few legitimate areas where psychology could enrich economics.

While the second chapter is rather general in its scope, the third chapter is more specific and examines in detail a particular application of psychology in economics, namely the psychological theories of business cycle (e.g., Shiller 2015; Akerlof and Shiller 2009). I point out a number of problems faced by such theories. In particular, I argue that they violate the proper methodology of economics; ignore important economic factors; appeal to psychological phenomena but do not adequately explain their genesis, their course, and why they should result in business cycles; assume a causal relationship from mental states to objective market reality, introducing changes in mental states as *diabolus ex machina*; do not adequately explain all features of business cycles; ignore the concept of the invisible hand and systemic (ecological) rationality; constitute ex post narratives about particular business cycles rather than general theories that allow for predictions; assume a dubious view of human nature. These issues seriously undermine the validity of the psychological theories of business cycle. Hence, based on a specific example of the use of psychology in economics, this chapter shows serious difficulties in making economics more psychological, strengthening the argument of the second chapter.

The fourth chapter analyzes claims that capitalism negatively affects the psychological well-being of people (e.g., Prins et al. 2015; Sell and Williams 2019; Eisenberg-Guyot and Prins 2022) and that GDP should be replaced or supplemented by some happiness index (Scitovsky 1976; Oswald 1997; Diener 2000; Jansen et al. 2004; Easterlin 2005; Layard 2005; Lee and Goh 2023; Agrawal et al. 2025). I argue that attempts to link some mental health outcomes to capitalism seems to be a gross over-simplification that does not take into account several crucial causal elements. The idea that happiness is an important factor for people is hardly controversial. However, I demonstrate that making happiness a social goal or a criterion for evaluating the economic system does not stand up to scrutiny.

The fifth and penultimate chapter is about the psychology of anti-market sentiment. It argues that the negative attitude towards the market-based economy held by many people, despite the enormous benefits of this economic system, can stem from three psychological factors. First, people can have tribal instincts (e.g., solidarity, in-group altruism, inter-group aggressiveness) that have enabled their small groups to function and survive in the past, but they have come to apply them inappropriately to the extended order of cooperation through markets (Hayek 1973, 1988). Second, according to many people, one of the biggest problems of market-based economies is (excessive) income and wealth inequality. But should not poverty be a more important social issue? It seems that egalitarianism can be motivated by envy (Hayek 1960; Nozick 1974; Schoeck 1987; Buchanan and Hartley 2000). Third, the idea of spontaneous order is not only intellectually but also emotionally challenging – it requires faith in impersonal market forces, while people could be evolutionarily adapted to live in hierarchical groups in which someone is 'in charge' (Hayek 1973, 1988). Thus, having the government in charge can offer a (false) sense of security and control. This chapter is the most speculative, but it shows that the concept of biases can be used not only to argue against the free market and for government interventions (since people allegedly suffer from biases, which lead them away from full rationality), but also to argue that anti-market sentiment can be a form of a bias itself.

The book concludes, in Chapter 6, by summarizing my analysis, offering theoretical and policy implications, and suggesting directions for further research on the intersection of psychology and economics.

# 1. Four concepts of rationality in economics

## 1. INTRODUCTION

The debate about rationality is among the most fascinating controversies in the social sciences, economics included (Vanberg 2004; Smith 2008; Zouboulakis 2014). The dispute has been so heated that it has even been labeled the *rationality wars* (Sturm 2012; Rich 2016). The issue is also one of the most confusing in economic discourse, as it raises many challenging questions, such as the following: What does it mean to be rational? Are people rational? Should economists assume that economic agents behave rationally, even if it turns out that they do not always act in such a way? What is the status of the rationality assumption? Is the *Homo economicus* postulate valid? And if it is, in what sense? Who is right about rationality: neoclassical or behavioral economists? Or maybe the Austrians?

As is often the case in the social sciences, confusion stems partly from the fact that the concept of rationality is understood and applied variously by different researchers. The aim of this chapter is to clarify the debate about rationality through appropriately classifying distinct notions of rationality.

I am not the first who has wanted to cut this Gordian knot. Agassi and Jarvie (1980, 127), for example, list a few levels of rationality: "[It] is either goal-directed conduct in light of given views, or the choice of views in light of a given standard of rationality, or the choice of views in light of the best available standard, or the choice of the best standard of choice among the available standards, or the interplay of all these and more factors in the style of the workshop."

Montesano (1993) notices two principal meanings of rationality in economics: there is a preference system and preferences are rational. According to the former notion, "an action is rational if it results from a choice which is determined in accordance with a criterion, i.e. a preference system" (p. 65), while according to the latter notion, "not only does there exist a preference system, but preferences are also required to satisfy some conditions of regularity" (p. 66). In a somewhat similar vein, Vanberg (2004) distinguishes between rationality principle, which asserts that "human action is rational, *given the purposes (or preferences) and beliefs (or theories) of the actor at the time of action*" (p. 2, emphasis in original), and rationality hypothesis, which asserts "*more* than just local subjective consistency of actions, preferences and beliefs" (pp. 2–3, emphasis in original).

Spohn (2002, 258) distinguishes between a normative theory of rationality and an empirical theory of rationality. The former answers the question, "What is the best thing to do?" while the latter is used for "the prediction and explanation of human behavior."

Smith (2003, 2008) sets up a dichotomy of constructivist and ecological concepts of rationality orders. The constructivist concept of rational order "applies reason to the design of rules for individual action, to the design of institutions that yield socially optimal outcomes, and constitutes the standard socioeconomic science model" (Smith 2003, 499), while the ecological concept is "an emergent order based on trial-and-error cultural and biological evolutionary processes" (Smith 2003, 500). Similarly, Rich (2016) and Gigerenzer (2021) differentiate between axiomatic rationality and ecological rationality. As Rich (2016, 90, emphasis in original) explains, "The *axiomatic approach* evaluates the coherence of behavior according to axiomatic criteria, while *ecological rationality* evaluates processes according to their expected performance."[1]

McKenzie (2010) describes three levels of meaning of rationality: purposefulness, a predisposition to reasoning, and maximizing behavior. The latter is the narrowest, as it is not just about people with purposes or who seek thoughtful discussions; it is also "a set of precisely cast presumptions, or premises, about human motivation, decision making, and behavior from which all logical steps in argument and the resulting deductions flow" (p. 3), that delineates the methodology of mainstream economics.

Rizzo and Whitman (2020, loc. 812–884) write that "rationality" has many meanings. It can mean: purposefulness; abstract approach to solving problems, applying universal systems of thought and inference, and following scientific methods; avoiding errors of logic and reasoning; revising one's beliefs in accordance with Bayes' Rule; having preferences that conform to certain axioms which guarantee the preferences are internally consistent and have a certain structure. They notice that in neoclassical economic theory, rationality

---

[1] Compare Gigerenzer (2021, 3547): "Axiomatic rationality is defined in terms of conformity to abstract axioms. . . . Ecological rationality can be seen as a formalization of means–end instrumentalist rationality." Dekker and Remic (2019) argue that the notions of "ecological rationality" used by Gigerenzer and Smith are distinct: the first refers to the use of cognitive strategies in real-world decisions, while the second refers to the rationality of cognitive systems consisting of multiple individuals, institutions, and social norms.

meant all of the above (loc. 812–816). Thus, they call it neoclassical rationality, or puppet rationality, as it "describes agents who always conform to a specified model of behavior" (loc. 821). They contrast it with ecological rationality, i.e., "successfully adapting to some task environment – that is, acting on the basis of beliefs, habits, and heuristics that function well in a specific environment to attain the agent's goal" (loc. 821). Rizzo and Whitman (2020) also propose their own type of rationality, termed "inclusive rationality," which means "purposeful behavior based on subjective preferences and beliefs, in the presence of both environmental and cognitive constraints" (loc. 828).

My classification is a bit different, although I acknowledge the value of the above contributions, with which mine partially overlaps. I would, however, suggest that my categorization is more exhaustive. I list below four general meanings of the word "rationality," distinguished by the aspects of reality to which they refer. These notions are, unfortunately, conflated by economists (isn't that irrational?).

First, there is individual rationality, in which rationality is treated as a normative or descriptive model of individual decision-making. In this sense, rationality is generally equated with logicality. Evans, Over, and Manktelow (1993) call it "rationality of process." The *Homo economicus* (hereafter "HE") model is occasionally applied in this sense, and when it is, it – rightly – draws behavioral economists' criticism. However, they are mostly criticizing a straw man, as the HE model was constructed as an analytical tool, not as a realistic model of human mental processes.

Second, rationality can be understood as a methodological tool, a core scientific principle that enables economic inquiry, as people's behavior would be inexplicable without it. I call this "methodological rationality" or refer to the "rationality principle" (Popper 1985). Most orthodox economists use the HE model in this sense. The Austrian school's praxeological approach, which equates rationality with purposefulness, also generally understands rationality in this sense (although there are certain differences). For Austrians, rationality is purely formal, and they adopt the concept of a formal means–ends structure to analyze human action.

Third, rationality can be understood in a metaphysical way in which all human actions (i.e., purposeful behavior) are rational, in contrast to "a reactive response to stimuli on the part of the bodily organs and of instincts, which cannot be controlled by volition" (Mises 1998 [1949], 20). Thus, people behave rationally because they use reason and are not unconditionally driven by impulses, so they stand above other living creatures.

Fourth, rationality can be treated as an assumption about an empirical tendency – namely, that people tend to choose the suitable means to achieve their goals. Although rationality of process also concerns the real world, this approach is more interested in an aggregate outcome, or systemic (ecological) rationality, than in individual rationality. The focus on the aggregate effect of the behavior of many people enables economists to avoid making assumptions about how individuals behave or to assume that they act *as if* they were rational in the first sense.

Sections 2–5 below analyze these meanings in detail. Section 6 concludes.

## 2. INDIVIDUAL RATIONALITY

Individual rationality is probably the notion that comes to mind first when people think about rationality, as it refers directly to the question as to whether individuals should and do behave rationally. In this sense, rationality is a normative and descriptive model of human behavior. Behavioral economists (and other critics of neoclassical economics) argue that the latter model is false, as human decision-making deviates from rationality due to heuristics, biases, and emotional influences. Often it leads them to the conclusion that people have bounded rationality or even behave irrationally (Jolls, Sunstein, and Thaler 1998; Mullainathan and Thaler 2000; Rabin 2002; Ariely 2009; Thaler 2000, 2015, 2016). Thus, the aim of behavioral economists is to increase "the explanatory power of economics by providing it with more realistic psychological foundations" (Camerer and Loewenstein 2004, 3). Alternatively, as Thaler (2016, 1578), puts it, "Behavioral economics simply replaces Econs [*Homo economicus* – AS] with Homo sapiens, otherwise known as Humans." However, behavioral economists seem to conflate rationality referring to human behavior in the real world, and rationality as the methodological tool used by economists in their scientific inquiry.

### 2.1 Rationality as Logicality

As the norms of rational behavior are usually logical axioms, individual rationality is often equated with logicality. In this approach, economic agents are rational if they think in accordance with formal logic and probability calculus. This concept, which can also be called "rationality as consistency" (Walsh 1996), thus pertains to people's decisions rather than their actions. Decisions are, of course, needed to take actions, but rationality as logicality refers to people's cognitive competence or their mental processes rather than the effectiveness of actions as means in relation to ends.

There are three problems with this approach. The first is that rationality as logicality is often equated with the HE model. But the HE model was created as and is still used as a rationality principle rather than as a model – either descriptive or normative – of human behavior.

The second controversial issue is that the "heuristics and biases" program of behavioral economics rejects the rationality-as-logicality concept as a descriptive model but still adopts it as a normative benchmark.[2] This gives rise to two further difficulties.

First, as Pesendorfer (2006, 717) asks, "[W]hy would humans go to the trouble of maximizing objective functions, formulating complicated beliefs only to get things systematically wrong?" And he continues,

> The assumption that humans have wrong, even systematically biased, beliefs seems plausible and strikes a cord with most readers. At the same time, it seems highly implausible that individuals would go to the trouble of solving a dynamic optimization problem when solving this problem has no clear benefit. In a standard model, maximizing a utility function is simply a concise representation of how the agent behaves. But once the model is interpreted as a mental process, we must imagine that the decision maker actually performs the optimization. Since the decision maker is systematically wrong about future behavior there is no obvious benefit from maximizing the objective function as opposed to taking some other (perhaps arbitrary) action. The metaphor of an operator of a broken machine comes to mind. Think of a car owner who operates a car with a defective steering and yet behaves as if the steering were in perfect working condition. He spends great effort learning how to drive on a perfectly working car only to crash his defective vehicle at every opportunity (Pesendorfer 2006, 717–8).

In other words, behavioral economists assume that people suffer from biases, but they still try to behave according to the HE model, despite these biases, which prevent optimization from being achieved. Hence, people do make mistakes, but cannot do anything with them; they cannot learn and improve their performance. They have broken machines and cannot fix them.

The second issue is that "real-life reasoning is not, in general, well modelled by laboratory reasoning tasks" (Evans et al. 1993, 170), as the relevant data (like probabilities) are not known or computations are too demanding in real-life economic problems.

Thus, the deviations from the benchmark do not necessarily mean that people are irrational. Rather, they undermine the concept of rationality of

---

[2] Interestingly, Davis (2018, 4) argues that behavioral economists "do not seem to have a clear understanding of what the positive-normative distinction (or the descriptive-normative distinction) involves," and that "it is rather behavioral economics that is normative, not standard rational choice theory as behavioral economists claim" (Davis 2018, 8). This is because behavioral economists, in order to make their nudging recommendations that are believed to be a Pareto improvement, "engage in counterfactual reasoning about choice behavior by describing it in terms of the choices that people *would* make *were* choice architects able to change their circumstances of choice" (Davis 2018, 8, emphases in original). However, Davis (2018, 9) claims that both behavioral economics and standard rational choice theory "are value-laden because they both advance explanations of behavior that depend on valuing freedom of choice."

logicality as the universal normative standard of human action, as it applies only to a narrow class of closed-ended problems, which are categorically different from the open-ended problems that are dominant in real life.[3] In a world of genuine uncertainty and scarcity of cognitive and willpower resources, following rules or heuristics can often be the best way to achieve goals (Rizzo and Whitman 2020, loc. 905–1002). Without them, "no one could get through the day under the burden of the self-conscious monitoring and planning of every trivial action in detail" (Smith 2008, 32), and our ability to make abstraction – which is possible only because of suppressing details – would be seriously impaired. Surely, relying on heuristics can lead to errors from time to time, particularly when making decisions about abstract choices, but it seems to be a small price for automating most of our activities – especially as it generally works correctly, at least in routine situations (Sieroń 2020). McKenzie (2010) argues that, from the perspective of neurobiology, and given the economizing problem of the brain, perfect rationality would be irrational. Thus, "the brain is likely to seek a rational level of rationality, as well as a rational level of irrationalities[. T]he brain can operate more rationality by accepting decision-making processes that lead to some irrationalities" (McKenzie 2010, xvi).

Given that ought implies can – what people ought to do must be something they can do (Hands 2014) – and given that the standard of human behavior should be realistic, rationality should not be equated with logicality. Please note that in real life, people have to rely on induction, which is prone to error. Thus, Lopes (1982, 626) rightly asks, "[F]or if induction cannot be justified rationally, then what criteria can be used to judge whether it is being done rationally?"

In other words, the fact that in some experiments people violate the axioms of normative decision theory, does not necessarily prove that people are not as rational as the axioms assume. It is possible that people *rationally* take into account factors that are ignored by the axioms or that are omitted in the laboratory setting. As Gul and Pesendorfer (2008, 23) point out, "many situations in which agents systematically make mistakes can be interpreted as situations where agents face subjective constraints on the feasible strategies that are not apparent from the description of the decision problem."

The issue with experiments is that the standards of rationality are abstract and formal, while "the material of an experimental investigation is necessarily concrete and framed in ordinary rather than formal discourse" (Kyburg 1983, 232). Pinker (2021) notices that, in a certain sense, logic is not rational. Due

---

[3] As Simon (1978, 12) notes, "A theory of rationality that does not give an account of problem solving in the face of complexity is sadly incomplete. It is worse than incomplete; it can be seriously misleading by providing 'solutions' to economic questions that are without operational significance."

to its formal character, it abstracts from the content – i.e., from everything except the set of symbols. However, in daily life, ignoring the content and what one knows about the world is not reasonable. Thus, as Smith (2005, 149, emphasis in original) puts it, "[M]y point is simple: when experimental results are contrary to standard concepts of rationality, assume not just that people are irrational, but that you may not have the right model of rational behavior. *Listen to what your subjects may be trying to tell you.*" Similarly, Lopes (1983, 141) notes in her discussion of the Ellsberg paradox,

> people who violate the axiom may simply and with good cause be trying to consider facts about the world that the axiom ignores. Whether they are correct in doing so is not for logic to decide but must depend on empirical effectiveness, a matter on which both normative decision theory and psychological decision theory tend to be silent.[4]

The third problem is that the argument that people are not rational because they deviate from the cognitive-competence benchmark rests on the assumption that this benchmark is the only legitimate way for people to reason. In reality, reasoning consistent with formal logic is only one of several possible definitions of rationality.[5] As Pareto (2014 [1906], 20) remarks,

---

4 Also, the behavioral experiments revealed the sensitivity of judgment to seemingly minor changes in the presentation of questions. However, subjects may not perceive the tasks as identical since content can hide structure or differing framings could make their meaning quite different, in the same way that the context of a passage affects the meaning of individual words and phrases, which reasonably leads to altered interpretations (Einhorn and Hogart 1981).

5 What is more, there is no one universally accepted concept of probability. Thus, although it would be difficult to dispute that elementary algebra or elementary propositional calculus is a useful basis of thinking in most cases, the focus on the Pascalian concept of probability in behavioral research is questionable (Cohen 1979). According to Cohen (1979, 385), "the Pascalian theory of probability is admittedly the only explicit and systematic theory of probability that currently forms part of a scientist's educational curriculum." He contrasts Pascalian with the Baconian concept of probability, writing, "the Pascalian judgment grades probability on the *assumption that* all relevant facts are specified in the evidence, while the Baconian one grades it by *the extent to which* all relevant facts are specified in the evidence" (Cohen 1979, 389, emphases in original). See also Gilboa (2015) on why rationality does not imply Bayesianism, and Lopes (1982) on the fact that randomness is not clearly defined and even people who are not naïve, such as mathematicians and philosophers, have problems to say exactly what randomness is. One of the problems with randomness is that it is a property of processes, but the randomness of processes cannot be observed directly.

> It should be noted, moreover, that nonlogical does not mean illogical; a nonlogical action might have been the best that could be found, given observed facts and logic, for adjusting the means to the end; but this adjustment was obtained by a procedure other than that of logical reasoning.

For Hayek (1967), rationality means primarily the ability to discover truth, not the ability to reason deductively from given premises. According to him, Cartesian rationality, which refers to the optimal choice between specific means to satisfy given ends, does not adequately describe the human world in which neither means nor ends are known in advance, and therefore people must use induction to learn which ends are worth pursuing and how to achieve them. For Hayek (1967, 90, emphasis in original), using Cartesian rationality

> implies the claim that man's intelligence is adequate to order his life successfully without availing himself of the aid which general rules or principles can give him, in other words, the claim that man is capable of co-ordinating his activities successfully through a full explicit evaluation of the consequences of all possible alternatives of action, and in full knowledge of all the circumstances. This, of course, involves not only a colossal presumption concerning our intellectual powers, but also a complete misconception of the kind of world in which we live. It treats out practical problems as if we knew all the facts and the task of coping with them were a purely intellectual one. I am afraid much of modern social theory also has been deprived of value by this same assumption. The crucial fact of our lives is that we are *not* omniscient, that we have from moment to moment to adjust ourselves to new facts which we have not known before, and that we can therefore not order our lives according to a preconceived detailed plan in which every particular action is beforehand rationally adjusted to every other.

In defense of behavioral economists, neoclassical economists do indeed sometimes use the HE model not only as an analytical tool but also as a description of how economic agents make decisions, mainly in rational choice theory and its applications. Rationality as logicality is used to describe decision-making in at least three ways.

First, in the theory of consumer choice, it is used as a description of people's preferences. Preferences are called rational if they satisfy certain axioms, such as completeness and transitivity. Consumers' behavior is called rational if they form preferences in a logical way (Mas-Collel et al. 1995). Second, in the expected-utility hypothesis, rationality as logicality is viewed as a description of people's choices under risk. Decisions are called rational when people choose between risky prospects by comparing expected-utility values (Friedman and Savage 1948). Third, in game theory, rationality as logicality is treated as a description of people's choices in games – i.e., in situations in which they interact with other people (players). Players' decisions are called rational in game theory when they are the result of maximizing payoff functions conditional on those players' expectations of other players' decisions (Von Neumann and Morgenstern 1944).

The problem with these theories and hypotheses is that they are highly formalized, to such an extent that "today's theory of value is nothing else but pure logic of choice" (Alter 1982, 150). By their nature, mathematical formalizations make relatively strict assumptions about the rationality of modeled agents. In formal mathematical models, agents have to be logical because otherwise the models would not work. For example, the axioms of completeness and transitivity are necessary conditions for a conventional utility function to exist, so they became norms of rational behavior, but the behavior is rational only in the sense that it can be modeled with a utility function. Hence, such norms are not *prescriptive* but *constitutive*.[6] Just as the rules of chess are constitutive of what it means to play chess, adherence to certain logical axioms is constitutive of what it means to be modeled in a neoclassical way. Luce and Raiffa (1957, 63, emphasis in original) similarly write about the game theory:

> [I]t is crucial that the social scientist recognize that game theory is not *descriptive*, but rather (conditionally) *normative*. It states neither how people do behave nor how they should behave in an absolute sense, but how they should behave if they wish to achieve certain ends. It prescribes for given assumptions courses of action for the attainment of outcomes having certain formal optimum properties. These properties may or may not be deemed pertinent in any given real world conflict of interest. If they are, the theory prescribes the choices which *must* be made to get that optimum.

Hence, the problem, as Rizzo (2017, 2) notes, is that

> economists—both neoclassical and behavioral—have confused the status of the axioms of rational choice. They have transformed the constitutive norms of economic theory into prescriptive norms. Agents who do not conform to the axioms are not simply failing to behave as "neoclassical agents", they are acting erroneously. In the neoclassical approach they always behave as if they conform. In the behavioral, they often do not and when that is the case, their decisions ought to change.

In other words, the behavioral economists do not properly understand the character of the standard rational choice theory. They use it as a benchmark in tests whether people behave as they 'should.' The problem is that theory only specifies how agents 'should' behave, if they are to behave in line with the model, not how they should behave in the real world. The axioms were used to made economic models mathematically tractable and to help construct useful

---

[6] Or, in a terminology used by Graziano (2013, 24–25), there are not norms "ought" but "ought in order to."

models, not to describe or dictate how real people do or should behave (Rizzo and Whitman 2020, loc. 1065–69, 2205).

The key to understanding the problem is to notice that properties of the model are not the same as the properties of the real world, and the evaluation criteria are also different. When one reads fiction, she does not evaluate it in terms of truthfulness but in terms of consistency. For example, readers do not debate whether the giant eagles in *The Lord of the Rings: The Return of the King* (Tolkien 1955) really existed but whether their appearance in the novel is in line with the logic of the plot. Similarly, models are not necessarily true, as they are used as a methodological device, not a description of reality. Hence, rationality as logicality is a feature of the model, not the modeled world. As Lagueux (2010) points out, the picture of rationality designed by economists and the rationality principle (in a sense that people are far from being stupid) itself are not necessarily the same. In other words, the rationality in the object (objective rationality) is something different from the rationality of the observer (Schumpeter 1984).

Furthermore, rationality in mathematical economic models refers to decisions rather than to actions, and it is different from rationality in real life. For example, the transitivity axiom is necessary for rationality in economists' models because the logical construct is timeless. But the axiom is not necessary for rationality in real life taking place in a temporal world, as in one moment a person can prefer apples to bananas but later she can prefer bananas to apples while remaining rational. The constancy of preferences is not desirable in case of free and learning entities acting in a temporal world (Mises 1998 [1949]).

Similarly, the majority of psychological experiments on risk have been run under static conditions that do not take properly into account the dynamic effects. In real world, decisions are not independent, but do affect future choices. It means that some actions that can seem irrational in static perspective can be perfectly rational in the context of the individual's goals and assessment of the future (Lopes 1983).

Hence, researchers should not conflate the notions of rationality as process (logicality) and as purpose (appropriateness of the means used for the goals pursued), as they concern different orders of reality. Logicality does not apply to actions, but only to reasoning.

This is because action "is a fact of will, not knowledge. The will presupposes reasoning, it is true, but action, which is the expression of will, cannot itself be qualified by adjectives such as 'logical' or 'illogical,' which pertain only to the application of reason" (Kirzner 1976, 169–70). Mises (1998 [1949], 103) writes similarly:

> One must not confuse the logical concept of consistency (viz., absence of contradiction) and the praxeological concept of consistency (viz., constancy or clinging to the same principles). Logical consistency has its place only in thinking, constancy has its place only in acting.
>
> Constancy and rationality are entirely different notions. If one's valuations have changed, unremitting faithfulness to the once espoused principles of action merely for the sake of constancy would not be rational but simply stubborn. Only in one respect can acting be constant: in preferring the more valuable to the less valuable. If the valuations change, acting must change also. Faithfulness, under changed conditions, to an old plan would be nonsensical. A logical system must be consistent and free of contradictions because it implies the coexistence of all its parts and theorems. In acting, which is necessarily in the temporal order, there cannot be any question of such consistency. Acting must be suited to purpose, and purposefulness requires adjustment to changing conditions.

Having said that, the point of economic models is not to model the real choice process of individuals but rather to predict the aggregate outcome and pattern of choice. I elaborate on this in section 5. Now, I would like to discuss two more understandings of individual rationality.

## 2.2 Informational Rationality

Some neoclassical models make unrealistic assumptions about the information sets of economic agents, equating perfect information with rationality. Perfect information can be understood in three ways. First, it can be viewed as an assumption in the perfect-competition model. In that model, markets are efficient, or rational, only if, among other things, all consumers and producers are informationally rational – i.e., they have perfect knowledge of market prices, utilities, and cost functions. However, as Hayek (1937, 45–49) notes, the assumption of perfect information as a condition of equilibrium is not only unrealistic, but it also sweeps the problem under the carpet and contributes nothing to the proper equilibrium analysis:

> The assumption of a perfect market then means nothing less than that all the members of the community, even if they are not supposed to be strictly omniscient, are at least supposed to know automatically all that is relevant for their decisions […].
>
> The statement that, if people know everything, they are in equilibrium is true simply because that is how we define equilibrium. The assumption of a perfect market in this sense is just another way of saying that equilibrium exists, but does not get us any nearer an explanation of when and how such a state will come about […].
>
> Instead of showing what bits of information the different persons must possess in order to bring about that result [equilibrium – AS], we fall in effect back on the assumption that everybody knows everything and so evade any real solution of the problem.

What is more, market participants can be rational even if they do not have full knowledge about the world. After all, differences in people's knowledge sets make it more or less probable that they will achieve their goals, but they do not affect whether the people are behaving rationally, in the sense that they use some means to achieve some goals. The information people possess affects the means they use, but deficient information does not rule out rationality in the formal sense of adherence to a means–ends scheme. As Rizzo (1982, 58) notes,

> The possibility that individuals will act in a mistaken fashion in no way compromises the assumption of rationality. Rationality is a purely formal relationship between means and ends and does not depend on the accuracy of the individuals' information.
>
> A decision can be optimal or rational relative to incorrectly perceived data. Such a decision could be called inefficient but never irrational.

For example, classical economists were clearly wrong in adopting the labor theory of value, although it was a rational attempt at explaining how the value of goods and services was determined. Another example might be the case of beginner chess players. They have less knowledge about openings, tactics, and strategy than grandmasters, but they still play rationally – i.e., they play in line with the rules of the game, trying to checkmate the opponent's king.

However, even if one agrees that people are irrational because they are not perfectly informed, markets can still be rational. Thanks to the process of competition and the price mechanism, which together generate and transmit information, individuals need not know much to take the right action. In other words, the effective operation of markets is not conditioned on a certain amount of knowledge on the part of market participants. On the contrary, some knowledge can be generated and gained only through the market process (Hayek 1945; Alchian 1950; Gode and Sunder 1993; Smith 2008).

Second, informational rationality can be understood in terms of the rational-expectations hypothesis (REH) used in macroeconomic models (Muth 1961; Lucas 1972). The general idea behind this assumption seems to be true: all the people cannot be fooled all the time. The outcomes people forecast cannot differ systematically from the market-equilibrium outcomes. However, the assumption is certainly false as a description of what people know and how they learn and formulate expectations. In particular, it is not true that people know the true economic model and its parameters (Snowdon et al. 1994).

Third, informational rationality is used as a description of asset price behavior. According to the efficient-market hypothesis (EMH), financial markets are efficient in the sense that asset prices are rational, meaning they reflect all available information so there are no market anomalies of which investors can systematically take advantage (Fama 1970; Malkiel 2003). As with the REH, the main idea behind the EMH seems to be true: it is impossible to systematically beat the market (or, in a sense that makes EMH very similar to REH, all the investors cannot be fooled all the time). Actual prices cannot differ systematically from market-equilibrium prices. However, the EMH is certainly false when it is used as a description of what investors know, how they learn, and how market prices are set. Two problems arise in particular. If asset prices always reflect all available information, how is new information incorporated into prices? And if all market participants have homogeneous expectations about future securities returns (if people are assumed to formulate rational expectations, they have to arrive at the same forecasts), then why should they engage in trade (Shostak 1997)?

The fundamental flaw of the view of rationality as perfect information is that it applies to equilibrium outcomes, not to the activity that generates those outcomes. In other words, it applies to decisions in the timeless world of models but not to the temporal market processes in real life. To put it another way, informational rationality conflates the order of scientific inquiry with the order of the subject of the scientific inquiry. To construct and solve models of competition, expectations, or asset prices, researchers have to know all the model parameters, but that does not imply that real-world subjects also have to possess full knowledge. The information set needed for researchers to describe subjects' behavior is different from the knowledge set of the subjects. As Hayek (1945, 530, emphasis in original) explains:

> The problem is thus in no way solved if we can show that all the facts, *if* they were known to a single mind (as we hypothetically assume them to be given to the observing economist), would uniquely determine the solution; instead we must show how a solution is produced by the interactions of people each of whom possesses only partial knowledge. To assume all the knowledge to be given to a single mind in the same manner in which we assume it to be given to us as the explaining economists is to assume the problem away and to disregard everything that is important and significant in the real world.[7]

## 2.3 Rationality as Maximization

The last notion of individual rationality I would like to describe is rationality as maximization. Economists often say that rational consumers maximize utility, while rational firms maximize profits. Depending on its exact meaning, this notion can be either true or false. On the one hand, maximization of utility is often used to mean that people are rational in a formal sense – i.e., that people choose means to achieve their goals and they direct these means towards

---

[7] See also Machlup's famous example of the different knowledge sets of drivers and of researchers formulating a theory of overtaking (Machlup, 1946, 534–35).

their most desired ends (Rothbard 2009, ch. 1). In this meaning, the notion that people maximize utility could be equated with the rationality principle (Mises 1998 [1949], 243).

On the other hand, maximization of utility can be understood literally to mean that people calculate the utility of alternative courses of action and choose the one with the highest numerical value. This notion stimulates much more controversy. This is because it is impossible to measure utility quantitatively (there are no *utils*), so maximization understood mathematically is impossible (Mises 1998 [1949]; Rothbard 2009). And even if we could calculate utility (just as we can calculate profits), we would have to know the whole utility (or profit) function, which is a too demanding assumption about people's information set.[8] In other words, maximization understood in a mathematical sense implies that we possess all the relevant information about revenues and costs in all possible scenarios, which is not true, as neither the objective function nor the constraints are given in the real world (Hayek 1945). To put it differently, rationality need not involve optimization – it can be reduced to solving an optimization problem, but only when the goals and the constraints can be expressed in terms of well-behaved mathematical functions, which is, usually, not the case (Hands 2015). Alternatively, rationality can be reduced to optimization from the scholar's perspective, or for didactic purposes, but not from the economic agent's perspective.

The notion that all agents maximize profits is also untrue, as people can get satisfaction from many things other than monetary profits (Mises 1998 [1949], 97–98; Rothbard 2009, 70–72). However, economists do not assume that people maximize profits; they say either that people maximize utility (without specifying the content of their utility) or that firms maximize profits (Machlup 1946; Mas-Collel et al. 1995).

Some caveats may be needed here. First, some entrepreneurs may be motivated by considerations other than monetary profits (Machlup 1946). But profits are wider terms than monetary profits and also include non-pecuniary rewards (Machlup 1946). Additionally, monetary profits are usually necessary to remain in the market and achieve other goals. Second, maximization should not be understood literally (mathematically), as uncertainty makes it meaningless (Alchian 1950).[9] Rather, profit maximization should be understood in

[8] And their cognitive powers as well. As McKenzie (2010, 261) notes, "the human brain is simply not constructed to make all decisions, and all behavioral responses, rational in the sense that all costs and benefits of all options are carefully and accurately weighed."

[9] However, even if firms may not consciously maximize profits, economists may analyze their behavior *as if* they do, because firms with no positive profits will not survive in the market in the long run (Alchian 1950).

a formal sense, similarly to utility maximization, as striving to achieve the highest possible satisfaction, but by the entrepreneurs (Machlup 1946; Mises 1998 [1949]).

# 3. METHODOLOGICAL RATIONALITY

## 3.1 Rationality Principle in Neoclassical Economics

John Stuart Mill (1844) is considered a creator of the HE model. But he made it clear that he did not believe individuals behave like HEs and that he adopted the model for methodological reasons:

> The science then proceeds to investigate the laws which govern these several operations, under the supposition that man is a being who is determined, by the necessity of his nature, to prefer a greater portion of wealth to a smaller in all cases .... Not that any political economist was ever so absurd as to suppose that mankind are really thus constituted, but because this is the mode in which science must necessarily proceed. (Mill 1844)

For Mill and other classical economists, the HE model was used to abstract from other motives than desire for wealth. For neoclassical economists, HE ceased to be the ideal type of people that seek to achieve only economic goals; the model became a fully formal analytical device, which abstracts from any motive or desire. The terms such as 'utility' or 'self-interest' are used without reference to any psychological content.[10] The latter "does not mean that people care only about themselves, but that they try to achieve their own goals, whatever they might be" (Sieroń 2020, 339).[11]

The HE model was never intended – neither for classical nor for neoclassical economists – to be a realistic psychological depiction of human behavior, but rather as "a *method* of analysis" (Becker 1993, 1, emphasis in original).

The rationality assumption, which is at the core of the HE model, can be considered the first principle of economic theory, the one without which

---

[10] Similarly, the law of diminishing marginal utility has nothing to do with the Weber-Fechner psychophysical law of diminishing satisfaction from stimulus (Mises 1998 [1949], ch. VII). In other words, "preferences are not assumed to be based on desire, happiness, or any life goal" (White 2014, 63).

[11] It is worth pointing out that for Smith (2008 [1776]), self-interest was related to sympathy and self-love, while the real foundation of the desire to trade was the desire to persuade, or to have consideration for other human beings. Hence, contrary to popular understanding, Smith's self-interest does not equate with egoism (Hayek 1948a;Sieroń 2020; Drakopoulos and Katselidis 2024, 21–25). See also McKenzie (2010, ch. 3) on Smith's invisible hands of markets and morality.

economic theorizing becomes impossible. Kirchgässner (2013, 7) sees the rationality principle as

> of similar importance for the social sciences as the 'principle of causality' for the natural sciences. In the same way as in natural sciences talking about natural laws does not become possible before accepting the principle of causality, in the social sciences the understanding of human actions is impossible if the distinction between preferences and restrictions, or purposes and means, embedded in the economic model of behavior is not accepted and if it is not presupposed that individuals use the means at their disposal in a subjectively rational way to reach their objectives.

Hence, the rationality principle does not describe the mental processes of human beings, or their motives, or their cognitive capacities, or their goals. It simply states that people have goals and try to accomplish them. In other words, people are seen as entities that act purposefully, so they adopt certain means to achieve their ends.

Although it may seem trivial, the rationality principle has been a fundamental principle of economic theory, the core element that makes economics scientific (Herfeld 2021). Without it, people's behavior would be inexplicable. Without the knowledge that people are purposeful creatures, it would be impossible to interpret insightfully descriptive material – i.e., to build economic theory. A good example is Mises's story about looking at Grand Central Station during rush hour, as discussed by Rothbard (1985, xvi):

> The 'objective' or 'truly scientific' behaviorist, he pointed out, would observe the empirical events: e.g., people rushing back and forth, aimlessly at certain predictable times of day. And that is all he would know. But the true student of human action would start from the fact that all human behavior is purposive, and he would see the purpose is to get from home to the train to work in the morning, the opposite at night, etc. It is obvious which one would discover and know more about human behavior, and therefore which one would be the genuine 'scientist.'[12]

In other words, without the rationality principle, people's behavior would follow no rules and we could not predict what they might do. No economic analysis would be possible, as economists would not be able to formulate economic laws. Thus, economic theorizing presupposes the rationality principle (Herfeld 2021, 3337).

McKenzie and Tullock (2012) point out that the rationality principle allows for people to learn from mistakes, adjust to changes, and push markets towards equilibrium. Denying the rationality principle entails denying that people improve their behavior or react in a predictable way to incentives (or nudges).

---

[12] See also Mises (1990, 48–49).

In other words, denying the rationality principle rules out a self-equilibrating mechanism, which means that people repeat the same irrational decisions or mistakes over and over again and are unable to correct them (Levine 2012, ch. 9).

As Friedman (1990) notices, the rationality principle introduces order into our thinking. The assumption that people are rational brings consistency and predictability into economic analysis. This is because the alternative would be an irrationality principle, and it is impossible to build a theory of irrational behavior, as irrational behavior follows no rules or patterns. The problem is that "since there is generally only one right way of doing things (or perhaps a few) but very many wrong ways, the 'rational' behavior can be predicted but the 'irrational' behavior cannot" (Friedman 1990, 4).[13] More generally, the problem is that we can deduce less from weaker premises, which implies that although premises allowing people to behave in any way could be more descriptively realistic (let us assume so for the sake of discussion), they could also be less useful, or even lead towards nihilism (Shearmur 1992).

What is important here is that the scientific explanation of a process is not the same thing as the actual process. As Machlup (1946, 535) puts it:

> The explanation of an action must often include steps of reasoning which the acting individual himself does not consciously perform [….]. To call, on these grounds, the theory 'invalid,' 'unrealistic' or 'inapplicable' is to reveal failure to understand the basic methodological constitution of most social sciences.

Pareto (2014 [1906], 21) makes a similar observation, providing an interesting example that nonlogical behavior (from the scientific point of view) does not mean illogical behavior:

---

[13] Cf. Lagueux (2010, 33): "More generally, were a significant number of people inclined to act in a stupid rather than in a 'rational' fashion, the prospects for explanation by the social sciences of phenomena resulting from human actions would be reduced dramatically." See also Weber (2012 [1908], 249, emphases in original): "Take the example of someone who emphasizes the necessity of taking into account the specific 'psychology of the stock exchange' *as a complement to* the purely abstract theory of price [formation]: the object of [such a 'psychology of the stock exchange'] which that person will have in mind will precisely be the influence of factors that are *irrational* from an economic point of view, in other words: 'disturbances' affecting the laws of price formation that are to be postulated theoretically." See also Becker (1962, 5), who notices that households are often said to be irrational because, on the one hand, they are allegedly impulsive and erratic, and, on the other hand, they are inert and habitual. He develops models of such irrational behaviors and shows that fundamental economic theorems are consistent also with these kinds of behavior.

> It is known, for instance, that the cells in a honeycomb end in the form of a pyramid, and that with a minimum surface, hence with the minimum outlay of wax, they achieve the maximum volume, that is, they can hold the largest quantity of honey. Nobody, however, supposes that this is so because the bees have solved a maximum problem by syllogisms and mathematics; it is obviously a nonlogical action, although the means are perfectly adjusted to the end, and consequently the action is far from being illogical. The same observation could be made about a great many other actions, which are usually called instinctive, either by men or by animals.

Weber and Schuetz also believe that the concept of rational action is a chief principle in all social sciences. For the former, rationality is not an assumption about the qualities of human life but a methodological device that enables social scientists to understand purposeful behavior. To him, including purpose in the scientific analysis of action "permits the grasping of the cause of an action through the understanding (*Verstehen*) of its motive" (Kirzner 1976, 157). Thus, without the rationality principle, which assumes a means–ends structure, human action would be meaningless:

> Only in this respect and for these reasons of methodological convenience is the method of sociology 'rationalistic.' It is naturally not legitimate to interpret this procedure as involving a rationalistic bias of sociology, but only as a methodological device [...]. Only in terms of such categories [means and ends] is it possible to 'understand' objects of this kinds. On the other hand processes or conditions, whether they are animate or inanimate, human or nonhuman, are in the present sense devoid of meaning in so far as they cannot be related to an intended purpose. That is to say they are devoid of meaning if they cannot be related to action in the role of means or ends but constitute only the stimulus, the favoring or hindering circumstances. (Weber 1978, 6–7)

For his part, Schuetz (1943) distinguishes clearly between the level of real life and the level of scientific inquiry about it. He argues that the rationality principle makes the latter level accessible – i.e., it enables researchers to theorize about and interpret the social world. This is because "only action within the framework of rational categories can be scientifically discussed. Science does not have at its disposal other methods than rational ones and it cannot, therefore, verify or falsify purely occasional propositions" (Schuetz 1943, 148). In other words, thanks to the rationality principle, we can develop scientific theories and acquire knowledge about the world – i.e., transform "an uncontrollable and unintelligible world into an organisation which we can understand and therefore master, and in the framework of which prediction becomes possible" (Schuetz 1943, 136).

The rationality principle does not say anything about the mental processes of human beings, simply because it is a methodological device, not a psychological one. As Rizzo (2017, 13) notes, "Rationality is a tool that social scientists use to understand the world. The term rational is not a description of a person but a way of looking at some or all of his actions, including the beliefs he holds." Economics cannot deal with individual mental processes, because it would lose its universal validity, as people think and react differently. Theory must be expressed in general terms, but mental processes are very personal and highly situation-specific. We can, of course, study what is going on in people's minds, but we would not then be engaged in theoretical economics (Schuetz 1967).

In other words, the rationality principle is a methodological tool that allows economists to work within their own mental limitations when they try to understand complex human interactions in the marketplace (McKenzie and Tullock 2012).[14] Thanks to this intellectual device, they can abstract from psychological, neurobiological, and other aspects of human action. As Weber (2012 [1908], 249, emphasis in original) puts it, "the theorems that constitute specifically economic *theory* [...] are only an instrument [...] for the analysis of the causal interconnections of empirical reality."

It should be clear now that researchers who question the rationality assumption in economics conflate different levels of reality: rationality referring to human behavior in the real world, and rationality as the scientific basis for the social sciences in general and economics in particular. This means that empirical findings of deviations from rational behavior are not enough to discard the rationality principle. As Kirchgässner (2013, 3) notes, "this does not necessarily imply, however, that such versions of the rationality principle should generally not be applied in economic analyses. In order to reject a theory it is necessary not only for it to be falsified but also for a 'better' theory to be available for the purpose at hand, a theory that has more explanatory power."[15]

However, the rationality principle is not an empirical statement that can be verified or falsified. It does not describe reality. Rather, it suggests how

---

14 McKenzie (2010, ix) points out the irony that we need the rationality principle only because we are not perfectly rational: "only when people, including economists, have analytical limitations does it make sense to simplify and sterilize the underlying behavioral assumption regarding human motivations."

15 Cf. Shearmur (1992, 107): "the correct question to ask concerning the premises from which economists argue is their role in explanatory models, rather than as descriptively correct accounts of the phenomena with which they are dealing. Accordingly, it seems to me that while psychology-inspired criticism of the assumptions of theoretical economics may be of use, three conditions need to be satisfied before it is telling: first, that it discloses to us some premises as being incorrect; second, that this turns out to be of explanatory relevance – that it makes a difference; and third, that we can replace our older model by one that takes into account the criticism, in such a way that we are left with something of at least as much explanatory power as we had before."

we should analyze human behavior: we should explain individuals' actions in terms of purposes and means. Economists should simply assume that people have reasons to act a certain way. As Kirchgässner (2013, 8) notes, the rationality principle "is a heuristic principle that gives us methodological guidance for the way we are conducting research in the social sciences. It tells us that whenever we want to explain human behavior, we should try to explain it as the rational actions of individuals or as the result of rational decisions, respectively." Similarly, as Popper (1985, 359–365) puts it,

> If you look upon the rationality principle from the point of view which I have here adopted, then you will find that it has little or nothing to do with the empirical or psychological assertion that man always, or in the main, or in most cases, acts rationally. Rather, it turns out to be an aspect of, or a consequence of, the methodological postulate that we should pack or cram our whole theoretical effort, our whole explanatory theory, into an analysis of the situation: into the model.
>
> If we adopt this methodological postulate, then, as a consequence, the animating law will become a kind of zero principle. For the principle may be stated in this way: having constructed our model, our situation, we assume no more than that the actors act within the terms of the model, or that they 'work out' what was implicit in the situation [...].
>
> The adoption of the rationality principle can therefore be regarded as a byproduct of a methodological postulate. It does not play the role of an empirical explanatory theory, of a testable hypothesis [...].
>
> The 'rationality principle' on the other hand has nothing to do with the assumption that men are rational in this sense – that they always adopt a rational attitude. It is, rather, a minimum principle (since it assumes no more than the adequacy of our actions to our problem situations as we see them) which animates all, or almost all, our explanatory situational models, and, although we know it not to be true, we have some reason to regard as a good approximation. Its adoption reduces considerably the arbitrariness of our models; an arbitrariness which becomes capricious indeed if we try to proceed without this principle.[16]

In sum, the critique of rationality in economics by behavioral economists is ill founded because the rationality principle does not constitute an economic theory but a grammar for arguing about it (Brennan 2007). Just as grammar allows us to organize our sentences within a 'subject–verb–object' framework and to effectively communicate with others (compared to mere articulating the sounds), the rationality principle provides a necessary structure for economic inquiry (compared to mere reporting of the facts) (Brennan 2007; Li 2020).

---

[16] Rizzo and Whitman (2020) seem to mock neoclassical economists, writing about 'puppet rationality', but – after reading the above quote from Popper (1985) – it should not be surprising that when economists create models, the actors (or puppets) are assumed to act within the terms of the model.

## 3.2 Rationality as Purposefulness in the Austrian School of Economics

The praxeological approach adopted by the Austrian school of economics explicitly equates rationality with purposefulness. Hence, all purposeful behavior is rational, in contrast to "a reactive response to stimuli on the part of the bodily organs and of instincts, which cannot be controlled by volition" (Mises 1998 [1949], 20). This approach has been criticized for being tautological, but it is not obvious *a priori* that action is of primary importance in economics and social sciences, and that the axiom of human action brings forth a fruitful research program (Rizzo 1982).

It should also be noted that the very concept of human action is meaningless without the reference to conscious individuals aiming at chosen ends. One can observe some behavior, for example that several people run erratically and kick the ball, but one can *understand* what they are doing only when one knows that they play a game called 'soccer,' so there are two teams who want to kick the ball into the opponent team's goal (Mises 2007 [1957]). This understanding what it means to strive after ends chosen, Mises (1990, 48) calls "the praxeological a priori." He writes about the individual, an acting being, as follows:

> There is something that distinguishes in his eyes the movements of germs in a liquid as observed in the microscope from the movements of the individuals in the crowd he may observe in the rush hour at New York's Grand Central Terminal. He knows that there is some 'sense' in a man's running around or sitting still. He looks upon his human environment with a mental equipment that is not required or, to say it more precisely, is downright obstructive in endeavors to explore the state of his nonhuman environment. This specific mental equipment is the praxeological a priori. The radical empiricism of the historicists went astray in ignoring this fact [...]. There is no human action that can be dealt with without reference to the categorical concepts of ends and means, of success and failure, of costs, of profit or loss. (Mises 1990, 48–49)

Moreover, equating rationality with purposefulness makes praxeology a truly formal science. In other words, Austrian economics endorses fully the formal nature of economics, thanks to which it can abstract from assumptions about the psychological motives or mental processes of people. The formal approach of the Austrian school is very similar to the neoclassical approach of treating rationality as a scientific principle. For Mises and his followers, the axiom of human action – i.e., that people behave rationally in the sense that they have purposes they want to achieve – is also the ultimate foundation of economics as a science. According to Rizzo (1982), the rationality postulate belongs to the Lakatosian hard core of the research program of the Austrian school of economics,[17] and that it was a methodological decision to make it non-falsifiable.

Hence, if the concept of HE is used as a rationality principle, which is an analytical tool, then it can be equated with the Austrian concept of *Homo agens*. However, Austrian economists usually contrast these two concepts and endorse the latter. This is because economics is seen in this approach as a theory of action rather than a theory of decision, which implicitly assumes only closed-ended problems (Huerta de Soto 1998). For the Austrian school, action is not identified with constrained maximization among given alternatives; it also includes discovery of the possibilities (Kirzner 2001).

Furthermore, HE is sometimes misused, especially by behavioral economists, as a model of people's decision-making. But in the Austrian approach, it does not matter *how* people make decisions or *why* they act in a certain way; what matters is that the particular action was taken. As Mises (1990, 24) explains,

> Economics does not deal with an imaginary *homo oeconomicus* as ineradicable fables reproach it with doing, but with *homo agens* as he really is, often weak, stupid, inconsiderate, and badly instructed. It does not matter whether his motives and emotions are to be qualified as noble or as mean. It does not contend that man strives only after more material wealth for himself and for his kin. Its theorems are neutral with regard to ultimate judgments of value, and are valid for all actions irrespective of their expediency.

In other words, the Austrian concept of rationality presupposes neither deductive competence, nor lack of logical errors,[18] nor decision-taking based only on logical reasoning and probability calculus (and not on impulses and emotions):

> To make mistakes in pursuing one's ends is a widespread human weakness. Some err less often than others, but no mortal man is omniscient and infallible. Error, inefficiency, and failure must not be confused with irrationality. He who shoots

---

[17] And the neoclassical school as well, although their research programs are obviously not the same (Rizzo 1982).

[18] Please note that we can often reduce the risk of one type of errors only at the expense of increasing the risk of committing another type of errors. The implication is that rationality does not imply being faultless, as some behavioral economists seem to believe. Some mistakes are more consequential for people than others. Thus, it is perfectly rational to, for example, set criteria of signal detection low and be exposed rather to false alarms than to more consequential misses (Lopes 1982). More generally, it is possible that occasional misjudgments are the price of having a powerful reasoning system, just as occasional misperceptions of visual scenes are the price of having a powerful visual system augmented by the expectancy-driven information (Lopes 1982).

wants, as a rule, to hit the mark. If he misses it, he is not 'irrational'; he is a poor marksman. The doctor who chooses the wrong method to treat a patient is not irrational; he may be an incompetent physician. The farmer who in earlier ages tried to increase his crop by resorting to magic rites acted no less rationally than the modern farmer who applies more fertilizer. He did what according to his—erroneous—opinion was appropriate to his purpose. (Mises 2007 [1957], 268)

Hence, Austrian economists fully abstract from psychological reasoning because for them rationality equals purposefulness, which implies that people use means to attain ends. What the ends are is irrelevant to economists. And how people use means is also irrelevant: they can use them wrongly and make mistakes, but they remain rational in the sense that they use reason to improve their situation. As Mises (1998 [1949], 11–12) puts it, "the field of our science is human action, not the psychological events which result in an action. It is precisely this which distinguishes the general theory of human action, praxeology, from psychology. The theme of psychology is the internal events that result or can result in a definite action. Theme of praxeology is action as such."

Thus, the Austrian school distinguishes between the formal aspect of action (the fact that people act and its logical implications) and the substantive aspect of action (the content of actions; the specific goals people pursue). Hence, praxeology provides only an "ultrarefined grammar" for thinking and communicating about social-scientific phenomena (Hutchison 1998, 68).[19] As Mises (2007 [1957], 271–272, emphasis in original) explains:

Praxeology is not concerned with the events which within a man's soul or mind or brain produce a definite decision between an A and a B. It takes it for granted that the nature of the universe enjoins upon man choosing between incompatible ends. Its subject is not the content of these acts of choosing but what results from them: action. It does not care about what a man chooses but about the fact that he chooses and acts in compliance with a choice made. It is neutral with regard to the factors that determine the choice and does not arrogate to itself the competence to examine, to revise, or to correct judgments of value. It is *wertfrei*.

*Why* one man chooses water and another man wine is a thymological (or, in the traditional terminology, psychological) problem. But it is of no concern to praxeology and economics.

[19] Cf. Hirshleifer (1985, 53) who notes that "economics really does constitute the universal grammar of social science." See also Gintis (2004, 38, 40), who writes, "Game theory provides a transdisciplinary behavioral lexicon for communication and model-building" and thus it is "a generalized schema that permits the precise framing of meaningful empirical assertions, but imposes no particular structure on the predicted behavior."

> The subject matter of praxeology and of that part of it which is so far the best developed—economics—is action as such and not the motives that impel a man to aim at definite ends.[20]

With such an approach, the Austrian school seeks to maintain scientific objectivity, as treating ends of the individuals as data assures that economists abstain from explaining them, which would require reducing them to the means and judging them in light of some arbitrarily chosen ends (Engelhard et al. 1996; Mises 1998 [1949]).

## 4. METAPHYSICAL RATIONALITY

Rationality can also be understood metaphysically. In this perspective, rationality means using reason in life, not merely being guided by impulses like animals.[21] Unlike animals, people act not impulsively but purposefully – i.e., they use reason in employing certain means to achieve chosen goals in order to improve their situation.[22] In other words, people are able to choose in the face of alternative options and to behave accordingly. As Mises (2007 [1957], 269) puts it,

> The fundamental thesis of rationalism is unassailable. Man is a rational being; that is, his actions are guided by reason. The proposition: Man acts, is tantamount to the proposition: Man is eager to substitute a state of affairs that suits him better for a state of affairs that suits him less. In order to achieve this, he must employ suitable means. It is his reason that enables him to find out what is a suitable means for attaining his chosen end and what is not.

---

[20] Knight (1969, 135, emphasis in original) adopts a very similar, formal view of economics: "There are no laws regarding the *content* of economic behaviour, but there are laws universally valid as to its *form*. There is an abstract rationale of all conduct which is rational at all, and a rationale of all social relations arising through the organization of rational activity."

[21] For Boland (1981), a statement is metaphysical, when it is deliberately put beyond question within the research program, and, for him, neoclassical maximization is such a statement. However, according to the classification adopted in this chapter, it would be rather an example of a methodological rationality.

[22] Ward (1893) notes that the method of rational man compared to the method of nature is teleological instead of genetic. As a consequence, "the existence of a rational faculty in man, which, while it does not render his actions any less subject to true natural laws, so enormously complicates them that they can no longer be brought within the simple formulas that suffice in the calculus of mere animal motives [...]. It is in rational man, therefore, that the first application of anything worthy of the name of economy is made. Nature has no economy. Only through foresight and design can anything be done economically" (Ward, 1893, 73–80).

Undoubtedly, humans share many instincts and impulses with animals. However, one cannot ignore the calculated self-interest as a factor in human behavior, or that people make judgements of value. Although survival and procreation impulses can explain animals' behavior quite nicely, referring to only impulses would be unsatisfactory when studying human behavior. As Mises (2007 [1957], 267) puts it, "If man were only an animal and not also a valuing person, he would always yield to the impulse that at the instant is most powerful. The eminence of man consists in the fact that he has ideas and, guided by them, chooses between incompatible ends."

The greater emphasis on philosophical foundations is the difference between the neoclassical rationality principle and the Austrian view of rationality as purposefulness. For Mises, rationality is not just an analytical tool adopted for pragmatic reasons; it has an epistemological and ontological basis.[23] More specifically, Mises (2007 [1957]) argues for methodological subjectivism in economics, and in general for methodological dualism, which holds that we should use a different methodology to analyze the actions of human beings from the methodology used in the physical sciences. The reason is that people have free will, so their actions are not determined but purposeful.

Schuetz (1943, 146) also believes in methodological dualism and argues that understanding social phenomena requires the analytical framework of means and ends:

> The real reason for this is that we cannot deal with phenomena in the social world as we do with phenomena belonging to the natural sphere. In the latter, we collect facts and regularities which are not understandable to us, but which we can refer only to certain fundamental assumptions about the world. We shall never understand why the mercury in the thermometer rises if the sun shines on it. We can only interpret this phenomenon as compatible with the laws we have deduced from some basic assumption about the physical world. Social phenomena, on the contrary, we want to understand and we cannot understand them otherwise than within the scheme of human motives, human means and ends, human planning—in short—within the categories of human action.

---

[23] However, Mises does not adopt it dogmatically, but rather because it has pragmatic value – i.e., it works. As he puts it, "But the same pragmatic proof that can be advanced in favor of the exclusive use of causal research in the field of nature can be advanced in favor of the exclusive use of teleological methods in the field of human action. It works, while the idea of dealing with men as if they were stones or mice does not work. It works not only in the search for knowledge and theories but no less in daily practice" (Mises 2007 [1957], 248).

Knight (1969, 120, emphasis in original) offers a similar view on the necessity to assume free will, or at least to adopt a teleological perspective when analyzing the behavior of living beings:

> It is impossible to construct in thought a world of real objects in purely objective terms; if objects are to have the qualities of consistent behaviour they are inevitably thought of as possessing rudiments of mind. We interpret the behaviour of the most material thing by to some degree putting ourselves in its place. Still more true is this when we come to consider the behaviour of living things. Purely mechanical biology remains an aspiration of the scientific intellect. Some sort of teleology is inevitable in speaking of the phenomena of life. The *will* to live and to increase is more than the *fact* of living and increasing, and we cannot account satisfactorily to ourselves for the facts of the lowest animal and plant life without recognizing an *element of striving*, as well as processes and results.

And so does Rothbard (2011, 73–74):

> On one point, and on one point alone, however, praxeology and the related sciences of human action take a stand in philosophical psychology: on the proposition that the human mind, consciousness, and subjectivity exist, and therefore action exists. In this it is opposed to the philosophical base of behaviorism and related doctrines and joined with all branches of classical philosophy and with phenomenology.[24]

Hence, for Austrians, the rationality principle is not only a heuristic principle or methodological tool but a metaphysical statement about human nature: people are rational entities that act on reason and will; they adapt to changed environmental conditions not in a passive or deterministic way but according to their own objectives or preferences. There is no obvious observable difference between the actions of people and the behavior of other entities; hence, assigning action to people and people only is a methodological decision (one that stems, among other things, from metaphysical beliefs).

The rationality principle allows researchers to understand and predict human behavior (at least in the aggregate) without adopting a deterministic stance. As Kirchgässner (2013, 18) points out, "One advantage of applying the (weak) rationality principle is that it makes two seemingly contradictory views compatible: the assumption of free will and the predictability of human behaviour." Similarly, Latsis (1976) notes that the rationality principle reconciles the doctrine of free will with deducibility, or it creates a connection between the actions and their preceding mental processes, avoiding both physicalism

[24] Allport (1955, 6–17) writes in this context about Lockean and Leibnitzian traditions in philosophical psychology: according to the former, people react to stimuli, while to the latter, they act purposefully in the direction of future possibilities.

and inexplicability of social phenomena. He writes: "The rationality principle bridges the logical gap between mentalistic and activistic propositions while *not* necessitating (in the same way as a natural law would necessitate) that the predicted action will take place" (Latsis, 1976, 6–7, emphasis in original).

This is not the only possible assumption about human nature. We could assume that people are driven purely by emotions or that their actions are completely determined by biological factors or societal norms and institutions (people are the product of their environment). And models based on such assumptions would be useful in some areas. It is obvious that emotions and social norms can be important constraints on human behavior. However, the success of the rationality principle or the HE model not only in economics but in other social sciences as well, especially when compared to the *Homo sociologicus* and *Homo psychologicus* models, is indisputable and suggests that it is a useful construct and that it will not be easy to replace it in the social sciences (Jensen and Meckling 1994).[25]

In other words – thanks to reason – people are "able to offset environmental, social, and biological forces that would otherwise determine what they do" (McKenzie and Tullock 2012, 8). They can set their own goals and try to reach them, instead of being driven by impulses. Hence, although we could also apply the means–ends framework to other entities, such as animals, we generally know in advance their goals (survival and reproduction).[26] To be sure, such a perspective does not fully explain all behavior of living creatures, especially higher mammals, but it generally works well empirically. However, assigning only these goals to human beings would be too narrow, as we know empirically that people also have goals other than propagation of their genes. Doing so would also contradict the principle of subjectivity.

## 5. RATIONALITY AS AN EMPIRICAL TENDENCY

As the previously discussed meanings of rationality indicate, rationality can be understood in a formal sense – as a methodological tool that provides a means–ends framework for scientific inquiry into economic activity. However,

[25] Gintis (2004, 38, emphasis in original) calls for more unity in the human behavioral sciences. He believes that they should be based on game theory and rational actor model, which "is a flexible tool that applies to all the human behavioral disciplines."

[26] For example, we could use the praxeological approach to study animal behavior and say that dogs bark at mail carriers because it increases their satisfaction, or it substitutes a state of affairs that suits them better for a state of affairs that suits them less. But we know with a high degree of probability the reason they bark: territoriality.

rationality can also be seen from a more empirical perspective referring to the content of human action. There are (at least) two variants of such an approach.

## 5.1 Rationality of Goals

The first concerns the rationality of goals pursued by individuals. Is it rational for John to drink alcohol on Friday night? Is it rational for Eve to marry Adam? Is it rational for Mark to buy a new Porsche? Is it rational for Kate to ascend the ranks in an international corporation? In this sense, rationality could be equated with reasonableness or appropriateness. The obvious problem with this approach is that evaluating the goals of other people contradicts the principle of methodological subjectivism, according to which actions are based on unique value scales known only to the individual agents (Hayek 1948b; Mises 1998 [1949]). To answer the above questions, one would need either to know the agents' preferences or to impose their own values. For example, to deem drinking alcohol as irrational, one would have to know that John values health and not having a hangover the next day more than having fun with friends and relaxing after the working week, or one would have to assume that health and sobriety are the goals that everyone should pursue. Knowledge of other people's scale of preferences (values) is impossible, while adopting one's own scale of preferences as universally valid contradicts the principle of freedom from value judgments and conflates economics and ethics. This is why economists accept individual preferences as given and agree that *de gustibus non est disputandum* (Stigler and Becker 1977).[27]

Of course, in daily life, or even in lectures on personal finance, people do say that certain kind of actions are not rational (or reasonable). There is almost universal agreement that living on credit, having unprotected sex, injecting heroin each morning, sleeping three hours per night, and insulting everyone around are not very reasonable actions. However, this is only because in our societies people share certain values, and implicitly assume them to be worthwhile. People tend to assess the above activities as irrational only because they implicitly assume health, prosperity, and good relations are values.

Importantly, if one assumes that people's goal should be or is maximization of wealth, one arrives at the caricatured version of HE, according to

[27] See Mises (1998 [1949], 14): "The ultimate goal of human action is always the satisfaction of the acting man's desire. There is no standard of greater or lesser satisfaction other than individual judgments of value, different for various people and for the same people at various times. What makes a man feel uneasy and less uneasy is established by him from the standard of his own will and judgment, from his personal and subjective valuation. Nobody is in a position to decree what should make a fellow man happier."

which individuals are egoistic and materialistic beings that exclusively thirst for wealth. But economists do not assume the content of utility – it might be wealth, but also any other values, including altruistic ones – and they treat preferences as given.[28]

Meanwhile, if one assumes that the goal is maximization of evolutionary success, one gets evolutionary rationality. This concept of rationality posits an almost universally acclaimed goal (namely, survival) and a less commonly shared but still widely accepted aim (namely, reproduction). It can also explain some allegedly irrational behavior among humans (such as loss aversion) pointed out by behavioral economists.[29] However, as Sieroń (2020, 361n29) notes, this approach is

> not fully satisfactory, as, first, the conditions that prevailed during most of the existence of human beings were radically different from the current environment and, second, some people decide to commit suicide or to not have children, which clearly does not grant an evolutionary advantage but can still be perfectly reasonable, given their particular scales of preferences. Hence the purely formal definition of rationality seems to be the most satisfactory, as it avoids excessively narrow notions or value judgments about the behavior of other people.[30]

---

[28] See Mises (1998 [1949], 14–15): "To establish this fact [the ultimate goal of human action is always the satisfaction of the acting man's desire – AS] does not refer in any way to the antitheses of egoism and altruism, of materialism and idealism [...]. There are people whose only aim is to improve the condition of their own ego. There are other people with whom awareness of the troubles of their fellow men causes as much uneasiness as or even more uneasiness than their own wants. There are people who desire nothing else than the satisfaction of their appetites for sexual intercourse, food, drinks, fine homes, and other material things. But other men care more for the satisfactions commonly called 'higher' and 'ideal' [...]. Praxeology is indifferent to the ultimate goals of action. Its findings are valid for all kinds of action irrespective of the ends aimed at. It is a science of means, not of ends."

[29] See Graziano (2013, xv) on a kind of rationality that could be named 'biological rationality' ("rational agents are biological organisms in an environment"), according to which "although agents in certain cases and contexts might systematically depart from standard models of rationality, this does not necessarily mean that humans cannot be considered rational animals."

[30] Hence, regarding the difference between our current environment and the previously prevailing one, people's inclination to eat as much as they can could be seen as perfectly rational (adaptive) when food was very scarce, although it causes significant problems in societies in which food is relatively plentiful. See Speakman (2013) on evolutionary perspectives on the obesity epidemic, and McKenzie and Tullock (2012, ch. 12) on economic perspective.

## 5.2 Rationality of Means

The second variant of rationality that refers to the content of human action is rationality as the appropriateness of the means used to pursue goals. In this sense, rationality can be defined as efficiency or simply as acting in a way that helps individuals to achieve their goals. This definition is the closest to the ordinary understanding of rational behavior as reasonable or consistent with common sense. What is important in this definition is that deductive competence can be helpful but is not necessary for acting rationally, as people can also use other methods to achieve their goals.[31]

For Mises (1998 [1949]), people always choose the most rational means to achieve their ends, given the state of their knowledge, as the mere fact of choosing these means indicates that people perceive them as the best ones; otherwise, they would choose other means. Hence, Misesian purposefulness can also be considered as ex ante rationality.

However, rationality can also be understood as ex post instrumental rationality – i.e., as the empirical tendency of people to use the correct means to achieve their objectives.[32] According to Friedman (1990, 3), this is the core assumption of economics: "Economics is that way of understanding behavior that starts from the assumption that people have objectives and tend to choose the correct way to achieve them." Economists assume that people tend to find the suitable ways to achieve their goals, not that people do this in a rational way; the latter is the assumption of rationality as logicality, the assumption that people make decisions using formal logic.

Another significant feature of the assumption of ex post rationality is that it refers to the aggregate outcome. It does not say that all people always choose the best means all the time, as that would be clearly false. Rather, it states that people generally tend to use the correct means to achieve their objectives and that the aggregate effect of many people's behavior is the same *as if* they were acting rationally.[33] Such an assumption seems to be justified, as economists often focus on the behavior of markets, not individuals. For example, price theory says that when the supply increases, the price will decline, *ceteris paribus*. This is also what is generally observed empirically, although it is possible that

---

[31] For example, Rich (2016) points out that heuristics can outperform more complex procedures.

[32] According to Kolodny and Brunero (2023), "someone displays instrumental rationality insofar as she adopts suitable means to her ends."

[33] Rizzo (1982) notes that the part of the research program of the Austrian school of economics is the presumption that there is a tendency towards coordination, not that there will be actual coordination at all times (such a statement would rather fit the simplistic neoclassical hard core).

in real life, when other things are never constant, some sellers do not trade at lower prices. It is worth mentioning here Machlup's comment on the statement that "If, because of an abundant crop, the output of wheat is much increased, the price of wheat will fall":

> It is, of course, probable that some sellers may decide to hold back and to wait until trade is better. It is even possible that other sellers may be willing, influenced by an adviser, to sell only a portion of their crop, provided they expect the others to do the same. But it is entirely improbable that all of a great many sellers do act in this way. If only a few producers should sell their whole increased output [...], more and more producers would follow suit and the statement would be proven to the hilt. (Machlup 1936, 42)

The possibility of a rational aggregate outcome, even if individual market participants do not act rationally, arises for a few reasons. First, insofar as irrational actions are random, their effects are likely to average out in the aggregate (Friedman 1990). For example, in response to a price change, some people may purchase too much of a good, while others may not buy enough, but overall demand will adjust to the price change *as if* everyone were reacting rationally.

Second, the market is a continuous process. As people can repeatedly interact with others in the marketplace, they can learn and improve the efficiency of their decisions. According to Hayek (1945), market prices transmit important knowledge. Hence, the aggregate outcome of the market process should be more rational than the one-off actions of individuals. Not surprisingly, in experiments in which subjects are allowed to play a game repeatedly, the outcomes improve (Smith 2008; Levine 2012).[34]

Third, market institutions allow individuals to bypass their own cognitive limitations. For example, retail investors can buy reasonable asset portfolios even if they do not analyze securities 'rationally,' as long as they can decode reputational signals and hire professional financial managers. In other words, markets can be seen as extended mind (Dekker and Remic 2024). Thus, it is hardly surprising that, in experiments where subjects have no access to any cumulative learning or cues embedded in market institutions, where "they have no solution technologies available to them except their raw brains" (Ross

[34] McKenzie and Tullock (2012) criticize behavioral economists for drawing too far-reaching conclusions from single experiments that do not allow subjects to learn. More generally, Binmore (1999) criticizes behavioral economists for drawing too far-reaching conclusions from experiments in which problems are not simple enough itself and to the subjects, the incentives are not adequate, and the time for trial-and-error adjustments is not sufficient, as in such conditions the economic theory should not be expected to predict achieving (immediate) equilibrium.

2014, 206), they make errors and do not always choose as if they follow modern utility theory or modern portfolio theory (Von Neumann and Morgenstern 1944; Markowitz 1952).[35]

Fourth, there is a selection mechanism in markets, which implies that economists "are often dealing not with a random set of people but with people who have been selected for the particular role they are playing" (Friedman 1990, 4–5). Irrational market participants who systematically make wrong decisions lose money and become increasingly unimportant in the market, while market participants who are consistently right have an increasing amount of money and influence on the market.

In other words, there is a self-regulatory mechanism built into markets that penalizes irrationality and promotes rationality. Thanks to this selection mechanism, the market outcome tends to be the same *as if* market participants behaved rationally; if they do not, they will be eventually drop out of the market (Alchian 1950; Friedman 1953).

Becker (1962) develops this argument and argues that negatively inclined market demand curves, which are the main implication of utility theory, do not depend on rational behavior, but on a general principle which includes a wide class of irrational behavior as well. Thus, he claims that "households can be said to behave not only 'as if' they were rational but also 'as if' they were irrational" (Becker 1962, 4). This general principle is that economic agents are subject to budget constraints and react to changes in the opportunity sets (through changes in incomes or relative prices). As a result, the market would act as if it was rational not only when households and firms were rational, but also when they were not explicitly adopting utility maximalization.

Last but not least, the focus on aggregate, systemic, or ecological rationality – and the associated assumption of ex post rationality on the part of market participants – is in line with the origin and nature of economics. After all, economics arose as a science mainly from amazement that people cooperate, that certain regularities occur in the economic sphere, that Paris gets fed (Bastiat [1850] 1996). The central question of economics is how social cooperation takes place among myriad self-interested strangers, or, put differently, how the invisible hand operates (Hayek 1937, 1945, 1955). Social cooperation is a fact, so the assumption that people tend to behave rationally is a reasonable one. By analogy, we know that traffic is generally smooth, so the assumption that drivers tend to drive rationally seems to be justifiable, even though some drivers

[35] According to McKenzie (2010, x), the existence of the embedded corrective feedback loops on decision-making in competitive markets is the reason why economists assume a level of rationality that is greater than the level that people manifest in socially unstructured settings of surveys or laboratory experiments.

drive carelessly or make mistakes and do not have an exact theory of driving (Machlup 1946).

## 6. CONCLUSIONS

Rationality can be understood in several ways. The most general notions presented in this chapter are as follows:

- Rationality as a description of the mental processes or reasoning of individuals.
- Rationality as a methodological tool, scientific principle, or framework for economical inquiry.
- Rationality as a metaphysical statement about human nature.
- Rationality as the empirical proposition that people *tend to* choose the suitable means to achieve their goals. The aggregate outcome is rational, and it is *as if* individuals behave rationally.

All notions of rationality are important, but the individual and metaphysical rationalities belong to the realms of psychology and philosophy, respectively, rather than economics. Methodological rationality provides an indispensable framework for economics as an scientific inquiry, while empirical rationality deals with the aggregate effects of individual's actions within the markets, which most economists focus on in their empirical research and predictions.

The problem with the debate about rationality in economics is that economists conflate these notions. In particular, behavioral economists oppose the concept of rationality, but they refer to rationality as a description of the behavior of individual agents, even though economists generally do not use rationality in this way.

The focus on individual rationality, although it could be interesting for psychologists, does not contribute too much to economics, as economics is interested in the effects of individuals' actions subject to budgetary constraints rather than how people reason. Explanations how people think in the laboratory cannot be easily extrapolated to their behavior, especially in a market environment. In other words, as Levitt and List (2008, 909) put it, "[T]here are many reasons to suspect that [...] laboratory findings might fail to generalize to real markets." And, as McChesney (2013, 76) summarizes behavioral economics, "to forsake analysis of markets in studying individuals' choices is to ignore the very essence of economics."

Thus, it seems that behavioral economists fit in a long tradition of criticizing economics without having a proper understanding of its methodology. They mistakenly believe that the rationality of the markets depends on the rationality of individuals, and oppose neoclassical economics as unrealistic, as they maintain that all assumptions should be descriptively realistic, which is a methodological flaw that conflates theoretical and empirical orders.[36]

Another conclusion is that – although they are some differences[37] – both the neoclassical school and the Austrian school generally accept the last three notions of rationality. In particular, they adhere to the rationality principle as an indispensable methodological tool in social science. This is because rationality of action is "at its most fundamental level, the logical structure of thought" (Rizzo 2015, 389). The rationality principle explains the success of economics as a science, because without it, economists would not, for example, be able to maintain that individuals react to incentives or, more generally, to understand people with (unobservable) values and beliefs different from their own. Adopting the rationality principle enables economists to preserve the principle of subjectivity of value while fulfilling the requirement of scientific objectivity (Rizzo 2015).

---

[36] Hence, the behavioral economists' critique resembles that of the Historical School. See Kirzner (1976, 15, emphasis in original), who writes, "According to the Historical School, economics seeks to describe the phenomena of the real, empirical economic world as it unfolds in its setting of time and space. According to the 'theoretical,' 'abstract' school of thought, on the other hand, the task of economics is not – or, rather, cannot be – to explain 'individual' (or particular) economic phenomena, but only to discover the regularities, the 'general' chains of cause and effect, that *underlie* the innumerably various forms that present themselves in economic history."

[37] Neoclassical economists are more interested in rationality as an empirical proposition, while Austrian economists write more explicitly about the metaphysical notion of rationality and focus more on methodological rationality, equating rationality with purposefulness. Another difference is that the Austrian school investigates theory of action rather than theory of decision and, together with the behavioral economists, criticizes neoclassical economics for some of its unrealistic assumptions. This is why they reject mathematical formalization and the view of rationality as logicality and as maximization (in the literal sense). The more thorough analysis of the concept of rationality within different economic schools goes beyond the scope of this book.

# 2. Should economics be more psychological?

## 1. INTRODUCTION

One of the most common criticisms of economists is that they do not give due consideration to the contributions of other social sciences in economic research. Indeed, economics is a relatively insular field with a significantly lower level of external citations (Fourcade et al. 2015; Truc et al. 2020; Cruz-e-Silva and Cavalieri 2022).

However, criticism of mainstream economics by behavioral economists goes further, as the latter claim that the *Homo economicus* (HE) model should be replaced by a new model of *Homo sapiens*—i.e., a more psychologically realistic depiction of human behavior that would take into account the bounded rationality, bounded willpower, and bounded self-interest of people (Jolls, Sunstein, and Thaler 1998; Mullainathan and Thaler 2000; Camerer and Loewenstein 2004; Ariely 2009; Thaler 2000; 2015, 2016). Rabin (2002, 658) argues in a similar manner: "economists should aspire to make our assumptions about humans as psychologically realistic as possible." In other words, behavioral economists believe that economists and psychologists use different models of human decision-making or study separate 'species,' and that one of them is clearly not descriptively realistic. This is what Kahneman (2011, 269) thinks:

> My economist colleagues worked in the building next door, but I had not appreciated the profound difference between our intellectual worlds. To a psychologist, it is self-evident that people are neither fully rational nor completely selfish, and that their tastes are anything but stable. Our two disciplines seemed to be studying different species, which the behavioral economist Richard Thaler later dubbed Econs and Humans.[1]

---

[1] See Thaler and Sunstein (2008, 6–7): "If you look at economics textbooks, you will learn that homo economicus can think like Albert Einstein, store as much memory as IBM's Big Blue, and exercise the willpower of Mahatma Gandhi. Really. But the folks that we know are not like that. Real people have trouble

In Chapter 1, I demonstrated that such claims are founded on a misconception according to which HE is a description of individual behavior, while it is an analytical device. I also showed that the notion of rationality used by behavioral economists to describe mental processes is different from the rationality principle used by mainstream economists as a methodological tool.

But one general question remains. Does economics abstract too much from psychology and, thus, should psychology play a more important role in economics? This has been suggested not only by behavioral economists and psychologists, but also occasionally by some mainstream economists, at least according to Thaler (2016, 1579), who cites Pareto (2014 [1906]) and John Maurice Clark (1918a, 1918b).[2] Answering this question is the purpose of this chapter.

In order to fulfill this aim, let us analyze some arguments for grounding economics more in psychology. For instance, Pareto (2014 [1906], 20), as cited by Thaler (2016, 1579), writes:

> The foundation of political economy and, in general, of every social science, is evidently psychology. A day may come when we shall be able to deduce the laws of social science from the principles of psychology.

---

with long division if they don't have a calculator, sometimes forget their spouse's birthday, and have a hangover on New Year's Day. They are not homo economicus; they are homo sapiens. To keep our Latin usage to a minimum we will hereafter refer to these imaginary and real species as Econs and Humans." See also Thaler (2015). Although this book is a pleasant read, Thaler (2015, ch. 1) describes Econs in a caricatured way, falling into a straw man fallacy. He writes, for example, "Econs would be perplexed by the entire idea of gifts" and "Econs do not have passions; they are cold-blooded optimizers. Think of Mr. Spock in *Star Trek*." Of course, the HE model does not preclude individuals from feeling emotions or having altruistic preferences (Becker 1976; Machlup 1978; Andreoni and Miller 2002). As Ross (2014, 202) points out, "There is no axiom in the formal theory of the economic agent, or in any standard formalization of game theory, that stipulates that agents are narrowly selfish in their concerns, let alone an axiom according to which people treat maximization of utility as equivalent to maximization of monetary gains." One might expect that social scientists had learned this lesson since Veblen's caricature of HE as a lightning calculator of pleasures and pains (Veblen 1898), but apparently not.

2 As one can see, attempts to improve theories of economics by adopting ideas from psychology were made long before the emergence of modern behavioral economics. Similarly, "the claim that economics is quite closely related to psychology is not new" (Rizzo, 2015, 364). Interestingly, Coats (1976, 57, emphasis in original) already almost fifty years ago noted, "[C]urrent complaints about the existing theory have an inescapable quality of *déjà vu* to those familiar with the literature reviewed." If this is the case, we are now experiencing the *déjà vu* of *déjà vu*.

However, it might be useful to cite the whole paragraph of Pareto (2014 [1906], 20), which Thaler (2016) unfortunately does not do:

> The foundation of political economy and, in general, of every social science, is evidently psychology. A day may come when we shall be able to deduce the laws of social science from the principles of psychology, in the same way that some day, perhaps, the principles of the constitution of matter will give us, by deduction, all the laws of physics and chemistry. But we are still very far from this state of affairs, and we must adopt another approach. We have to start from certain empirical principles to explain the phenomena of sociology, as well as those of physics and chemistry. At a later date, psychology, by extending the chain of its deductions, and sociology, by going back to principles that are more and more general, may combine and form a deductive science, but these hopes are still far from being realized.

As one can see, the whole paragraph is much less convincing than its beginning, in that Pareto thought psychology should play an important role in economics, as Thaler (2016) suggests. Rather, Pareto noted that if we know fully the principles of the constitution of mind, we should be able to deduce the laws of social science from the principles of psychology.[3] However, he also noticed that we were very far from such a situation, so we had to adopt another approach.[4] Thus, Pareto justifies why we need an approach other than deductions from the laws of psychology rather than expressing the need for a greater role of psychology in economics, as claimed by Thaler (2016). Given that the shift to displace psychological notions from economic theory is known in the literature as the 'Paretian turn' (Drakopoulos and Katselidis 2024), the choice of the person quoted is rather unfortunate.

Let us investigate now what Clark (1918a, 4) said:

> The only way in which the economist can keep his studies from duplicating the psychologist's work is by taking his psychology from those who have specialized in that field. To rely on the mere fact of choice, regardless of the kind of motives behind it, might seem to take economics out of all dependence on psychology, but it does not really do so, save at the cost of becoming utterly meaningless. The

---

[3] Neuroeconomics seems to have such an aim (Camerer et al. 2005). According to Graziano (2013, 40), there are some neuroeconomists who claim that "just the measurements of cerebral activity during decision-making allows us to verify economic notions." For a critique of such belief, see Gul and Pesendorfer (2008). For a reply, see Camerer (2008). For a more nuanced view of neuroeconomics, see Harrison and Ross (2010).

[4] Bruni and Sugden (2007, 154) cite Pareto's letter from 1897 to the philosopher Adrien Naville: "It is an empirical fact that the natural sciences have progressed only when they have taken secondary principles as their point of departure, instead of trying to discover the essence of things… Pure political economy has therefore a great interest in relying as little as possible on the domain of psychology."

> economist may attempt to ignore psychology, but it is a sheer impossibility for him to ignore human nature, for his science is a science of human behavior. Any conception of human nature that he may adopt is a matter of psychology, and any conception of human behavior that he may adopt involves psychological assumptions, whether these be explicit or no. If the economist borrows his conception of man from the psychologist, his constructive work may have some chance of remaining purely economic in character. But if he does not he will not thereby avoid psychology. Rather he will force himself to make his own, and it will be bad psychology.[5]

The main argument here is, thus, that economics is – just like psychology – a science of human behavior. The conclusion that follows is that economics uses a conception of human nature involving some psychological assumptions – the only question is whether it does explicitly and thoughtfully or implicitly and *ad hoc*. According to this view, economics is actually not insufficiently psychological, but is based on faulty, unrealistic psychology. Thus, the economists should find simply a sounder psychological basis, which would enable them to better understand human behavior.

Hence, the calls for grounding economics more in (proper) psychology are not new (Lewin 1996; Bondo and Presskorn-Thygesen 2022; Drakopoulos and Katselidis 2024). There was dissatisfaction with hedonistic preconceptions present in economic analysis in the late 19th and early 20th century.[6] However, mainstream economics not only departed from hedonism and utilitarianism (Bentham 1823 [1780]; Jennings 1855), but additionally it started to view its discipline as "science about the logic of means and ends rather than about the psychology of utility" (Langlois 1998, 56).[7] This shift is said

---

5 Cf. Camerer and Loewenstein (2004, 43, emphasis in original): "All economics rests on *some* sort of implicit psychology. The only question is whether the implicit psychology in economics is good psychology or bad psychology. We think it is simply unwise, and inefficient, to do economics without paying *some* attention to good psychology."

6 Mitchell (1914) provides not only an interesting survey of literature of his time about human behavior and economics, but also a final passage that is a good example of such views: "It was because hedonism offered a theory of how men act that it exercised so potent an influence upon economics. It is because they are developing a sounder type of functional psychology that we may hope both to profit by and to share in the work of contemporary psychologists. But in embracing this opportunity economics will assume a new character, it will cease to be a system of pecuniary logic, a mechanical study of static equilibria under non-existent conditions, and become a science of human behavior" (Mitchell 1914, 47).

7 Robbins (1932, 83–86) admits that some of the founders of subjective theory of value, such as Gossen, Jevons, and Edgeworth, invoked hedonistic postulates. However, he notes that these hedonistic preconceptions were never present in the Austrian economics. He also claims that these "hedonistic trimmings of the

to have been initiated by Pareto and completed by Slutsky, Hicks, Allen, and Samuelson (Giocoli 2003; Bruni and Sugden 2007; Muramatsu 2009; Hands 2010; Drakopoulos and Katselidis 2024).[8] According to Giocoli (2003), economists decided to escape from psychology in order to preserve an instrumental view of rationality and to base the discipline upon an observed behavior, which was considered a more solid empirical basis than psychological theories.[9]

Economics is also often criticized for being tautological and lacking any meaningful psychological content. This is how some researchers perceive the rationality principle, according to which people maximize their utility – i.e., they choose means to achieve their goals and they choose the means in such a way that it gives them the highest possible satisfaction. In light of this principle, economists can explain all possible actions simply by indicating that they had to provide the highest utility to the acting individual – otherwise he or she would not do it. If economists see, for example, that a lady drinks coffee, they can declare that she acts rationally, as she maximizes, determined by her individual scale of preferences, the subjective perceived utility. But if she instead drinks tea, or does not drink anything, it would be an equally rational act, as she still maximizes utility, according to her scale of preferences, which in this case is simply different. Hence, for economists, every action is a rational action – in a sense that people act the way they do, because they have some reason for it. The lady had some reason for choosing coffee over tea, even if it is unknown to external observers.[10]

A related argument is that such tautologies cannot be tested empirically. Economics is believed, thus, to be too deductive. As Clark (1918a, 5) notes,

---

works of Jevons and his followers were incidental to the main structure of a theory which—as the parallel development in Vienna showed—is capable of being set out and defended in absolutely non-hedonistic terms" (Robbins 1932, 86; see also Mises 1998 [1949], ch. I). In this way, he attacks the critics of economics who do not see beyond the façade. This critique may be applied to the authors who make claims that economics should be more psychological based on the allegation that psychological concepts, like these hedonistic preconceptions, were present in economics since its beginnings and were removed only by some neoclassical economists (Crespo 2017; Drakopoulos and Katselidis 2024).

8 See, e.g., Pareto (2014 [1906]); Slutsky (1915); Hicks (1946), Hicks and Allen (1934), Samuelson (1938, 1948).

9 Hands (2010) argues that the escape from psychology was not successful. However, he seems not to understand that the fact economics examines the realm of subjective meaning does not mean it involves mental-state psychology (Hayek 1948b, 2017 [1952]; Bylund 2023).

10 In Fisher's words: "Each individual acts as he desires" (Fisher 1926, 11).

> A hypothesis capable of fitting any state of facts is one on which no predictions can be based. It is as true and means as much as the statement that white is white. Of this sort is the assumption that men seek their interests in purchases for consumption. Lacking further information, one would be utterly at a loss to devise means of putting this statement to the test, especially when told that the consumer's purchase is itself the evidence from which to infer what his interest is, and that men's interests are continually changing.

This inability of many researchers to understand that some unfalsifiable assumptions are necessary in any science (Hodgson 2012, fn. 14) and how economics can yield substantive truths by means of logical deduction, led to the idea that economics either should be grounded more in psychology, or it should become a science of observed behavior, without any reference to subjective categories (Rothbard 1956). Such views can be called *psychologism*[11] and *behaviorism*, respectively. It seems that behavioral economics combines these two strands, as it wants to make economic research more based in psychology, while adopting experimental methodology similar to that of behaviorism.

In particular, economics is criticized for not taking into account the psychological factors believed to be non-rational aspects of behavior, such as emotions or customs. For example, Smith (1999, 203) writes:

> People like to believe that good decision-making is a consequence of the use of reason, and that any influence that the emotions might have is antithetical to good decisions. What is not appreciated by Mises and others who similarly rely on the primacy of reason in the theory of choice is the constructive role that the emotions play in human action.

But no Austrians nor mainstream economists believe that emotions do not play a role in human action. The maximization framework does not preclude emotions (or customs), it only asserts that people behave purposefully, because we can study economics only within such a framework. As Schuetz (1943, 148) puts it "[O]nly action within the framework of rational categories can be scientifically discussed." The rationality principle is a *methodological* statement, not a claim about decision-making *in reality*. Hence, economists do not argue with the psychological or neurobiological findings about the importance of emotions in decision-making (Damásio 1994). Thus, the behavioral

---

11 See Schumpeter (2006 [1954], 25): "As regards psychology, there is the view that came first to the fore in the eighteenth century, and hence has been sponsored intermittently, that economics like other social sciences deals with human behavior. Psychology is really the basis from which any social science must start and in terms of which all fundamental explanation must run. This view, which has been defended as strongly as it has been attacked, we shall denote by the term Psychologism."

economists conflate the level of real life with the level of scientific inquiry about it.

In other words, for economists, the starting point of analysis is simply human action, and they are interested in explaining its consequences. The psychological causes of human actions – whatever they are and however motivated – are simply irrelevant for economic analyses. Thus, it is not true that economists *omit* certain motives of behavior – they *abstract* from all motives, either reasonable or not (Lachmann 1977). For example, the fact that men occasionally buy flowers for women can be determined by custom (or passion) and can be seen as irrational in a certain sense (flowers are so impractical!), but it certainly has an economic effect, affecting the market for flowers.[12]

To sum up this part, the orthodox economics, with its core model of HE, has been the object of critique for either bad psychology or abstracting too much from psychology for a long time. As Coats (1976, 48) notes,

> When the defenders denied – as most did – that marginal utility presupposed hedonism, the critics merely shifted their ground and attacked the 'hard core' of economic theory, in particular the conception of the 'economic man'. Economic theory, it was said, assumed that the individual consumer possessed a stable and consistent scale of preferences, and was able and willing to make the requisite rational calculations of satisfactions depicted in the marginalists' conception of equilibrium – that he possessed, in J. M. Clark's words, an 'irrationally rational passion for dispassionate calculation'. These assumptions were flatly in conflict with the findings of recent psychological research, which demonstrated that human behaviour was seldom rational, and often impulsive, instinctive, inconsistent, and in other respects unstable.

However, the HE model, or the rationality principle, is not psychological, but formal, methodological device. Thus, it cannot be a bad psychology, because it is not a psychological model at all. It is true that it abstracts from psychology, but methodological (and metaphysical) assertions are devoid of any empirical content, psychological or any other. According to Latsis (1976, 12), economists (who are methodological conventionalists) adopt the psychologically anonymous ideal type – i.e., a theoretical construct that concentrates on an individual with a minimal internal structure and characteristics, and in 'single-exit' situations, which do not commit the economists to any particular psychology of the individual.

Let us now investigate the differences between psychology and economics in order to provide a thoughtful answer to the question as to whether economics should be more psychological.

---

12 And, by the way, such a gift can be a perfectly rational course of action, from the perspective of a man who aims to use flowers to win a woman's heart.

## 2. DIFFERENCES BETWEEN PSYCHOLOGY AND ECONOMICS

What are psychology and economics? Let us start with the former. It is not easy to define psychology precisely, as it can be argued that it is a collection of several sub-disciplines rather than a unified discipline (Henriques 2004). However, the most established definition asserts that psychology is a science of the mind and behavior (American Psychological Association 2016; Pérez-Álvarez 2018). Its goal is to explain how the mind works and how different mental processes translate into various behaviors.

And what is economics? Although economics also has some sub-disciplines, it seems to be a more unified discipline than psychology, with a well-established definition. Since Robbins (1932, 15), economics has been widely defined as, "[T]he science which studies human behaviour as a relationship between ends and scarce means which have alternative uses."

What are, thus, the differences between psychology and economics, if these disciplines allegedly investigate the same matter—i.e., human behavior? Well, one might say, especially in light of Robbins' definition of economics, that economics studies behavior, but in a very specific context of economizing. When there is no choice – i.e., when people do not have to allocate scarce resources between alternative ends – there are no economic problems. However, such a situation can occur only in the Land of Cockaigne (Mises 1998 [1949], 525), so the context of economizing is actually quite large in the real world – although the scope of human choices and actions is necessarily narrower than human behavior, which also includes, on the one hand, reflexes, emotional responses, etc., and, on the other hand, determining the ultimate goals. As Ross (2014, 249, fn. 12, emphasis in original) puts it, "[P]sychologists study many phenomena that are not choice phenomena. Economists study *only* choice phenomena."

Although both economics and psychology seem to investigate human behavior, they ask different questions. As Lachmann (1977, 174) puts it, "It is not the nature of our empirical material, but the nature of the questions we ask of our material, that determines the boundaries between sciences." What distinguishes psychology and economics is that the former tries to explain internal events that can result in particular action, while the latter deals with action as such (Mises 1998 [1949]). This means that, while psychologists want to explain *why* people choose certain ends, economists treat goals simply as *given*, and study only the *implications* of human actions. In Schuetz's terminology, psychology deals with how and why people come to have particular *because-motives*, while economics is about how people act to achieve their *in-order-to-motives* (Kurrild-Klitgaard, 2001, 132). Or, as Lachmann (1977, 168) puts it, "[T]he economic consequences (implications, if you like) of the choice once it is made, not the psychological causes, belong to the province of Economics."

In other words, economics analyzes actions, and abstracts from the motives behind them (Fisher 1926). It pays attention only to what people do, without speculating about what is happening inside agents' heads. It concerns itself not with the inner, mental states, but with the external conduct to the external conditions of existence, with the use of the categories of ends and means (Binmore 2009; Weber 2012 [1908]).

Hence, economics is *contentless* – i.e., it is a science that deals with the *formal* implications of the fact that people have some goals and use certain means to achieve these goals, while psychology studies the *content* of people's actions. Thus, the economists do not need to account for the origin of wants, as they are interested only in the facts of choice, and their business "is to study the means of satisfying them, and the conditions under which they may be satisfied" (Dickinson 1919, 378). Or, as Rothbard (2009, 73, emphasis in original) puts it,

> Since all these disciplines deal with the subjective decisions of individual human minds, many observers have believed that they are fundamentally identical. This is not the case at all. Psychology and ethics deal with the content of human ends; they ask, *why* does the man choose such and such ends, or *what* ends *should* men value? Praxeology and economics deal with *any* given ends and with the formal implications of the fact that men have ends and employ means to attain them. Praxeology and economics are therefore disciplines separate and distinct from the others.

For example, people smoke cigarettes although they know that these are unhealthy. Psychologists try to understand why people engage in such an activity (e.g., they claim that smoking is primarily a manifestation of nicotine addiction) (Jarvis 2004), but for economists the reasons behind smoking are irrelevant. They simply notice that there is a demand for cigarettes – so people, for whatever reasons, want to smoke them – and analyze it, together with the supply side of this market, and how it affects the prices of cigarettes.

The contentless character of economic theory makes it similar to grammar. As Li (2020, 63) puts it, the rationality principle "establishes a universal but contentless grammatical rule for economists to represent human behaviour in a structured way, often called as 'the economic way of thinking.'" However, just as we can fill the grammatical structure with sentences about the actual world (e.g., Bob likes dogs) that can be true or not, we can fill the means–ends structure with some empirical content that can be true or not (e.g., people achieve utility only from selfish actions) (Brennan 2007; Li 2020).

Hence, one can argue that economics and psychology not only ask different research questions; they also give different answers or adopt distinct perspectives on ways of thinking. According to Stigler and Becker (1977, 76), psychologists study and explain people's tastes and could be satisfied with change in tastes as an explanation of some changes in behavior, while economists continue "to search for differences in prices or incomes to explain any differences or changes in behavior."

And, as Becker (1976, 5) puts it, "I believe that what most distinguishes economics as a discipline from other disciplines in the social sciences is not its subject matter but its approach." Indeed, economics studies human behavior under the means–ends framework or in light of the rationality principle (Popper 1985). Thus, the contemporary HE model, so widely criticized by the behavioral economists, is not a psychological description of entities studied by economists, but a methodological device (Kirchgässner 2013). Hence, it is incorrect to claim that economists and psychologists study separate species. They try to understand the same species, while using distinct perspectives (McKenzie and Tullock 2012). The difference is that economists look at the people and their actions through rational-tinted glasses.

Another important difference between economics and psychology lies in the approach to the existence of the mind, to human agency, and to the issue of subjective and objective phenomena. For some psychologists, mind either does not exist, or – if it does – it is only a socially sculpted virtual structure, or an information-processing system, as the brain (Ross 2023). For others, what really matters are only mental states and subjective variables, such as happiness (albeit they are often assumed to be objectively measurable). On the one hand, in some psychological perspectives, people are seen as non-unitary beings with inconsistent goals and preferences, driven by competing brain processes or 'selves' (Saint-Paul 2011).

On the other hand, economists do not study merely behavior, but action – i.e., a purposeful behavior. Human beings are, thus, not treated as driven by instincts or stimuli, but as unitary beings who have unique utility functions and act with their own interests (Saint-Paul 2011), or as conscious beings who have free will and use reason in life in employing certain means to achieve chosen goals in order to improve their situation, in contrast to being merely guided by impulses like animals (Knight 1969; Mises (2007 [1957]; Rothbard 2011).[13]

13 Gul and Pesendorfer (2008, 21) seem to disagree: "standard economics takes no position on whether a particular decision represents a manifestation of free will or a succumbing to biological necessity. Rationality in economics is not tied to physiological causes of behavior, and therefore, the physiological mechanisms cannot shed light on whether a choice is rational or not in the sense economists use the term." However, they later admit that economists decided "to view the individual as the unit of agency and investigate the interaction of the purposeful

What is important here is that economics is neither purely subjective, nor purely behavioristic. It is objective science of subjective value (Bylund 2023). Economics studies phenomena that are mind dependent,[14] or the realm of subjective meaning (O'Driscoll and Rizzo 1996; Rizzo 2015), but are interested in objective variables such as incomes, prices, etc.[15] The key element here is action, through which people's subjective valuations "are mapped onto objective reality" (Bylund 2023). This is why economists study revealed preferences – i.e., subjective valuation but revealed through actions in objective reality. In this way, they avoid the pitfalls of both psychologism and behaviorism that I mentioned in the previous section.

Economists focus on purposeful behavior for methodological reasons, as without purposes there would be no problem of allocation means towards goals, and no problem of scarcity. In other words, if people cease to be rational – i.e., surrender to the blind force of external stimuli and uncoordinated impulses – "the *raison d'être* of Economics disappears" (Robbins 1932, 141).

An important implication is a different approach to environmental factors. Some psychologists would consider these as *determinants* of human behavior. However, the economists view "factors such as the immediate environment as *constraints* within which the individual's preferences can operate" (McKenzie and Tullock, 2012, 8, emphasis added).

Another reason behind economists' focus on purposeful behavior is the fact that the social world examined by economists is a structured world of purposes and actions.[16] This is how individuals interpret the world in which they act. As Natanson (1962, xxxv, emphasis in original) puts it (describing Schultz's ideas),

> Men in their daily life interpret their world from the outset as a meaningful one[. T]he acts of other beings] are similarly treated as the conduct of a purposeful creature. Motives and goals are as inescapably part of the other's behavior as they are of our own. When I encounter a man acting in the world, I know I must understand him as a human being, and this means that his actions mean something to him as

---

behaviors of different individuals within various economic institutions" (Gul and Pesendorfer 2008, 34).

14 For instance, money is not just a physical object; it is a mental construction (a physical object is money only if it is perceived as a common medium of exchange) that would not exist without human minds (O'Driscoll and Rizzo 1996; Rizzo 2015).

15 This is why, as I write in the conclusion to this chapter, Gul and Pesendorfer (2008) argue for mindless economics.

16 Why this is the case, is another question. One possible answer is that mind is a meaning-making 'mechanism,' which classifies all external stimuli in some meaningful patterns (Hayek 2017 [1952]).

> well as to me […]. But this knowledge is itself taken for granted by me as well as by him; its being taken for granted by *us* is precisely the typification which makes intersubjectivity possible.

Hence, economics is a teleological science, while psychology (or at least some of its fields) is relatively more behavioristic, and closer to natural sciences (Stangor 2010).[17] This is because psychology tries to explain human behavior by referring to mental processes—and, perhaps ultimately, by the activity of the brain (Barrett 2009)—while economics treats the causes of human action as given or irrelevant. Thus, economists cut off causal reasoning on the very fact of human actions, treating them as not caused by anything but each individual's goal-orientated free will.

Last but not least, although economics and psychology allegedly investigate the same matter—i.e., human behavior—they focus not only on distinct *kinds* of behavior, but also on different *variables* that influence behavior. Economics is not interested in psychological (or physiological) data about the individual's decision-making process, but in market variables such as prices, quantities, etc. After all, "[E]conomic models are evaluated by their success at explaining economic phenomena" (Gul and Pesendorfer 2008, 33). And, as Coyle (2018, 2) notes, "[T]he market outcome is the result of changes in the opportunity set and relative prices. The individual cognitive process is not relevant."[18] In other words, what really matters is not how people behave, or what decision rule they use, but the fact that people's opportunities are restricted to budgetary constraints. As Becker (1962) shows, "not only utility maximization but also many other decision rules, incorporating a wide variety or irrational behavior[s], lead to negatively inclined demand curves because of the effect of a change in prices on opportunities." This is because the decisions of irrational households and firms, just as of rational agents, are limited by budgetary constraints, and, in consequence, they would be also, in a sense, "'forced' by a change in opportunities to respond rationally" (Becker 1962, 12).

Economists' focus on market variables results not only from their interest in aggregated market results, but also from the nature of psychological and economic data. The data about how people think or feel are not easily

---

[17] As Barrett (2009, 326) writes, "[F]rom its inception in the early 18th century (as an amalgam of philosophy, neurology, and physiology), psychology has always been in a bit of an identity crisis, trying to be both a social and a natural science."

[18] Coyle (2018, 2) points out some biological experiments (e.g., Herbranson and Schroeder 2010), in which many types of entities other than humans, including fungi and bacteria with no neurons and cognitive capacities, seem to act in line with the HE model. These results suggest that not cognitive processes but rather the context of resource scarcity is responsible for optimizing behavior.

applied to economics. The psychological variables, which may be observable in experimental settings, are often unobservable in economic (field) data. As Pesendorfer (2006, 713–714) points out, "[A] prominent example of this is the reference point in prospect theory. The reference point can be manipulated in experimental settings but is essentially unobservable outside the laboratory. This makes it difficult to adapt prospect theory to economic contexts." Meanwhile, economic data is such that economists focus on revealed preferences. As Gul and Pesendorfer (2008, 8) explain:

> Economic data can—at best—reveal what the agent wants (or has chosen) in a particular situation. Such data do not enable the economist to distinguish between what the agent intended to choose and what she ended up choosing; what she chose and what she ought to have chosen. The standard approach provides no methods for utilizing nonchoice data to calibrate preference parameters. The individual's coefficient of risk aversion, for example, cannot be identified through a physiological examination; it can only be revealed through choice behavior. If an economist proposes a new theory based on nonchoice evidence, then either the new theory leads to novel behavioral predictions, in which case it can be tested with revealed preference evidence, or it does not, in which case the modification is vacuous. In standard economics, the testable implications of a theory are its content; once they are identified, the nonchoice evidence that motivated a novel theory becomes irrelevant.

To sum up, according to Gul and Pesendorfer (2008), economics and psychology answer distinct questions, adopt unlike abstractions (or perspectives), have different objectives, and also address various types of empirical evidence. Economists and psychologists also differ in their perspectives on human dysfunction. As Levine (2012, 125), puts it, "[M]uch of the goal of psychology [...] is to help people become more functional. However, most people are quite functional most of the time." Hence, economists are not therapists and they focus more on the marvel of social cooperation that is constantly occurring in the marketplace (Bastiat 1996 [1850]; Smith 2008 [1776]; Hayek 1945).

## 3. WHY ECONOMICS SHOULD NOT BECOME MORE PSYCHOLOGICAL

Now we are ready to answer the title question of this chapter. Of course, all definitions are, in a sense, arbitrary. Hence, we could define economics, or psychology, in such a way that both sciences would be more integrated with each other. However, there are strong arguments for the two fields of social science to remain separate and for economics not to become more psychological.

First—to reiterate the previous section—while psychology investigate the content of people's action, i.e., the motivations behind the choices, economics studies only the formal implications of the fact that people act, so it is contentless. And it is not interested in why people have particular preferences, as it treats these as given, focusing rather on the consequences of actions. The problem here is that theories of psychology or behavioral economics, which focus on biases or motives, "are difficult to connect to economic data because their main insights are about psychological variables, that is, how the person thinks (i.e., deals with biases) and feels" (Pesendorfer 2006, 714).

Second, thanks to its formal nature, economics can formulate *general* theories that accommodate the infinite diversity within the human race. This is exactly because economics *abstracts* from psychological factors. As Machlup (1936, 45) notes, "the statements of 'pure economic theory' are the statements which assume the most general and anonymous types of behaviour. They allow us, therefore, to proceed in the economic analysis without restating and reiterating the assumptions again and again."

This way, economists explain human action *regardless* of people's motivations—by making economics more psychological, one would reduce the generality of its models, which are formalisms for eliminating all irrelevant details of the context (Gintis 2004; Gul and Pesendorfer 2008; Rizzo 2017; Shostak 2022). This is because psychological theories (or propensities) are context dependent and, thus, are not particularly subject to generalization.[19] Meanwhile, economic phenomena—such as economic growth, inflation, business cycles, etc.—are the effects of actions of many individuals. Hence, as Rizzo (2015, 372) puts it,

> Economics strives for a fairly high degree of generality. We do not wish to develop a separate theory for every concrete action. Therefore, we abstract from much detail about how real-world agents actually behave. We focus on those motivations and beliefs that are relevant to explaining the particular actions under investigation.

Third, economics is more interested in studying the *effects* of human actions rather than their *motives*, and on *aggregate* outcomes rather than *individual* behavior. Economists focus on the behavior of markets, not individuals, as they are interested in directional changes on the margin in response to changes in the environment, rather than how particular individuals react (Friedman 1990; McKenzie and Tullock 2012; McChesney 2013). As Ross (2014, 249) puts it, "[I]f one wants to learn about human behavioral variation at the scale of individual idiosyncrasy, psychology is the discipline to consult. If one wants to learn about the structures of markets under different conditions, one should turn to economics."

---

[19] Cf. Pesendorfer (2006, 720): "Behavioral economics emphasizes the context-dependence of decision making. A corollary of this observation is that it is difficult to extrapolate from experimental settings to field data or, more generally, economic settings." I write more on this topic in sub-section 2.3 of Chapter 3.

In other words, economics can be seen as a science of spontaneous order. As such, it wants to explain not the conscious actions of individuals, but the undesigned results of groups of people interacting (Levine 2012, 125). One of the reasons for this approach is precisely the fact that most of the phenomena investigated by economists are the results of human action, but not of human design (Hayek 1967). Thus, we can say that, while psychologists focus on the issue how men really behave, economists are more interested in the question as to how the markets select and coordinate human actions (Carver 1918).[20] Please note that even if we have the perfect explanation of individual behavior, it would not be enough to explain the functioning of the groups or markets due to the interactions between individuals; simple extrapolation would easily result in a fallacy of composition (Levine, 2012, 127).[21]

One can even claim that, if all social phenomena were simply the intended results of individual actions, perhaps all social sciences could be reduced or based in psychology. As Hayek (1955, 39) puts it,

> It is a mistake, to which careless expressions by social scientists often give countenance, to believe that their aim is to explain conscious action. This, if it can be done at all, is a different task, the task of psychology. For the social sciences the types of conscious action are data and all they have to do with regard to these data is to arrange them in such orderly fashion that they can be effectively used for their task. The problems which they try to answer arise only in so far as the conscious actions of many men produce undesigned results, in so far as regularities are observed which are not the result of anybody's design. If social phenomena showed no order except in so far as they were consciously designed, there would indeed be no room for theoretical sciences of society and there would be, as is often argued, only problems of psychology. It is only in so far as some sort of order arises as a result of

---

20 See also Hands (2015, 4–5, emphasis in original): "It should be noted that much of economics, even standard microeconomics, goes beyond RCT [rational choice theory]. The characterization of *individual economic agents* is in terms of RCT, but most of the things that economists want to explain – like market prices – are not the result of the actions of a single economic agent; they are the result of the *interactions* of a number of rational agents interacting within the context of a specific institutional structure and subject to various social-level constraints. For example, the key economic concept of Adam Smith's invisible hand involves a social result – an increase in the wealth of nations, or the efficient allocation of scarce resources – that was not a goal of any individual agent. Economic explanations almost always involve RCT, but only in the first (individual action) part of the explanation; the heavy explanatory lifting is often done by the relevant institutions/rules for interaction of the individual agents and the particular solution (some version of an equilibrium) that is imposed on, or emerges from, that interaction."

21 For example, Hwang and Bowles (2012) show that too high a level of altruism among individuals can reduce the level of cooperation.

> individual action but without being designed by any individual that a problem is raised which demands a theoretical explanation.

In other words, the idea that economics is, just as psychology, the science of human behavior, ignores the emergence—i.e., the fact that the individual actions coordinated through the markets lead to the social order that no one chose and that cannot be reduced simply to the sum of individual actions. As Hudík (2011, 150) puts it, "It is precisely for this reason that psychology is irrelevant to social theory – explaining why someone chose to do what he did is of no help in explaining a phenomenon that no one chose." Thus, economics is not the science of human behavior, but of coordination or lack of coordination of individual behaviors between many people (O'Driscoll 1977). Popper (1964, 158) provides a nice example of differences between psychological and coordination issues that are at the core of economics: "[A]lthough some people may claim that a liking for mountains and solitude may be explained psychologically, the fact that, if too many people like the mountains, they cannot enjoy solitude there, is not a psychological fact; but this kind of problem is at the very root of social theory."

The fact that psychology focuses on the situational factors makes it inherently a partial equilibrium science and implies that it will always need economics—which is about general equilibrium—to provide a framework for understanding the supply of framing, influence, and situation, and to explain aggregate outcomes, i.e., patterns of behavior over time and space (Glaeser 2004). As Glaeser (2003, 10) puts it,

> One way to think about this seeming paradox—that it is through psychology's insistence on the primacy of social influence that economics' influence is assured—is that the great achievement of economics is understanding aggregation. Our discipline has always been about the wealth of nations, not individuals, and as psychologists are the first to emphasize, aggregates do not merely sum up individuals.

Fourth, it is not the case that economic perspective without more generous use of psychology is not complete (or vice versa). After all, no psychological insight refutes the core principles of economics that people respond to incentives and that returns tend to be equalized across activities (Glaeser 2004). Rather, both economics and psychology offer distinct, complementary views and explain different levels of reality. Hence, even if economists have perfect knowledge about the psychological motivations of people in a given society, they would still select some of them—as well as some important non-psychological factors affecting people's preferences and actions—to understand the effects of interactions between individuals that product particular economic phenomena, and to construct a proper theoretical explanation (Shearmur 1992).

To illustrate this point, let us ask a simple question: why did John eat his dinner? John himself would be surprised by such an inquiry, as, for him, the reason was simple: he was hungry. This is also the answer that probably most psychologists would give, although some of them might say that in this way he wanted to cope with negative emotions or to improve his mood. The evolutionary biologists, however, would say that John ate his dinner to sustain his body in order to be able to pass on his genes in the future. This is true, even if John certainly does not think about reproduction and his evolutionary success while eating. Similarly, economists could say that John ate his dinner simply because it was a means to satisfy his goal that offered him higher utility than any alternatives. Of course, John is not thinking in these terms when deciding about eating his dinner.

However, although from the individual perspective the case is simple—John eats dinner because of hunger (or some other motives interesting for psychologists)—it does not mean that the answers given by evolutionary biology or economics are wrong. The fact that individuals do not think in terms of reproductive success or utility, does not invalidate evolutionary biology or economics. These disciplines just offer different, complementary perspectives, which are simply much more interested in *ultimate* rather than *proximate* motives, or in how individual actions create more complex structures (Binmore 2009).

Please also note that, while psychologists are interested in explaining the direct motives behind people's actions, for evolutionary biologists or economists, the maximization of reproductive success or utility is not the realistic description of human behavior, but rather an assumption *as if*—for them, the end result (ecological or economic equilibrium) is *as if* individuals intentionally maximize chances of survival and reproduction or utility. As Binmore (2009, 12–13, emphases in original) puts it,

> Since a gene is just a molecule, it can't *choose* to maximize its fitness, but evolution makes it seem as though it had. This is a valuable insight, because it allows biologists to use rationality considerations to predict the outcome of an evolutionary process, without needing to follow each complicated twist and turn that the process might take. When appealing to rationality in such an evolutionary context, we say that we are seeking an explanation in terms of *ultimate* causes rather than *proximate* causes. Why, for example, do songbirds sing in the early spring? The proximate cause is long and difficult. This molecule knocked against that molecule. This chemical reaction is catalyzed by that enzyme. But the ultimate cause is that the birds are signalling territorial claims to each other in order to avoid unnecessary conflict. They neither know nor care that this behavior is rational. They just do what they do. But the net effect of an immensely complicated evolutionary process is that songbirds behave *as though* they had rationally chosen to maximize their fitness.[22]

[22] Similarly, drivers or billiard players do not need to be well versed in physics to overtake other cars or to make good shots. Nor do economic agents need

It should be clear now that neither the evolutionary principle nor the rationality principle has ever been constructed as a psychologically faithful description of human decision-making; these principles are the scientific tools used to organize thinking, namely methodological devices. Hence, the content of human thoughts (or decisions and actions in real life) and the content of scientific thoughts about human thoughts (or decisions and actions in real life) are different levels of reality, which should not be conflated.

## 4. WHAT ARE THE REASONS BEHIND THE CALLS TO MAKE ECONOMICS MORE PSYCHOLOGICAL?

The criticism of economics as not being psychological enough or psychologically accurate stems from several reasons. The major one seems to be lack of understanding with regard to the methodological differences between psychology and economics, and the nature of the latter. This confusion can be easier to grasp if we remember that economics is a relatively young discipline that managed to escape from psychology (Giocoli 2003)—i.e., to free the discipline from any mental variables or psychic concepts such as pleasure, pain, motivations, etc.—only relatively recently, i.e., in the first half of the 20th century, and has been criticized from its very beginning.

An important point here is that economics is, to a large extent, a logical rather than an empirical science (Giocoli 2003),[23] which perhaps explains why behavioral economists and psychologists—who have a more positivist and empirical approach—face challenges in grasping the methodology of economics. They do not understand properly the scientific role of metaphysical assertions or *a priori* knowledge, and that there can be laws of human behavior independent of people's psychological disposition (or any empirical content) (Mises 1998 [1949], ch. II; Herfeld 2021).

In other words, economics could become emancipated as a separate, value-free discipline of scientific thought only through abstracting from ethical, religious, philosophical, political, or psychological considerations. Thus, the lack

---

to use marginal analysis to act in the marketplace. They all just do what they do. However, we can formulate physical theories of overtaking and of playing billiards, or economic theories of consumer and firm behavior, in which the economic agents behave *as if* they know theoretical explanations (Machlup 1946; Friedman 1953).

[23] Giocoli (2003) writes in such a way about neoclassical economics. But given its prominence, my generalization concerning economics probably would not be an exaggeration, especially that it covers, then, the Austrian praxeological approach.

of psychological foundations is not a fatal defect of economics, as described by its critics, but is actually its great achievement. After all,

> the whole point of the homo economicus model is not to provide a theory of true behavior, but to sidestep the need for one. Analyzing action in terms of the true cognitive processes rather than the abstract model of homo economicus is naïve, as various mental procedures, judgments, and heuristics are very situation-specific and can hardly be expressed in general terms, which is what theory, in contrast to mere description, requires. (Sieroń 2020, 340)

People who criticize economics for abstracting from psychology also do not understand that the rationality principle provides a universal grammar of economic explanations—since then it would be obvious that the critique is misguided. After all, no one attacks grammar (or logic) for abstracting from psychological content.

Behavioral economists seem to believe that we need to understand human nature to conduct proper economic research and study economic systems. This view can be called methodological psychologism, which probably results from thinking about economics and psychology in very broad terms, i.e., as disciplines that have the same goal – to explain human behavior (Gul and Pesendorfer 2008)—and from "the false belief that [it] is a necessary corollary of a methodological individualism" (Popper 1964, 157). However, economists can be methodological individualists, i.e., in trying to understand collective phenomena as a result of actions of individuals, without accepting methodological psychologism and understanding the psychological reasons behind each individual action.

The calls for grounding economics more into psychology stems also from the fact that, for some social scientists, the economic point of view is too limited, almost esthetically repelling. It overlooks the social context and does not take into account emotions, culture, institutions, norms, etc. (e.g., Polanyi 1944; Skidelsky 2020). Hence, these social scientists believe that economics should draw from other fields, such as anthropology, sociology, political science, and, of course, psychology—because only then would it be possible to paint descriptively accurate picture of human nature (Crespo 2017).[24] They seem to complain about economics because it is just economics and does not take into account all the richness of human life in society; and also because it is, well, economics, and not another social science, which investigates more interesting things than money, financial system, fiscal deficits, etc.[25]

---

24 Colander (2014) calls for more pluralism not merely in economics but in all social sciences, through blending them together.

25 Davis (2018) goes further and argues that psychology's successful reception in economics, at least in the emergence of behavioral economics, stems from the

What is more, some behavioral economists seem to not fully understand the issues of subjectivity and utility in economics. If they have, they would not have been surprised that people can treat physically the same good differently, depending on the intended use of this good—i.e., use *mental accounting* (Thaler 1985). People can mentally attach different values not only to homogenous units of money, but to homogenous units of any good, as this is what the subjective theory of value and the law of diminishing marginal utility are all about (Böhm-Bawerk 1930; Mises 1998 [1949]; Rothbard 2009).

Consistent adherence to the subjective theory of value can also explain the *framing effect* (Tversky and Kahneman 1981). According to the behavioral economists, making different choices depending on how the problem was framed constitutes a cognitive bias, as people should be invariant to equivalent descriptions of alternatives. However, the ultimate objects of choice are *not* certain physical objects that are independent of the description, but *objects that are subjectively perceived by the agents*. It is not the case that people already know in advance what they truly desire, what are their 'true' preferences—e.g., that they would rather have surgery than not have it—so any description of the problem choice is irrelevant. The key matter is that the alternatives must be somehow presented and apprehended by the people. As Rizzo and Whitman notice (2020, loc. 2033), "[T]here is no rigorous meaning to 'options independent of their description.' Options are only perceived as such through their descriptions." Descriptions can be considered equivalent by researchers, but—in line with the subjectivism—what are the relevant characteristics of a good are those the individuals perceive as such. Hence, people can consider information about the risks of surgery in terms of survival and mortality rates differently, despite their mathematical equivalence.[26]

Behavioral economists would not be surprised either that individuals can value more goods that they own, relative to the goods that they do not own. When a person owns a coffee mug, it is already satisfying some of her wants,

---

fact that both these social sciences make a conception of freedom central to their explanations of behavior, and that behavioral economics offers an understanding of freedom that can be seen as both descriptively and normatively superior.

[26] Levine (2012, 80) also believes that framing effects is not strange at all: "Framing refers to the fact that the answer to a question often depends on the way the question is framed. As I pointed out above 2.2 times 75 is a more difficult question than what is 2 times 75 plus 10 percent although they are in fact the same question. By the same token, if I ask you whether you would prefer to vote for the candidate who dropped out of Harvard or the one who founded Microsoft, you will probably choose the latter, even though both are Bill Gates. Put this way, framing is hardly controversial."

even if it is only the want of having a coffee mug.[27] Thus, a coffee mug a person owns is more valuable than a coffee mug she does not own; or, in other words, the additional utility of the second unit of a good is lower than that of the first unit of a good. Hence, the fact that subjects in the experiments are eager to sell mugs at higher prices than they would be willing to pay for them does not necessarily indicate a mysterious *endowment effect* (Kahneman et al. 1990)—it is rather the law of diminishing marginal utility in play (Bylund 2011).[28]

To generalize, the phenomenon that behavioral economists call *loss aversion* (Kahneman and Tversky 1979) does not represent a great mystery for the adherents of the subjective theory of value. As I mentioned above, it should be clear that the value of a unit of good that the person already has and that satisfies some of her wants is necessarily higher than the value of an additional unit of this good, as it would be able to satisfy only less urgent wants. Thus, losing the unit of the good she already owns would reduce the value by more than the gain of the additional unit of the good (Böhm-Bawerk 1930; Mises 1998 [1949]; Rothbard 2009). Hence, the fact that losses weigh more than gains in terms of utility is something one can easily deduce from the law of diminishing marginal unity—introducing extra psychological concepts is not necessary here.[29]

Last but not least, many researches erroneously treat utility, value, or preference scales as if they existed separately from real action. It is often said that, for example, John drank tea, because he preferred this action to drinking coffee, or because the utility of drinking tea was greater than drinking coffee, or because drinking tea was the highest on John's scale of preferences. However, such an interpretation constitutes something that Binmore (2009, 19, emphasis in original) calls 'causal utility fallacy':

> In revealed-preference theory, it isn't true that Pandora chooses *b* rather than *a* *because* the utility of *b* exceeds the utility of *a*. This is the Causal Utility Fallacy. It isn't even true that Pandora chooses *b* rather than *a* because she prefers *b* to *a*. On

---

27 Please also note that owning a mug allows the person to use it in the future to fulfill some of her needs, even if she does not know them yet.

28 One can also ask whether buying at low prices and selling at high prices is really such a strange behavior. Do currency exchange offices and financial institutions exhibit the endowment effect or try to make profit on bid–ask spread? See Plott and Zeiler (2005) and Levine (2012, 80–81) on the methodological shortcomings of experimental research on the endowment effect.

29 To be clear, I do not argue that people like or easily accept losses. I am simply pointing out that the finding that a loss of a certain amount of a good has a greater utility loss than the utility increase of a comparable gain *does not* constitute an anomaly in light of the subjective theory of value.

> the contrary, it is because Pandora chooses *b* rather than *a* that we say that Pandora prefers *b* to *a*, and assign *b* a larger utility.[30]

The key point here is that utility or preferences are not independent entities to be found in mental world; they are rather a methodological concept used by economists to describe people's action. As Mises (1998 [1949], 95) notes:

> [O]ne must not forget that the scale of values or wants manifests itself only in the reality of action. These scales have no independent existence apart from the actual behavior of individuals. The only source from which our knowledge concerning these scales is derived is the observation of a man's actions. Every action is always in perfect agreement with the scale of values or wants because these scales are nothing but an instrument for the interpretation of a man's acting.

Rothbard (2009, 260, 310, emphasis in original) puts it in a similar way:

> [E]conomics deals with the universal aspects of real action, not with the actors' inner psychological workings. We deduce the existence of a specific value scale on the basis of the *real act*; we have no knowledge of that part of a value scale that is not revealed in real action (...) we are interested in preference *as revealed through choice* and not in the *psychology* of preferences.

Utility is not something that lies in the goods before individuals make them objects of choice. It is a result or a reflection rather than a determinant of the action. The choice reveals how the individual values given goods. When economists teach economics, they talk *as if* people had already determined preferences or calculated utilities of competing goods. But this is only done for didactic reasons or for theoretical representation of the process—in real life, the action reveals to the individual how he or she values the object. As Fetter (1915, 18–19), puts it:

> In case of a choice of a thing by a person for his own use the valuation is simply the resultant of choice; it is the arithmetic expression necessarily involved in the action and reveals to the person himself what he has done, how he values the object, rather than determines his action (...) [. Value] is not to be thought of as something in a thing before man makes it an object of choice. The logical order is: first, choice; secondly, a valuation by necessary implication; third, value—the quality imputed

30 Similarly, Luce and Raiffa (1957, 32, emphasis in original) point out a few fallacies about the modern utility theory that stem from the failure to understand that actions *precede* utilities. Describing one of them, they write, "[T]he point is that there is no need to assume, or to philosophize about, the existence of an underlying subjective utility function, for we are not attempting to account for the preferences or the rules of consistency. We only wish to devise a convenient way for *represent* them."

> to the object. Yet in real life these are but three phases, absolutely contemporaneous, of the same thing.

Buchanan (1982, 12 emphasis in original) also believes that utility or preferences do not exist independently of choices:

> Individuals do not act so as to maximize utilities in *independently existing functions*. They confront genuine choices, and the sequence of decisions taken may be conceptualized, *ex post* (after the choices), in terms of 'as if' functions that are maximized. But these 'as if' functions are, themselves, generated in the choosing process, not separately from such process.

Please note that treating utility, value, or preference scales as if they existed separately from real action, is the fundamental, although mistaken, view held by behavioral economists who are in favor of nudging (Thaler and Sunstein 2008). The idea is that people do not act rationally, because they do not really do what is best for them, or they exhibit some inconsistences of choices and preferences. In other words, people have some interests that they are unaware of, or they do not satisfy their 'true' preferences.[31] Thus, the task of the researchers or policymakers is to make people aware of them, or to 'nudge' people towards their best interests. This idea is problematic for several reasons, the discussion of which is beyond the scope of this book.[32] I would just like to point out here an often raised and valid argument that policymakers are not able to discover people's 'true' preferences (White 2013; Lecouteux 2016).[33]

---

31 This is the second of two assertions that constitute 'neuroeconomics' according to Gul and Pesendorfer (2008, 3): "What makes individuals happy ('true utility') differs from what they choose. Economic welfare analysis should use true utility rather than the utilities governing choice ('choice utility')." As one can see, the erroneous belief that utility exists independently from real action is common for behavioral economists and researchers on happiness economics. So I return to this topic in sub-chapter 4.6. The first assertion is, "Psychological and physiological evidence (e.g., descriptions of hedonic states and brain processes) is directly relevant to economic theories. In particular, it can be used to support or reject economic models or even economic methodology" (Gul and Pesendorfer 2008, 3).

32 See, e.g., White 2013; Abdukadirov 2016; Rizzo and Whitman 2020. See also McKenzie (2010, 220, 262), who rightly asks how supposedly irrational people can engage in rational discussion with behavioral economists or respond to nudges if they are not rational enough to respond effectively to market incentives.

33 See White (2013, xv): "[P]olicymakers simply have no information regarding people's true interests. Instead, they judge people's choices to be bad ones based on the interests assumed and imposed by the policymakers, and then nudge people into making choices that the policymakers want them to make." Lecouteux (2016, 196) notes that "the existence of true preferences [...] forces us to accept a

However, if one drops the idea of preferences existing somewhat separately from action, the whole justification behind nudging, or libertarian paternalism, collapses, as people do not have 'true' preferences to elicit by policymakers and by which they could judge people's choices and fix the inconsistences (Rizzo and Whitman 2020).

Hence, what is left is the 'standard' paternalism—i.e., the idea that some people know better than others what is best for them. Such a notion contradicts the idea of subjective preferences and assumes a level of knowledge that cannot be possessed (Rizzo and Whitman 2020).

The list of fallacious instances of treating preferences as independent entities would be very long, so I will end this section simply by referring to paradoxes that are often invoked to invalidate the axioms of rational-choice theory, such as the Allais paradox (Allais 1953; Grüne-Yanoff 2012). But the fact that these axioms are invalidated says something about the mathematical formalization of human actions, not about the human actions themselves. For example, the fact that preferences may not be constant is problematic for the atemporal world of mathematical formalization, but not for the temporal world of real people (Mises 1998 [1949], ch. V). The fact that the exponential form of discounting leads to the time inconsistency is problematic for the use of the exponential form of discounting (Rabin 2002)—which is not a prescriptive norm, but a modeling one (Rizzo and Whitman 2020)[34]—but not for the very time preference. Economic theory only states that, *ceteris paribus*, people prefer to get the same, subjectively perceived, good sooner rather than later (Mises 1998 [1949], ch. XVIII; Rothbard 2009, ch. 1). But it does not say anything about the strength of this preference or that it must be the same in the whole horizon—i.e., that incremental delays in getting the good must be discounted in the same way, no matter when these delays are situated in time.

## 5. CONCLUSIONS

The complaints that economics either abstracts too much from psychology, or that it should adopt a more psychologically realistic model of human behavior, have accompanied economics almost from its beginnings. Interestingly, I have not encountered the opinions that psychology abstracts too much from

---

reductionist account of human beings as a rational agent trapped in a psychological shell, and to treat psychological characteristics as alien elements to our true self."

34 Ross (2014, 238) is skeptical about the experiments of behavioral economists suggesting that people discount hyperbolically: "If most people frame their individual choices in a way that leads to hyperbolic discounting, why aren't most interest rates in the neighborhood of 1,000 percent or more? These are the sorts of rates implied by the discounting experiments typically emphasized by behavioralists."

economics or that it should adopt a more economically realistic model of human behavior.

I believe that, in this chapter, I have shown that—although both seem to study human behavior—economics and psychology are separate fields of social science with different research questions and perspectives, and that they should remain separate fields, respecting each other's methodology. I think that I have also demonstrated that economics should not become more psychological, as this would deprive it of its unique character, and I have explained why—in Popper's words (1964, 142)—"psychology can be treated, not as the basis of all social sciences, but as one social science among others."

However, this does not mean that psychology has nothing to offer to economics (or vice versa). As Ross (2014, 19) notes, both sciences "need to borrow one another's insights if they are each to offer contributions to an internally consistent scientific picture of objective reality."

Psychological insights can be useful in economic modeling. In this chapter (and the whole monograph), I do not question it, but rather defend economics from behavioral imperialism, according to which economics is essentially applied psychology and should reject its fundamental constructs to have more realistic psychological underpinnings or to become more psychological or 'mindful.' As Gul and Pesendorfer (2008, 3) write in a piece aptly titled, "The case for mindless economics":

> Neuroeconomics goes beyond the common practice of economists to use psychological insights as inspiration for economic modeling or to take into account experimental evidence that challenges behavioral assumptions of economic models. Neuroeconomics appeals directly to the neuroscience evidence to reject standard economic models or to question economic constructs.

What are the legitimate areas where psychology could enrich economics?[35] This topic needs a separate study, so here I am forced to merely signal a few

[35] It should be clear that economics could enrich psychological inquiry as well. The starting point is Becker's claim (1976, 14) that "the economic approach provides a useful framework for understanding all human behavior." In line with this view, he used an economic approach to explain a variety of non-market behaviors, such as discrimination, crime, marriage, and fertility. In this vein, I believe that we could adopt the economic approach for understanding some human behavior that was traditionally explained by psychologists, and that we can put certain psychological theories into the framework of an economic model. For instance, when one inserts sex and death instincts into utility function, we could perhaps obtain a simple Freudian model, while when one inserts meaning into utility function, we could obtain a simple model of Frankl's psychological approach (Freud 1922; Frankl 2004). And, of course, the economic way of thinking could be helpful

applications. First of all, economics treats people's goals or wants as given. But knowledge as to *why* people choose certain ends, or what are their motives behind particular purchases, could be useful at times—not only for the entrepreneurs, but also for the economists. In other words, in the economic approach preferences are given and stable. However, the knowledge of how people form particular preferences—including time, risk, and leisure/labor preferences—and how they change over time is also relevant for understanding human behavior (Becker 1976), and could possibly enrich economics (although at the level of applied economics rather than the fundamentals of economic theory). As Dickinson (1919, 387) notes,

> The psychology which is of use to economics is that which relates to the motives, or springs to human action [...] it is only by adding significantly to our knowledge of motives that the psychologist can help us with our own theory; and here only so far as our explanations do imply certain incentives to economic conduct – not throughout the whole of economic theory.

Second, the standard maximization model in which individuals maximize their utility subject to constraints could be enriched by some psychological insights. Research on social preferences and other insights from social psychology could be fruitful (Fehr and Schmidt 2006). For example, Becker (1976) incorporated altruism into the economic framework by adding the consumption of other people into the individual's utility function. Others included the costs of gathering and processing information or cognitive limitation of the mind into the constraints (Downs 1957; Simon 1957; Stigler 1961),[36] while Akerlof and Dickens (1982) created a model with beliefs and cognitive dissonance playing an important role.

Third, confidence is inherent in economic life (Zak and Knack 2001), which implies that psychology could help us to understand some economic

---

also in applied psychology and in positive economic psychology (Hart and Hart 2025). After all, some norms of rational behavior could improve people's financial and economic well-being. In particular, the concept of sunk costs could be useful, as it could help people to realize that they should not stay in certain projects only because they invested a lot of time, effort, and resources to maintain them (Rego et al. 2018). Another interesting example of the application of economic analysis to psychology could be the use of standard economic tools to understand the formation and spread of cognitive errors (Glaeser 2004). Last but not least, behavioral patterns in individuals could be modeled as equilibria of games among sub-personal agents (Harrison and Ross 2010).

[36] Cf. Leibenstein (1976) and his idea of selective rationality, according to which, people select degrees of rationality they want to use or manifest (Leibenstein 1976).

phenomena. For instance, price bubbles and business cycles are undoubtedly economic phenomena. However, as Mises (1998 [1949], 560) puts it, "[A]ccidental institutional and psychological circumstances generally turn the outbreak of the crisis into a panic." Another example might be bank runs—economists can say that banks that operate under the fractional system are prone to the bank runs (Diamond and Dybvig 1983; Huerta de Soto 2006). But, as Mises notices (1998 [1949], 433), "[H]ow far the bank can go on increasing its issues of fiduciary media without arousing distrust, depends on psychological conditions." Similarly, one of the most important economic laws says that the increase in the money supply leads to the price inflation (Mises 1998 [1949], Huerta de Soto 2006; Rothbard 2009; Machaj 2024). However, how much the money supply can increase without triggering distrust of the currency and inflation spiraling out of control, also depends on psychological conditions. As Mises (1998 [1949], 424, emphasis added) writes,

> The tendency toward a fail in purchasing power as generated by the increased supply of money is intensified by the general propensity to restrict cash holdings which it brings about. Eventually a point is reached where the prices at which people would be prepared to part with 'real' goods discount to such an extent the expected progress in the fall of purchasing power that nobody has a sufficient amount of cash at hand to pay them. The monetary system breaks down; all transactions in the money concerned cease; *a panic makes its purchasing power vanish altogether.* People return either to barter or to the use of another kind of money.

Fourth, psychology could be helpful in explaining the formation of expectations and shared mental models and ideologies, which are key factors in shaping institutions and resulting incentive structures for economic actors (Denzau and North, 1994). As Kurrild-Klitgaard (2001, 138) formulates the Schuetzian's message to economists, "[T]he more empirically oriented the analysis, the more the scientist will need to incorporate assumptions about a number of issues, e.g., the particular form of reasoning of the agent, his beliefs, knowledge, expectations, etc."[37]

[37] Other interesting areas of use of psychology in economics could be: elasticity of demand and demand for money; propensity to save; how people acquire knowledge and learn from experience (Hayek 1937); how to motivate people and encourage them to work efficiently (management); how to make them buy certain goods and services (marketing), etc. See Lea and others (1987) on this subject.

# 3. Psychological theories of the business cycle: a critique

## 1. INTRODUCTION[1]

Along with the development and growing popularity of behavioral economics in the 21st century, references to psychology in explaining business cycle phenomena have also gained popularity, especially after the global financial crisis of 2007–2009. Two publications by Shiller in particular stand out: *Irrational Exuberance* (2015; first published in 2000) and, jointly with Akerlof, *Animal Spirits* (2009).[2] There has also been a surge of interest in Minsky's (1992) financial instability hypothesis and in sunspot models, in which changes in market psychology are important exogenous shocks explaining deviations from competitive equilibrium (Azariadis 1981; Cass and Shell 1983; Farmer and Woodford 1997; Farmer 2013).[3]

However, it should be noted that psychological explanations of economic phenomena, including business cycles, have always been formulated (Rötheli 2021). In fact, it can be said that they were part of the folk psychology (Hutto and Ravenscroft 2021) and pre-economic reasoning, which did not see any regularities in human behavior, but saw it as driven by impulses, emotions, illusions, and superstitions. The best example of such an approach is Mackay's

[1] This chapter is a translated modification of my Polish article "Krytyka psychologicznych teorii cyklu koniunkturalnego" (Sieroń 2024).

[2] Shiller (2015, ch. 1) defines *irrational exuberance* as "unjustified optimism," which is "the psychological basis of a speculative bubble." Akerlof and Shiller (2009, 1–4) do not provide a clear definition of the animal spirits, but they write about them as "the thought patterns that animate people's ideas and feelings," or "noneconomic motivations" (such as feelings, impressions, passions, changing confidence, temptations, envy, resentment, illusions) that make people irrational or misguided.

[3] It is also worth mentioning De Grauwe (2013), who creates a behavioral macroeconomic model based on the standard New-Keynesian model. Milani (2011) also builds a New-Keynesian model that includes a potential role for psychological forces.

(1852) book *Extraordinary Popular Delusions and the Madness of Crowds*, which puts financial bubbles in the same category of "madness of crowds" as witch mania, the crusades, alchemy, fortune-telling, magnetisers, etc.

Haberler (1946) places psychological theories in one of the few major categories of business cycle theories (along with monetary, over-investment, underconsumption, cost-of-production, and agricultural theories). According to him, psychological factors were most strongly emphasized by Taussig (1911), Lavington (1922), and Pigou (1926). The latter argued that business cycles are caused by changes in people's mental states, and more specifically that booms and recessions result from waves of optimism and pessimism and related herd behavior. He even wrote, "[T]he varying expectations of business men [...] and not anything else, constitute the immediate and direct causes or antecedents of industrial fluctuations" (Pigou 1926, 33).

It is also worth mentioning here John Stuart Mill (1844) and Marshall (1923). The former described the business cycle as a succession of ups and downs, precisely under the influence of psychological factors such as unreasonable hopes and fears. The latter believed that rising prices translate into an increase in expected profits and optimism and thus an expansion of economic activity (Geiger 2016).

One cannot, of course, overlook Keynes (2018 [1936]), who emphasized the role of psychological factors ("animal spirits") in changes in investment demand and in economic fluctuations, stating that the marginal efficiency of capital is ultimately determined "by the uncontrollable and disobedient psychology of the business world" (p. 282).[4] According to Newman (2021), Keynes' recourse to psychological explanations was inspired by the work of Jevons (1878), in which he sought to explain changes in market psychology – which John Mills (1867) had previously written about – by changes in solar activity affecting the agricultural production.

---

[4] However, the very passage in which the phrase 'animal spirits' is present can be interpreted to mean that Keynes (2018 [1936]) was referring to the willingness to act, take risks, and make decisions under conditions of uncertainty, when the probability of success cannot be calculated (Koppl 1991). According to Keynes, rational beliefs exist only in a state of pure knowledge, while in a situation of uncertainty, subjects necessarily act based on irrational beliefs. This is a flawed dichotomy, which I will address in this chapter's conclusions. Also, Barens (2011) questions the great importance of 'animal spirits' in Keynes' theory attributed to him by some scholars, pointing out that the section, in which the famous term is present, ends with these words: "We should not conclude from this that everything depends on waves of irrational psychology. On the contrary, the state of long-term expectation is often steady, and, even when it is not, the other factors exert their compensating effects" (Keynes 2018 [1936], 142).

Although the concepts of different authors differ in detail, psychological theories of the business cycle can be reduced to the statement that business cycles are caused by alternating waves of optimism and pessimism. They lead entrepreneurs to make erroneous expectations about future conditions, which generate cycles in investments and economic activity in general. Consequently, according to Haberler (1946), the response of economic agents to changes in market variables, determining, for example, the amount of investment demand, is stronger than purely economic theories would suggest, which explains the business cycle.

The source of all psychological explanations of business cycles is the opposition to the concept of HE, and the assumption that people do not behave fully rationally, which is supposed to prevent the economy from continuously following an equilibrium path. Psychological theories therefore introduce certain assumptions about the reactions of individuals, in which they deviate from rational behavior and throw the economy out of equilibrium (Akerlof and Shiller 2009; Milani 2011).[5]

The purpose of this chapter is to examine psychological theories of the business cycle as an example of a specific misapplication of psychology in economics. In the next section, I discuss several problems faced by such theories. Then, I move on to the conclusions, in which I argue that psychological theories of the business cycle should not be endorsed by economists.

## 2. PROBLEMS CONCERNING THE PSYCHOLOGICAL THEORIES OF THE BUSINESS CYCLE

I see a number of problems with the above psychological theories of the business cycle. I start with methodological shortcomings, before moving on to more substantive issues.

### 2.1 Economists Should Seek Economic Theories

Economists' recourse to psychological explanations represents a confusion of levels of analysis or an unwarranted departure from the discipline of economics. Any social phenomenon can be described from the perspective of both economics and psychology (as well as sociology, etc.) – but *replacing* one

---

[5] It is telling that publications on psychology in economics almost never present the psychological mechanisms that lead to rational actions (or the psychological aspects of government interventions), but rather draw attention to the irrationality of individuals.

perspective with the other does not *increase* our knowledge.[6] For example, trade can be explained as the exchange of oppositely valued goods by individuals wishing to increase their utility and by appealing to the law of comparative advantage (Rothbard 2009), but one can also, for example, appeal to the inherent propensity of human nature to truck, barter, and exchange (Smith, 2008 [1776]).

One can see here the danger of appealing to psychological explanations – they can often contribute as much as *virtus dormitiva* (dormitive power) to explaining why opium puts people to sleep (Molière 1926). In a similar manner, people trade because they are characterized by the propensity to trade. The economy is cyclically thrown out of equilibrium because people are characterized by certain propensities (such as excessive optimism and pessimism) that lead to the business cycle.[7]

While not devaluing psychology, economists – if they want to conduct economic research – should focus on economic explanations. By their very nature, economic explanations appeal not to people's mental states,[8] but to their actions in the context of scarce resources and responses to incentives, in the form of, for example, changes in the structure of relative prices. Similarly, all accounts of business cycles and financial booms and busts are incomplete without references to changes in interest rates, money supply, and credit conditions.

In other words, before appealing to the not fully rational or even irrational aspects of human behavior or market valuations, economists should first try to find reasonable explanation from the economic point of view. As Garber (1990, 35) puts it:

> Before economists relegate a speculative event to the inexplicable or bubble category, however, we must exhaust all reasonable economic explanations. While such explanations are often not easily generated due to the inherent complexity of economic phenomena, the business of economists is to find clever fundamental market

---

[6] I am not saying that the interdisciplinary approach is wrong. To understand something in its complexity, we need different perspectives. What I argue is that *replacing* economic theory with a psychological theory is of no value for economics.

[7] It is worth noting here another danger of adopting a psychological perspective. While it may provide valuable insights, researchers may fall into the trap of treating psychological factors as objectively measurable variables that exist independently of the economy and exert an exogenous influence on it (Bassie 1955).

[8] "The teachings of praxeology and economics are valid for every human action without regard to its underlying motives, causes, and goals. The ultimate judgments of value and the ultimate ends of human action are given for any kind of scientific inquiry; they are not open to any further analysis" (Mises 1998 [1949], 21).

> explanations for events; and our methodology should always require that we search intensively for market fundamental explanations before clutching the "bubble" last resort.[9], [10]

It is worth noting that psychological theories of the business cycle assume a dubious view of human nature. This is because in order to justify sudden changes from extreme moods, it is necessary to assume that people are impulsive and reactive. Certainly emotions, moods, or instincts are important factors in people's lives, but people also have reason and the ability not to succumb to moods or to act in spite of them (Kirzner 1976). As Mises (1998 [1949], 16) puts it, "However unfathomable the depths may be from which an impulse or instinct emerges, the means which man chooses for its satisfaction are determined by a rational consideration of expense and success." Every action *has* a psychological component, but it is not the case that every action is *determined* by it.

## 2.2 Using Psychological Concepts Does Not Explain Anything

Explaining crises by referring to errors does not enrich our knowledge, because that is how a crisis can be defined – as the result of previously accumulated entrepreneurial mistakes. As Hayek (1975 [1939], 141) puts it:

> Every explanation of economic crises must include the assumption that entrepreneurs have committed errors. But the mere fact that entrepreneurs do make errors can hardly be regarded as a sufficient explanation of crises. Erroneous dispositions which lead to losses all round will appear probable only if we can show why entrepreneurs should all simultaneously make mistakes in the same direction. The explanation that this is just due to a kind of psychological infection or that for any other reason most entrepreneurs should commit the same avoidable errors of

---

[9] Indeed, as I explained in Chapter 1, rationality in economics does not serve as an assumption about human behavior, but as a key methodological postulate that brings consistency and predictability to economic analysis and enables the social sciences to explain social phenomena. After all, the alternative would be the principle of irrationality, which would be a poor basis for theoretical reasoning.

[10] Balcerowicz (1995, 12) gives a similar methodological recommendation for comparative analysis: "With respect to how to explain systematic differences in performance, I believe another rule should be followed. An explanation in terms of the interplay between different institutional factors and human invariants should have priority over the explanation in terms of some psycho-social peculiarities. In other words, only if the first explanation proves to be unsatisfactory (and the reference to other easily identifiable factors fails, too) is one justified in searching for an explanation in terms of some peculiarities. But, again, this is only justified if it is empirically possible to establish their existence."

> judgment does not carry much conviction. It seems, however, more likely that they may all be equally misled by following guides or symptoms which as a rule prove reliable.[11]

More generally, it is not clear what the appeal to optimism and pessimism adds. If, for example, optimism means that during a boom banks are more willing to lend and entrepreneurs are more willing to borrow and invest, then one does not need the concepts of 'optimism' and 'pessimism' at all, as referring to investment demand and credit conditions will be entirely sufficient.

## 2.3 Psychological Theories Are Strongly Context Dependent

The next methodological problem with psychological theories of the business cycle is the same as with all psychological theories: they are strongly context dependent, and it is difficult to generalize where they are concerned. Different people tend to act in various ways, and on top of that, people act in various ways across diverse settings (Mises, 2007 [1957]; Kagan 2012; Sunstein and Rizzo 2021). Thus, the same economic events can trigger various mental states in individuals, which in turn can translate into different actions. For example, a sustained rise in the price of a particular asset can trigger both expectations of further increases and expectations of a price correction, and these expectations, and the accompanying emotions, can lead to different actions in different people, depending on other factors (budget constraints, etc.).

It is worth emphasizing here that only certain mental states translate into actions, or, in other words, action is the result of conflicting psychological motives occurring in a certain environment imposing different constraints (Robbins 1932). People may feel shame and guilt for continuing to smoke cigarettes, but they keep doing it anyway. They may desire to go on a vacation abroad, but not have the money to do so. They may hate their jobs, but still not quit them. They may think that prices of real estate are too high, but buy a home anyway to have a shelter. Hence, the influence of emotions or beliefs on economic reality is limited. This is why, among other things, economics abstracts from mental states and focuses on actions. Unlike in psychology, economists can analyze economic phenomena without delving into the motivations or other psychological determinants of human behavior, and analyze the unintended social consequences of individual actions.

---

[11] See also Rothbard (2000) and Ross (2014, 265): "Of course most people do have confident expectations during booms and pessimistic expectations during recessions; but this is precisely what we want business cycle theory to explain in the first place."

While it is possible to try to describe a given business cycle by referring to psychological concepts, it is difficult to have a general psychological theory of the business cycle, that could additionally account for the differences between business cycles (if the same psychological mechanisms are always at work, why do cycles differ?).[12] Meanwhile, economics strives for general theories, and is able to generate them due to its formal nature and abstracting from psychological factors (Rizzo 2015, 2017).[13]

Thus, psychological explanations of business cycles, if they aspire to be general theories, will have to assume the existence of certain tendencies that will not be universally true. In other words, psychological theories are, so to speak, doomed to be *ad hoc* explanations – in the sense that a different but similarly convincing narrative can almost always be formulated.

For instance, over-optimism and over-pessimism are most often cited as explanations for booms and recessions, but the rise in the equity prices accompanying the post-Great Recession recovery is widely regarded as 'the most hated bull market' (Hoffmans 2012), because the mood was rather pessimistic. Economic crashes are supposed to be caused by excessive pessimism and self-fulfilling expectations, but they are often unexpected and surprising, occurring during the height of euphoria during the boom.

Another example: according to Minsky's financial instability hypothesis, booms are caused by optimistic expectations and escalating speculative behavior, while crises are the result of a sudden revaluation of expectations and thus of asset values (Minsky 1992, 2008, 2015).[14] However, Gordon (1987) argues that when entrepreneurs have experienced a series of successful years, they tend not to engage in more speculative behavior, but to become more risk averse in order to protect the wealth they have accumulated during those good years – a slump is therefore supposed to be caused by a reduction in borrowing activity and an increase in savings. Schumpeter (1939) also disagreed with the view that excessive optimism suddenly turns into excessive pessimism, as he noted that entrepreneurs generally remain optimistic for some time after the onset of a downturn.

---

[12] See Sieroń (2019, ch. 6) on the so-called secondary features of business cycles and the Cantillon effect as their possible explanation.

[13] It does not mean that economists see people as entities devoid of mental states – rather, they consider individuals without specifying their mental states, treating them as given (Long 2006; Mises 1998 [1949]).

[14] Minsky accepts Keynes' idea of the inherent instability of investment decisions (Minsky 2008). Minsky (2015, 65) writes that the instability that an economy with private debts exhibits "follows from the subjective nature of expectations about the future course of investment." Thus, it seems that he links the instability to human psychological propensities (Drakopoulos and Katselidis 2024, 104).

## 2.4 Psychological Analyses Are Ex Post Narratives Rather Than Theories

Psychological explanations represent a collection of anecdotes or ex post rationalizations of given economic events rather than a scientific theory that allows the formulation of predictions (Chicago Booth Review 2016).[15] This is especially true of concepts based on (self-fulfilling) expectations – any economic event can be explained as the result of the economic agent's expectations. On these grounds, Ross (2014, 65) argues that social psychology does not have a general theory that would allow for prediction of the timing of public mood swings, and that the animal spirits theory of business cycles is not a causal hypothesis (at least with no statistical evidence for its support), but rather just a redescription.

This matter is related to the following problem: psychological concepts are based on the assumption that economic agents display exaggerated pessimism or excessive optimism, such as mistakenly expecting further increases in real estate prices. However, whether a given expectation is 'excessive' or 'exaggerated' cannot be determined ex ante; it can only be determined with certainty ex post. After asset prices have fallen, it is easy to criticize buyers as having earlier unreasonable price expectations due to, for example, an availability heuristic. But as long as the price increase continues, the expected value of staying in asset could be greater than the expected losses, so it is difficult to make the same criticism (McKenzie 2010, 232). According to some researchers, the so-called price bubbles can be justified by appealing only to rational factors (Garber 1990), or "individual irrationality cannot be deduced from collective irrationality" (McKenzie 2010, 232).

On top of this, some buyers who are skeptical about the further price increases, may purchase the asset based on the belief that they will have time to resell it to others (Zou 2018), or that, if anything, the central bank or government will intervene to counteract excessive price declines. Moral hazard is an important factor that – along with monetary factors – makes it possible to explain the formation of so-called price bubbles, without referring to psychological (irrational) factors (Mueller 2001; O'Driscoll 2008; White 2009). These monetary factors are the loose monetary policy of central banks and increases in the supply of money and credit, which are increasingly mentioned in the economic literature as being inseparable from the formation of price bubbles (Kindleberger and Aliber 2005; Sieroń 2019, 95).

---

[15] Interestingly, although Akerlof and Shiller (2009, p. x) consider thinking in terms of narratives as animal spirits, they write that the goal of their book *Animal Spirits* is "to give its own story about how the economy behaves."

## 2.5 Psychological Theories Just Undo the Question By One Stage

Theories that refer to mental states do not actually explain the origins of business cycles, but merely undo the question by one stage, since one now has to explain the sudden changes in the mental states of market participants. As Mises (2006 [1928], 101) puts it, psychological theories of crisis "amount to no more than tracing one unknown factor back to something else equally unknown." Referring to, for example, 'animal spirits' does not explain anything. One must explain the mechanisms behind the cyclical transition of economic agents from excessive optimism to exaggerated pessimism.

This is because psychological theories of business cycles do not adequately explain several fundamental issues: (1) why there are sudden changes in people's mental states at all; (2) why these changes occur under specific circumstances of time and place; (3) why they are cyclical in nature; (4) why they are widespread, i.e. they affect the majority of entrepreneurs or investors, rather than being randomly distributed in the population (in the sense of why some entrepreneurs do not display excessive optimism and some exaggerated pessimism); (5) why these changes in mental states lead to erroneous expectations and actions (in the sense of why, stereotypically, coldly calculating and hard-nosed entrepreneurs, who are criticized for their heartless pursuit of profits, suddenly fall prey to psychological impulses and make errors); (6) why they do not level out these mistakes or why they are not corrected by profit-driven entrepreneurs (arbitrageurs); and (7) why these errors lead to systemic crises and not to isolated bankruptcies.

Here we touch on a very important methodological issue raised by Becker (1976), namely the assumption of stable preferences in economic analysis. Such an assumption, according to the Nobel laureate, is supposed to provide a solid basis for generating predictions about the reactions of economic agents to various changes, and to prevent the researcher from succumbing to the temptation to appeal to changing preferences in order to 'explain' all apparent contradictions with his or her predictions. Appealing in economic analysis to changes in mental states of individuals is a violation of Becker's postulate. This is because any behavior can be 'explained' by appealing to changes in the mental states of individuals (e.g., an increase in supply can be explained not by an increase in prices, but by better sentiment among producers, just as an increase in demand can be explained not by a decrease in prices, but by better sentiment among consumers).

It is not difficult to see that appealing only to mental states ignores the objective reality of the market, the impact of economic incentives on people's (optimizing) behavior, and the institutional conditions that ensure equilibrium tendencies in the market. This is puzzling, since modern psychology emphasizes the influence of the environment on behavior (Funder and Ozer, 1983).

If economic phenomena are explained by appealing to mental states, then of course there is no guarantee of the existence of a tendency towards market equilibrium, which is inconsistent with the observed reality that markets tend to balance (Bastiat 1996 [1850]). Psychological theories ignore the profit-and-loss mechanism by which accurate predictions and actions are rewarded with profits, while misguided ones lead to losses. This objective market test helps eliminate psychological errors (Rothbard 2000). As Wiśniewski (2019, 10) notes: "[I]f giving in to 'animal spirits' were the norm rather than the exception in financial markets, these markets would soon cease to exist, as the capital of their participants would be quickly and irreversibly squandered."

One can even risk the thesis that psychological theories of the business cycle question the existence of economic laws – after all, if economic reality is determined by the mental states of economic agents, which appear in an unspecified way, it is difficult to have any predictable regularities in the social world.

Here we touch on the very important issue of the formation of expectations. Logically, they can change either under the influence of changes in objective market data, or independently of them. In the first case, then, it is difficult to consider changes in expectations as *causes of* business cycles, since they are an effect rather than a cause. The second possibility, on the other hand, assumes that changes in the mental content of individuals appear like *diabolus ex machina* (Koppl 1991). The question that arises here, however, is why they would occur in such an exogenous way and lead entrepreneurs to make mistakes if objective market data have not changed. This contradicts the signaling and coordinating functions of the price mechanism, which generally properly guides the actions of market participants (Hayek 1944).

## 2.6 Psychological Theories Do Not Explain Important Properties of Business Cycles

Business phenomena are cyclical, but nevertheless each cycle is unique; the supply of money and credit in the economy fluctuates procyclically, while the interest rate fluctuates countercyclically; business cycles represent economy-wide changes, but there are wider fluctuations in sectors that produce capital goods than in industries that produce consumer goods (Rothbard 2000; Huerta de Soto 2006).[16]

[16] Changes in common sentiments or expectations could theoretically explain economy-wide cycles, but it is unclear why entrepreneurs in different industries would succumb to the same sentiment and to similar degrees – or why entrepreneurs in sectors that produce capital goods would experience greater swings in sentiment.

It is worth stopping at the last point – because it indicates that business cycles are not simply about over-investment during a boom and under-investment during a recession. If this were true, one could try to explain business cycles through over-optimism and over-pessimism. The problem during an expansion is not just over-investment, but also malinvestments (Mises 1998 [1949], ch. XXII; Salerno 2012). Thus the theory of the business cycle should explain why entrepreneurs make erroneous investments – a wave of optimism can perhaps 'explain' the increase in the volume of investments, but not necessarily their erroneous structure; in this case, an explanation referring to distorted economic calculation is needed. Moreover, the business cycle theory should explain not only financial crises (stock market crashes, bank panics) – which is the focus of some researchers referring to psychological factors (Barberis 2013) – but also disturbances in the real structure of production.

Business cycle theories that refer to monetary factors and malinvestments, in particular the Austrian business cycle theory, which draws attention to the lowering of the interest rate below its natural level, and the resulting effects on the profitability of investment at various stages of the production structure, seem to explain the above properties of business cycles much better (Hayek 2008 [1935]; Mises 1998 [1949]).

## 2.7 Psychological Theories Reverse the Causal Link between Mental States and Reality

Psychological theories of business cycles seem to take symptoms for causes (just because relative pessimism *characterizes* a recession, it does not mean that it is a *cause*) or even reverse the causal relationship that exists in reality. After all, the mental states, including the expectations, do not arise in a vacuum as sources of economic phenomena, but rather are caused by objective events. As Bassie (1955, 11–12) puts it,

> the whole psychological theory of the business cycle appears to be hardly more than an inversion of the real causal sequence. Expectations more nearly derive from objective conditions than produce them. The businessman both expands and expects that his expansion will be profitable because the conditions he sees justify the expansion [...]. It is not the wave of optimism that makes times good. Good times are almost bound to bring a wave of optimism with them. On the other hand, when the decline comes, it comes not because anyone loses confidence, but because the basic economic forces are changing. Once let the real support for the boom collapse, and all the optimism bred through years of prosperity will not hold the line.[17]

[17] See Salerno (2012), who writes that when recession reveals the entrepreneurs' errors (made because of the distorted interest rates and economic calculation), their confidence diminishes, which, in turn, may *prolong* recession.

## 2.8 Psychological Theories Assume Dormant Factors

The literature points to various psychological factors that cause or affect the business cycle. However, some of them are constantly present in economic reality – thus, if the psychological factors were the causes of business cycles and financial bubbles, these phenomena "would have happened continually, *ad infinitum*, throughout history" (French 2009, 106, emphasis in original) which is clearly not the case.

The question then arises why the psychological factors should have an effect only at a certain moment, and not earlier. For example, to explain the US financial system's supply of sub-prime mortgages, such psychological phenomena as cognitive dissonance, over-confidence, naïve extrapolation of the past, representativeness heuristics, groupthink, loss aversion, and ambiguity, etc., are mentioned (Barberis 2009, 2013). Certainly, these phenomena are important psychological factors, but they have been present in American financial system also before, without leading to the housing bubble and the business cycle. To declare them as causal factors, one would have to demonstrate that in the first half of the 21st century, people became more inclined to, e.g., groupthink.

## 2.9 Psychological Theories Ignore the Invisible Hand

The psychological approach assumes that to explain economic imbalances it is sufficient to demonstrate that certain psychological factors are responsible for the irrational actions of individuals. However, one of the fundamental achievements of economics is to show that an economic system can achieve equilibrium even if not all its members behave in a psychologically 'optimal' way (whatever that means). According to the concept of invisible hand, even actions that could be described as selfish, greedy, or not fully rational, will lead to economic equilibrium and social harmony, if they occur under certain institutional conditions (Smith 2008 [1776]; Hayek 1945; Salerno 1991).[18]

## 2.10 Psychological Theories Assume that People in Government are Less Irrational

A frequent political implication of psychological theories of business cycle is that government should protect us from our animal spirits or intervene (invest) when the private sector displays excessive pessimism or fear (Keynes 2018

[18] More generally, as I showed in Chapter 2, it can be argued that economics as science exists only because the market is a spontaneous order, otherwise psychological analysis would suffice (Hayek 1955).

[1936]; Akerlof and Shiller 2009). However, no one has ever shown that the individuals who make up the government are less susceptible to the influence of emotions or moods.[19] It can even be argued that market participants have a stronger incentive to overcome their instincts or biases than regulators, since their decisions involve their own money and are subject to the profit-and-loss mechanism (Hirshleifer 2008; McKenzie 2010).

## 3. CONCLUSIONS

The major conclusion of this chapter is that psychological theories are not satisfactory theories of business cycles, especially for economists. This is because: (1) they violate the proper methodology of economics, which postulates the rationality of individuals and stable preferences; (2) they ignore important economic factors (profit-and-loss mechanism, the signaling and coordinating functions of prices, the effect of incentives on behavior, economic calculation, etc.); (3) instead, they appeal to psychological phenomena, but do not adequately explain their genesis, their course, and why they should result in business cycles; (4) they assume a causal relationship from mental states to objective market reality, introducing changes in mental states as *diabolus ex machina*; (5) they do not adequately explain all features of business cycles; (6) they ignore the concept of the invisible hand and systemic (ecological) rationality; (7) they constitute ex post narratives about particular business cycles rather than general theories that allow for predictions; and (8) they assume a dubious view of human nature (that people are impulsive and reactive, and that this nature is different depending on whether an individual works within the private or the public sector).

The criticism presented in this chapter casts doubt on the validity of constructing psychological theories of business cycles or of seeing in psychological factors the causes of business cycles, and – more generally – on the validity of making economics more psychological.[20]

The following question arises: why do economists continue to appeal to psychological factors, despite the questionable theoretical basis for such an

---

[19] When it comes to cognitive biases, Berggren (2011) shows that 95.5 percent of articles in behavioral economics that propose paternalist policy action do not contain any analysis of the cognitive ability of policymakers.

[20] However, this chapter has not addressed the question of whether (and how) psychological factors can potentially amplify the course of business cycles. It also ignores whether the phenomenon of recurrent expansions and economic recessions, as well as certain factors accompanying them, can affect the psychology of markets and their participants (Huerta de Soto 2006) – these issues are beyond the scope of this chapter.

approach? This is perhaps a topic for a separate (psychological?) study – but let me suggest some possible answers.

First, the reference to psychological factors may stem from a belief that economics must be grounded in psychology to be fully scientific. However, economics is not empty without psychology and is not a mere generalization of psychological tendencies in the context of economizing of scarce resources (Long 2004). Thus, economics is a separate scientific discipline (Mises 1998 [1949]) and economic theory can abstract from psychological factors.[21]

Second, referring to psychological factors may be the result of a misinterpretation of methodological subjectivity. The fact that both economics and psychology studies mind-dependent phenomena does not mean that economics should adopt a similar research methodology (Rizzo 2015).[22]

Third, recourse to psychological factors may stem from a desire to know the ultimate causes of economic phenomena. However, it is impossible to know the ultimate cause of everything, because at some point we reach the ultimate data unavailable for further analysis. Therefore, every scientific discipline operates within certain limits, and for economics the data not subject to further analysis are specific value judgments and ultimate goals of individuals. One can speculate as to why individuals behave in this way and not in that way, but until one has knowledge of how specific mental states lead to specific actions, the rationale for treating psychology and economics separately and for rejecting psychological theories of business cycle will not disappear (Mises 1998 [1949]).[23]

Fourth, recourse to psychological factors may stem from Keynes' (2018 [1936]) view that rational behavior can occur only under conditions of risk, when one can calculate probabilities of events, while under conditions of uncertainty one is left relying solely on 'animal spirits'. This will only be the case if one defines 'rational behavior' as behavior based on calculating probability-weighted utility. However, as I showed in Chapter 1, this is not the only possible definition of 'rationality.' For some researchers, 'rational' behavior is

---

21 It does not mean that one can do so when trying to understand social phenomena holistically.

22 I write more on this topic in sub-chapter 2.2. In Chapter 2, I also write more about the first answer.

23 While Mises (1998 [1949]) does not rule out that advances in knowledge will someday enable us to treat economics as applied psychology or neurobiology, Hayek (2017 [1949], 358) stresses, "[I]t will never be possible for us to explain or predict why we think exactly as we do rather than differently, or why the human mind under certain circumstances will lead us to certain actions rather than to others." Gul and Pesendorfer (2008) are also skeptical about the revolutionary potential of psychology and neuroscience for economics.

equated with 'purposeful' behavior, and such will also occur in an environment of uncertainty (Mises 1998 [1949]). And it can be argued that the uncertainty of the future is contained in the very notion of action – that is, rational behavior. Without uncertainty, that is, "if man knew the future, he would not have to choose and would not act" (Mises 1998 [1949], 105).

However, even if one does not share Mises' view, we can note that uncertainty precludes the existence of a world of error-free economic calculation, but it does not preclude the existence of rational economic calculation as such. Entrepreneurs will inevitably make mistakes, but the profit-and-loss mechanism will reward accurate actions with profits, while punishing inappropriate ones with losses, thus correcting errors. Thus, we are not wandering in the darkness – the price system makes rational economic calculation possible (Mises 1998 [1949]).[24]

–And the last point: appealing to psychological factors, and in particular drawing attention to the incomplete rationality or irrationality of market participants, may result from a tendency to paternalism and a desire to feel superior by pointing out the irrationality of other people, or from a focus on finding deviations from rational behavior (Lopes 1991). The problem of erroneously treating the HE model as a descriptive model of human behavior returns here. Gigerenzer (2018) writes in this context about *bias bias* – i.e., the tendency to see cognitive biases even when there are none in reality. The obvious question here is how the psychological theory of the business cycle connects to the theory of economic growth; namely, given all of humanity's irrationality, manias, panics, and madness of crowds, how is it that civilization not only persists, but even thrives economically?

---

[24] Melberg (1998) also points out that uncertainty does not necessarily automatically imply instability, as market actors can rely on custom, and known probabilities do not necessarily lead to stability if those probabilities fluctuate.

# 4. How does economic life affect psychological well-being?

## 1. INTRODUCTION

It is a trivial observation that psychological factors affect the economic well-being of households and whole countries. The abilities to regulate emotions and to overcome the desire for instant gratification seem to be particularly important psychological ingredients of a successful life (Mischel et al. 1989). For example, Moffitt and others (2011, 2693) showed that "childhood self-control predicts physical health, substance dependence, personal finances, and criminal offending outcomes."

It is similarly clear that economic life affects the psychological well-being of people. Economic hardship and poverty are negatively related to the mental health outcomes (Ridley et al. 2020). Also financial worries are associated with higher psychological distress (Ryu and Fan 2023).

However, some researchers pose a more nuanced thesis – i.e., that capitalism negatively affects the mental health of people (Prins et al. 2015; Sell and Williams 2019; Eisenberg-Guyot and Prins 2022).

The aim of this chapter is to analyze these claims and consider whether capitalism can really be blamed for negative mental health outcomes. So far, I have been examining calls for economics to become more psychological; in this chapter, I analyze suggestions that economic systems should be assessed in terms of their impact on psychological or subjective well-being.

## 2. ARGUMENTS ABOUT THE NEGATIVE IMPACT OF CAPITALISM ON MENTAL HEALTH

How is capitalism supposed to negatively affect people's mental well-being? The starting point in this line of argumentation is a simple observation of correlation between socioeconomic status and indicators of mental well-being: "it has been firmly established that there are disparities in both mental and physical health across traditional measures of socioeconomic status (SES) such as income, educational attainment and other indicators of social rank"

(Prins et al. 2015, 1352). As correlation is not causation, a causal link from socioeconomic status to mental health is asserted. In their chapter in *Oxford Textbook of Social Psychiatry*, Eisenberg-Guyot and Prins (2022, 195) state, "[R]esearch consistently finds that capitalism harms workers' mental health and exacerbates inequities. It does so through at least three mechanisms: alienation; exploitation; and domination." Prins and others (2015, 1354) list initially only two of the above factors:

> [S]ocial position is not simply a function of individuals' inherited or achieved attributes, but arises from processes by which certain groups control productive resources by i) excluding other groups from access to those resources and controlling their labour activities (domination), and ii) appropriating the fruits of that labour (exploitation).

However, they add later alienation as well, writing: "The alienation of workers from production and the products of their labour is thought to diminish self-efficacy and result in a sense of powerlessness (...) and self-estrangement, that is, engagement in activities that are not intrinsically rewarding" (Prins et al., 2015, 1354–1355).

Kokorikou and others (2023, 2) blame income inequality, claiming, "[T]he link between inequality and mental health is well-documented." They admit that the precise mechanism between these two phenomena is uncertain, but they suggest that social rank, discrimination, stress, and weak relations with other people could be important here.[1]

The last element of this argumentation is the definition of capitalism. Eisenberg-Guyot and Prins (2022, 195) consider it "a socio-economic system characterized by the private ownership of the means of production and the exploitation and domination of wage labour for profit." Prins and others (2015) do not define capitalism explicitly, but they see it as a system that comprises distinct classes with different levels of domination and exploitation.

---

1 Sell and Williams (2019) also point out inequality, but they add many other channels, such as poverty, transnational capital, global markets, corporate market power, harmful products, climate change, pollution, neoliberal ideology, etc. Discussing all these issues would significantly increase the length of this chapter, so I will just say that this list does not seem to be properly substantiated. Historically, capitalism reduced poverty, while socialist economies in Central and Eastern Europe were characterised by the dominance of industry and large companies, as well as a low level of environmental protection compared with market-based economies (Balcerowicz 1994).

## 3. DOES CAPITALISM LEAD TO ALIENATION, EXPLOITATION, AND DOMINATION?

This kind of argumentation does not stand up to scrutiny. First of all, the argument is tautological – i.e., the conclusion is contained in the premise. This is because when one defines capitalism as a socio-economic system characterized by exploitation and domination, and if exploitation and domination negatively affect the mental health of the majority of people, then it follows than capitalism has detrimental effects on the mental well-being of individuals.

Traditionally, capitalism is defined as a system of the private ownership of the means of production (Mises 1998 [1949]). Then, the existence of exploitation and domination under capitalism should be demonstrated, not assumed. It would not be an easy task, as already Böhm-Bawerk (1898) has debunked the theory of exploitation (Gordon 1991). Employees are remunerated – and wages correspond to their marginal productivity (Borjas 2010) – which means that they chose to perform the given work, with all its potentially psychologically unpleasant features, in exchange for their paycheck. The implication is that they perceive the voluntarily agreed remuneration as more valuable than all the dissatisfaction of work.

What is more, labor contracts are concluded voluntarily, while the social classes are not castes: anyone can become a capitalist. There is an organizational hierarchy within companies (and other institutions), but locations within these hierarchies are not fixed. The rights and obligations of each member of the hierarchy are agreed upon the contract and either party can exit the relationship. Hence, one can hardly argue that there is inherent exploitation or domination under the capitalist system (Nozick 1974; Mises 1998 [1949], 308–311).

The notion of 'alienation' is also an assertion that could be very difficult to prove, especially in the modern, service-based economy. There are, for sure, employees who do not like their jobs (to put it euphemistically), but there are also people who enjoy their work. They are even individuals addicted to their work. Workaholism is actually a serious social problem, with an estimated prevalence rate of 15.2 percent and of 14.1 percent, after a trim-and-fill adjustment for publication bias (Andersen et al. 2023). And, although some workers may feel 'alienated' from their production, they can generally participate in production in many more and varied ways than in the pre-capitalistic society. There are many activities based on interpersonal relationships that seem to be not only monetary, but also intrinsically (psychologically) rewarding (Mises 1998 [1949], ch. XXI).[2]

What is more, being a worker is only one aspect of participating in the capitalist economy. All of us are also consumers (and some of us are landowners, entrepreneurs, or capitalists) – and it is practically self-evident that modern capitalist economies create enormous value for consumers.[3] The utility of goods and services, the range of choices, and the ease of purchases can be thought of as generating rather more positive than negative psychological externalities.

Data do not confirm bold claims of critics of capitalism. First, U.S. job satisfaction has not shown a constant decline, but rather an U-shaped movement since 1987, with a steady rise since the bottom during the Great Recession (The Conference Board 2023). Also in many other countries there has been a rise in the self-reported satisfaction over the last few decades (Ortiz-Ospina and Roser 2013).[4] The survey of Gallup and Wellbeing for Planet Earth Foundation conducted in 2021 revealed that the majority of workers liked their work: "[O]n average, more than eight in 10 people worldwide who work full time or part time, for an employer or for themselves, said they enjoy the work they do" (Clouet and Lai 2022).

Second, the average working hours declined dramatically for workers in developed economies since the Industrial Revolution. For example, in the United Kingdom, the annual working hours decreased by almost 40 percent – from 2,755 hours in 1870 to 1,670 hours in 2017 (Giattino et al. 2020).

Third, the unemployment reduces the well-being (Gedikli et al. 2023), which is probably not what we should see if the workers would be heavily alienated, dominated, and exploited.

Fourth, in countries that experienced transformation from socialistic economy into market-based economy, the self-reported happiness generally increased. For example, Frijters and others (2004) found that average life satisfaction in East Germany increased considerably following reunification and the resulting improvement in real household incomes, personal freedom, and

---

[2] Please note that workers consider many job characteristics beyond earnings and some of them prefer jobs that pay less (or even nothing in case of volunteer work), while offering non-monetary benefits, including psychological ones (Smith 2008 [1776]; Rosen 1986).

[3] The consumer welfare is greater than the GDP, because GDP does not include some important valuable goods and services. For example, Brynjolfsson and Oh (2012) estimated that the welfare gain from free internet services averaged over $100 billion per year in the U.S. alone during the period of 2007–2011.

[4] With, of course, some exceptions of countries that suffered from economic crises, such as Greece (Ortiz-Ospina and Roser 2013).

public services. Meanwhile, in Poland, in the period 1991–2015, there was a 56 percent fall in unhappiness and an increase in mean happiness by 13.4 percent; also, the average intensity of symptoms of depression declined (Czapiński and Panek 2015; Brzezinski 2019).[5]

Fifth, capitalistic countries differ significantly in terms of the self-reported life satisfaction and mental health (Ortiz-Ospina and Roser 2013; OECD 2020, Figure 5.5; OECD Better Life Index 2023). This fact indicates that the causes of mental health problems cannot be reduced to a single factor, such as the type of economic system.

Sixth, richer countries tend to have higher average happiness levels and richer people within countries tend to be happier than poorer people in the same countries (Stevenson and Wolfers 2008; Deaton 2013; Ortiz-Ospina and Roser 2013). If we agree that capitalism makes countries and people richer – and it would be difficult to argue with the increase in the income per capita and reduction in poverty since the Industrial Revolution (Roser et al. 2023) – then we have to admit that it also makes them happier.

Last but not least, capitalism – thanks to its productivity and overall economic success – created more opportunities for dealing with psychological problems. People gained not only more income but also more free time for their mental health compared with how these matters were in the past (Fogel 2000). The range of psychological health services has been wider, while their availability is greater than in the past or in socialist countries. One can also argue that because other needs have become relatively well satisfied under capitalism, people have started to be more aware of and interested in pursuing psychological or subjective well-being.[6] The so-called Generation Z is more aware of and accepting of mental health issues than older generations in America (APA 2018). And the stigma surrounding mental illness has been weaker than in the past or in socialist countries. For example, as Petrea and Haggenburg (2014, 159–160) note about mental health care during the Soviet period,

---

5 Please also note that literature mentions "the happiness gap," which is a significant and persistent difference between average happiness in Eastern Europe and Western countries, as well as between East and West Germany (Ortiz-Ospina and Roser 2013; Brzezinski 2019). The causes of this gap are not perfectly clear, but it might partially be a remnant of communism. The caveat is that one should not draw far-reaching conclusions from happiness measurements. In sub-chapter 6, I write about the problems with happiness as social policy's goal.

6 Foulkes and Andrews (2023) claim that the rising awareness about mental health problems inadvertently led to an increase in reported rates of such problems.

> The Russian Association of Psychiatrists supported the view that mental illness was characteristic of capitalist societies and would eventually disappear under the communist regime [...]. People who could not fit in with socialist standards because of their mental health problems were seen as incompletely developed and faced stigma and discrimination.

How people feel is important – and treatment of depression and other mental disorders is a valuable goal – but it is far from obvious why we should consider people's mental states when evaluating economic systems. One problem is that different people experience distinct mental states even under the same conditions. More fundamentally, the fact that some people feel depressed or stressed under capitalism does not *necessarily* say anything meaningful about capitalism.[7] In particular, the fact that some people *feel* exploited under capitalism does not necessarily mean they *are* exploited – and exploited *because* of the capitalism. As Hayek (1988, 131, emphasis in original) notes,

> Most individuals who now make up the proletariat could not have existed before others provided them with means to subsist. Although these folk may *feel* exploited, and politicians may arouse and play on these feelings to gain power, most of the Western proletariat, and most of the millions of the developing world, owe their existence to opportunities that advanced countries have created for them.

To sum up, in order to rationally discuss capitalism one should define it properly – not simply as the economic system one lives in right now, but as the economic system in which means of production are privately owned. Then, to assess its impact on people's subjective well-being, one should compare how people feel under such a system and under the economic system in which means of production are owned by the state (i.e., socialism), or under older socio-economic systems (like feudalism). Such comparisons are methodologically challenging, but all the cues we have indicate that people are better off

---

7 This is because "sense of well-being is an attribute of human experience that derives from people's perceptions of their contemporary situation" (Campbell 1981, 23), which implies that how people feel may also result from their perception of reality rather than objective circumstances. To be clear, I do not downplay the actual conditions in which people live. On the contrary, in section 6, I argue that pursuing happiness as a social goal could neglect disadvantaged people who remain content with their situation. What I argue here is that sometimes how people feel might say something about the psyche of these people and how they perceive or cope with the external world, but not necessarily about the external world itself, not to mention the economic system. Proving such a causal link would be a very complex task, as I have attempted to demonstrate in this section.

under capitalism, or at least that they prefer to live under capitalism, taking all things into account.[8]

## 4. SHOULD WE BLAME CAPITALISM FOR ALL SOCIAL ILLS?

A general problem with blaming capitalism for its allegedly negative effects of psychological or subjective well-being is confusion between inherent and adherent features of capitalism, or between features of capitalism and features of complex social systems as such (Haviland et al. 2011). It is true that the following phenomena are present in the capitalistic world: stress, a relatively quick pace of life, a consumerist lifestyle, differences in socio-economic status, income and wealth inequality, anxiety, depression, suicides, addictions, loneliness, etc. (Dattani et al. 2023). Thus, it might be tempting to blame all social problems on the existing economic system, especially as it is true that the environment in which people live has an influence on their psychological or subjective well-being.

However, to argue that capitalism – i.e., the economic system in which the means of production are privately owned – negatively affects people's psychological or subjective well-being seems to be a gross over-simplification. When one analyzes complex systems, such as modern societies, the monocausal explanations are rarely true. Capitalism has many aspects that could affect people's well-being in many ways. Pointing out only these unpleasant and stressful factors seems to be a significant methodological error. And, as Balcerowicz (1995, 12) points out, "[I]n analysing the impact of institutional variables, one must go beyond such conventional notions as 'capitalist economies', as they mask many differences in the institutional frameworks of these countries."

The reality is much more complex than monocausal explanations suggest. There are actually several different theories explaining problems related to mental health, ranging from child development and unsatisfactory parenting (Stewart-Brown and Schrader-Mcmillan 2011) through the increase in use of

---

[8] Please note that in modern market-based economies, people do not have to realize one central plan, but they can realize their individual goals (Hayek 1945, 1988). In other words, they are free to pursue happiness on their own. Of course, whether they will succeed is not guaranteed, but at least they are not constrained in their attempts, which is of enormous value, probably not adequately captured in simple comparisons. This issue is, however, beyond the scope of this chapter.

social media (Braghieri et al. 2022) and erosion of social relationship (Lane 2000) to lack of purpose in life (Kagan 2012; Koenig 2012).[9]

Some contemporary psychological challenges faced by people living in developed economies might be attributed to rising incomes, urbanization, or other societal changes (e.g., increase in divorce rate) rather than to the kind of economic system in which they live. Hamermesh (2004) points out that people with higher incomes feel more rushed for time, because they have higher opportunity costs of the time. It suggests that being more stressed about time is not related to some ‘capitalistic forces,’ but rather to the changes in individuals’ valuation of time in a response to higher income. Meanwhile, Kagan (2012, 27) notices that “the incidence of mental illnesses is usually greater in large cities than in rural areas or small towns because social supports are more common in the latter settings.”

More fundamentally, as Inglehart and Welzel (2005) argue, in modern high-income countries, people adopt post-materialist goals, which emphasize self-expression, personal autonomy, and the quality of life. The obvious downside of autonomy from social customs and traditional social roles is that people now have to find their own recipe for a good and happy life. As Lane (2000, 165) argues, “[T]oo many life choices [...] and lack of constraint by custom, [and] demands for self-actualization, that is, demands to discover or create an identity rather than to accept a given identity, and, as mentioned, the requirement to make friends rather than relying on kin and neighborhood for companionship all add to the stress.”

The fact that negative psychological and social problems exist in modern capitalist economies does not mean that they are *caused* by capitalism or are *inherent* to this economic system. In any social system, people struggle with difficult emotional states and mental disorders, including addictions, which can lead to aggression or suicide. They result from disorders in the human development process, traumatic life events, etc., not from the fact that factors of production are privately owned.[10] Stress is also universally present, as it is “a state of worry or mental tension caused by a difficult situation” (WHO 2023) or “any environmental or physical pressure that elicits a response from an organism” (Britannica 2023). Also, hierarchy and differences in social position and prestige are present in all societies. It means that societal life, or

---

9 The latter can be partially linked to secularization. Most research shows that religion and spirituality is positively associated with different aspects of mental health, such as higher life satisfaction and meaning, and lower prevalence of anxiety, depression, and suicidal tendencies (Koenig 2012).

10 The only way to get rid of negative emotions is “not to value the uncertain things of human life at all and to care only for one’s own inner states” (Nussbaum 2008, S94).

living in civilization, entails certain psychological costs, no matter the economic system embraced by the given society (Freud 2002).

Hence, the criticism of capitalism (and its impact on people's mental health) seems to be actually the criticism of the scarcity of goods and the resulting necessity to work – which is the inherent feature of the world present in each possible economic system – and seems to grow out of Rousseau's appeal for a return to nature and the life of the noble savage. The complaints on the alleged alienation, exploitation, and domination, as well as on stress, anxiety, etc., could be seen as the demands for liberation from the burdens of civilization (Hayek 1988).[11]

However, although the tribal life can be more gratifying to innate human instincts, it is not devoid of psychological challenges – they are simply of a different kind. In such groups, their members have to follow common goals and obey the commands of a headman. Their lives are subordinated to the interests of the group or a despot, which can certainly create strong psychological pressure (Hayek 1988; Mises 1998 [1949]). Meanwhile, in socialism, shortages of goods, the possibility of becoming denounced, the complete lack of opportunity for development not in line with the Party, political repression and terror (Courtois et al. 1999), etc., also negatively affects the psychological or subjective well-being of individuals.

What is important here is that the question of which of these sets are better or worse is probably unanswerable, as we cannot objectively compare the (dis) utility of being member of different societies. However, when people are given the choice, they usually choose living under capitalism rather than socialism (or outside of civilization), despite all its possible negative aspects. In other words, people's choices reveal that certain psychological tensions could be a price worth paying for living under capitalism, or in a high-income country compared to a low-income country. According to Berg and Besharov (2016), migration to developed countries, largely for economic gain, constituted about 70 percent of all migration, while the Word Migration Report 2022 reveals that, in 2021, 67 percent of migrant workers were residing in high-income level countries, 29 percent in middle-income countries, and 4 percent in low-income countries (McAuliffe and Triandafyllidou 2021).[12]

The relatively fast pace of life and consumerism are more characteristic of capitalism, though they are not its inherent features, but lifestyles adopted

---

[11] However, according to Crespo (2017, 99), Smith (1976 [1759]) already noted that commercial society provides the freedom and security that promote happiness (understood as tranquility and enjoyment) and prevents misery.

[12] It is worth pointing out that people can voluntarily migrate from poorer to richer countries, even if their relative income in the country of destination would be lower than in the country of origin (Becker and Rayo 2008).

by people, according to Huelsmann (2016) in response to credit expansion and inflation. One can live under capitalism and not subscribe to a consumerist lifestyle. And, as Wilkinson (2007, 33) points out, "[C]apitalist consumer societies—and markets in general—don't require materialistic monomania in order to operate. They require only that people want things, for good reasons or bad, and that they are willing to trade what they have produced to get them."

What is more, the modern consumer culture is believed to have begun after the Second World War (Higgs 2021), which clearly indicates that it is not the inherent feature of capitalism. Historically, capitalism has been associated with the misers (Marx 1976 [1867], 254–255), literally depicted as Ebenezer Scrooge. After all, mass consumption beyond mere subsistence could emerge only after some time thanks to the increase in incomes that was possible due to the development of capitalist economy (Lucas 2002). Interestingly, Inglehart and Welzel (2005) show that with rising incomes in developed countries, there has been a shift from materialist to post-materialist values in recent decades. For example, in 1972, materialists outnumbered post-materialists by 24 percentage points in the U.S., while in 2000, the latter outnumbered the former by more than 10 percentage points (Inglehart and Welzel 2005, 97–107), which suggests that consumerism can be a characteristic of a certain phase of socio-economic development rather than an inherent feature of the market-based economy.

Additionally, those who criticize consumerism either express their subjective opinion that other people buy too many goods or complain about natural human tendency towards improving living conditions and economic progress. As Mises (2008 [1956], 4) writes,

> It would be idle to lament this insatiable appetite for more and more goods. This lust is precisely the impulse which leads man on the way toward economic betterment. To content oneself with what one has already got or can easily get, and to abstain apathetically from any attempts to improve one's own material conditions, is not a virtue. Such an attitude is rather animal behavior than conduct of reasonable human beings. Man's most characteristic mark is that he never ceases in endeavors to advance his well-being by purposive activity.

It might be true that the pace of life was slower in the past, but this was because of economic stagnation and lack of opportunities for productive work or sophisticated leisure. People could indeed work less during winters, but this was related to being dependent on weather and climate, as well as to lack of food and the need to conserve energy during harsh conditions. It is doubtful whether anyone would agree for fewer working hours, but with real chances of malnutrition or worse. Being in torpor frees people from the need to work, stress, and the multitudinous burdens and anxieties of life, but this is probably not the kind of liberation imagined by the critics of capitalism (Reiss 2017).

It is tempting to believe that there was some time or place in which human beings were not troubled by the need to work, and by anxiety, depression, and unpleasant feelings. However, there is a lack of evidence that such a community ever existed. What is known is that life in the past was shorter, poorer, and more brutal (Pinker 2018). People often feel nostalgic about the past, but society should not base the scientific discussion on nostalgia.

## 5. DOES INEQUALITY NEGATIVELY AFFECT PEOPLE'S PSYCHOLOGICAL WELL-BEING?

Probably the most famous recent attempt to link income and wealth inequality to the deterioration of mental health can be found in Wilkinson and Pickett (2009), who argue that inequalities generate anxiety and tension. This is because occupying subordinate places in the social hierarchy causes chronic stress, which has a negative impact on physical and mental health.[13]

However, the claim of Wilkinson and Pickett (2009) is doubtful. First, in some sense, the observation that being at the bottom of the socio-income hierarchy is correlated with worse physical and mental health is not especially illuminating. This is what is expected and this is the reason why the economic growth is supported by practically all countries. However, although economic growth can take people out from poverty, there will always be people poorer than others, and there will always be people who are lower in social hierarchy, at least in certain aspects, as the society of perfect equality is a utopia.[14] What is here important is that it can be shown that more affluence is actually associated with more equality instead of inequality (O'Connell 2010).

---

[13] Their book fits into literature about the role of status and households' relative position in the social hierarchy, relative income, positional economy and arms race, interdependent preferences, etc. (Veblen 1918; Duesenberry 1949; Hirsch 1976; Leibenstein 1976; Scitovsky 1976; Frank 1985, 1999; Clark and Oswald 1996; Layard 2005; Clark et al. 2008).

[14] See Nozick (1974, 243, emphasis in original): "It might appear obvious that if people feel inferior because they do poorly along some dimensions, then if these dimensions are downgraded in importance or if scores along them are equalized, people no longer will feel inferior [...]. But it may well be that other dimensions would replace the ones eliminated with the same effects (on different persons). If, after downgrading or equalizing one dimension, say wealth, the society comes generally to agree that some *other* dimension is most important, for example, aesthetic appreciativeness, aesthetic attractiveness, intelligence, athletic prowess, physical grace, degree of sympathy with other persons, quality of orgasm, then the phenomenon will repeat itself."

Second, the methodology adopted by Wilkinson and Pickett (2009) is highly questionable. Their book is based on correlational studies, which are rather low in the hierarchy of evidence (O'Connell 2010). It also suffers from selections bias, as the authors include only the countries and 'social ills' that support their argument, as pointed out by Jason (2017). For example, the deaths of despair are also relatively high, or even higher than in the U.S., in several different countries that one would not perhaps describe as conducting 'neoliberal' policies, such as South Korea, Finland, or Russia (OECD 2020, Figure 5.5).[15] The authors also ignore time series, as historical analysis would show that several variables (e.g., life expectancy) have improved in most of the developed countries, irrespective of their levels of income and wealth inequality.[16]

Third, the main argument has also poor theoretical underpinning, as the alleged link from inequality to health is not sufficiently examined. It is far from clear that people know what is the level of inequality in the country and that it affects their decision-making or mental and emotional life.[17] If inequality affects the level of stress, it should be correlated with the prevalence of heart diseases, which is not the case (Lynch et al. 2001). Also, if stress results from living at the bottom of social hierarchy, perhaps we should see worse conditions in hierarchical societies (like Japan), which is also not the case. And it is difficult to reasonably use hierarchical stress as explanation of such variables as foreign aid or recycling (Jason 2017).

Fourth, Wilkinson and Pickett (2009) do not seem to understand that people as primates are hierarchical creatures for whom the desire for status lies deep

---

15 The deaths of despair has increased in the United States over the past several years, partially caused by the opioid epidemic (Case and Deaton 2020). Some authors argue that this increase in deaths from suicide, alcoholism, and drug overdoses is due to 'neoliberal' economic policies and ideologies (James 2008). The main culprits pointed out are reductions in social services, income and wealth inequality, mass incarceration, and job insecurity, as well as a change in ideology favoring individualism, materialism, and competitiveness (Zeira 2022). This is an interesting narrative, but it lacks convincing arguments, especially that neoliberalism is a buzzword (Eagleton-Pierce 2016), while the welfare state has, in many respects, intensified (IMF and Our World in Data 2025). Excluding the pandemic period, the U.S. labor market, when measured by the unemployment rate, has been improving since the Great Recession (U.S. Bureau of Labor Statistics 2025). It was even argued that the U.S. labor market has become tight or even overheated in the 2020s (Bernanke and Blanchard 2025).

16 See Mackenbach (2002, 1), who writes, "Now that good data on income inequality have become available for 16 western industrialised countries, the association between income inequality and life expectancy has disappeared."

17 After all, people do not compare themselves with the society as a whole or with the richest, but with their peers (Johns and Ormerod 2007, 70).

in the desire to attract mate and reproduce. Hence, one can always critique social hierarchy, affluence and status seeking, and the resulting inequality, but it might have actually a deep, evolutionary justification, which goes beyond the particular (neoliberal) ideology (Jason 2017). The process of status seeking (or, more generally, social categorization) is not tied to any particular economic system. It is just a human nature, or the reality of the human condition which is present in all societies (Berger 1966; Tajfel 1974; Koski et al. 2015; Becker and Murphy 2000, ch. 8).[18]

What capitalism does, however, is that it changes the possible way to achieve status from warfare into peaceful trade in the marketplace, and makes the quest for status more available for the wider population (Oppenheimer 1926; Mises 1998 [1949], ch. XXXIV; Wilkinson 2007).

In other words, the social researchers who focus on the importance of relative income for human well-being and negative effects of positional competition, ignore the role of culture and institutions in mediating human nature, generating positive externalities, and transforming behaviors that potentially create zero-sum (or even negative-sum) games into positive-sum games. As Wilkinson (2007, 25) points out,

> Whether we happen to be locked in zero-sum or positive-sum games is more a matter of culturally transmitted institutions (norms of interaction and coordination, explicit or tacit) than of brute facts about our genetic constitution. The question, then, isn't whether we are status seeking. The question is how our culture and institutions harness, suppress, or amplify our natural tendencies.

What is important here is that the status-seeking within market-based economy is a positive-sum game, as competition for social status implies benefits for society in the form of more entrepreneurial, scientific, artistic, or athletic production (or any other type that is associated with social recognition) (Hume 1987 [1777]). One can even argue that without the motivation of enhanced status, there would be under-investment in certain activities that are socially beneficial but risky or relatively low paid. As Becker and Murphy (2000, 124) note, "[G]reat scientists and outstanding entrepreneurs receive enormous prestige and status precisely in order to encourage scientific and startup activities."

It is true that some narrow status-seeking domains can be seen as a zero-sum game. There might be only one dominant company in the steel industry or only one richest entrepreneur in the world. However, focusing on *competition*

---

18 Becker and Murphy (2000, 125) point out that "status is distributed unequally in essentially every society that has been studied, regardless of culture or stage of economic development." The nationalization of the means of production will not eliminate it.

among entrepreneurs neglects the fact that it is happening within broader *social cooperation* under the division of labor, which means that entrepreneurs compete in delivering something valuable for consumers. Smaller companies from the industry and less wealthy entrepreneurs can be also value-generating, successful and profitable. As Mises (1998 [1949], 274) puts it, "[I]n a totalitarian system social competition manifests itself in the endeavors of people to court the favor of those in power. In the market economy competition manifests itself in the facts that the sellers must outdo one another by offering better or cheaper goods and services and that the buyers must outdo one another by offering higher prices."

And what about the non-business competition? It is true that there might be only one World Chess Champion and only one winner of the International Chopin Competition. However, the non-winning participants can still generate value for the viewers. And there is no limit to the possible forms of excellence, fame, or generating value for the customers. People can participate in other competitions and they even do not have to play chess or the piano; they can choose chess boxing, form a rock band, start a business outside the steel industry,[19] or create a completely new status dimension game (Wilkinson 2007). Markets continually find new means of satisfying consumer needs and also of "accommodating and attracting fame-seeking" (Cowen 2000, 102).

It is worth pointing out here that status has many dimensions (knowledge, skills, fame, character, appearance, etc.). Thus, focusing on relative income as the main dimension of status-seeking seems to be unjustified, especially that people do not always know how much their peers earn. As Wilkinson (2007, 26) notes, "[S]urfer dudes don't compete with Star Trek geeks for status [...]. Struggling artists do not necessarily doubt their superiority in the face of successful accountants."

## 6. SHOULD NATIONS PURSUE HAPPINESS INSTEAD OF ECONOMIC GROWTH?

On a more general level, one can ask whether the economic system or the society should be organized towards achieving subjective well-being or happiness, as the Kingdom of Bhutan attempts to do (Balasubramanian and Cashin 2019). It may sound strange, but it can actually be related to utilitarian ideas about bringing the greatest happiness for the greatest number of people (Bentham 1823 [1780]; Layard 2005; Driver 2022).

---

[19] As Mises (1998 [1949], 276) notes, "Competition does not mean that anybody can prosper by simply imitating what other people do. It means the opportunity to serve the consumers in a better or cheaper way without being restrained by privileges granted to those whose vested interests the innovation hurts."

Such an idea gained support in the empirical findings called the Easterlin's paradox. Apparently, Easterlin (1974) showed that, despite the positive correlation within and among countries at a given moment, happiness was not increasing with rising national incomes over time.[20] On this basis, some researchers started to suggest that societies should focus on increasing directly the subjective well-being or happiness rather than income, and supplement or even replace GDP with happiness as social goal (Scitovsky 1976; Oswald 1997; Diener 2000; Jansen et al. 2004; Easterlin 2005; Layard 2005; Lee and Goh 2023; Agrawal et al. 2025).[21] Are such claims justified?

First of all, subsequent research, that used better data and methodology, disproved Easterlin's findings (Hagerty and Veenhoven 2003; Veenhoven and Hagerty 2006; Ortiz-Ospina and Roser 2013). Kahneman and Deaton (2010) demonstrated that increased income translates into greater happiness among Americans, but only up to earnings of $75,000 per year. However, they only showed that *emotional well-being* does not improve after reaching a certain income level. But they also indicated that *life satisfaction* increases steadily with income. As Deaton (2013, 57) comments on research by Stevenson and Wolfers (2008), "[W]ith properly comparable data, economic growth within countries improves life evaluation in exactly the way that we would expect from the differences in life evaluation between rich and poor countries." What is here important is that this refers to *percentage* increases in income. While an *absolute* increase in income in dollars has a lesser impact on life satisfaction of a wealthy person than for a poor person, the same *percentage* increase in income results in a similar increase in life satisfaction. It is this erroneous focus on absolute values that led to the formulation of the Easterlin's paradox (Kagan 2012, 104–105; Deaton 2013).[22]

---

20 It should be clear that this is a statistical paradox, not an economic one. From the praxeological point of view, "the utility of X units of a good is always greater than the utility of X – 1 units" (Rothbard 2009, 25), as larger stock of means is capable of rendering more service to individual in her attempts to achieve a given goal. Hence, increase in income would lead to increase in utility. However, utility does *not* equal happiness and there is no economic law that says the increase in income (or in any other variable) must lead to the increase in happiness.

21 An overview of the literature on happiness economics can be found, for example, in Diener (2000), MacKerron (2012), or Clark (2018). The detailed discussion of this entire field is beyond the scope of this sub-chapter.

22 Johns and Ormerod (2007) point out that there is no temporal correlation between happiness and several social indicators other than income, such as longevity, crime, leisure time, infant mortality, income inequality, depression, etc. Given that these things should be expected to affect happiness, the lack of any meaningful relationship questions the validity of timeline happiness data and the Easterlin's paradox.

Second, let us note that the market-based economy is the impersonal self-ordering process that does not strive for any particular objective, such as the happiness or the highest possible pace of GDP growth, etc. It just allows people reaching their own goals, or attain happiness in their own way, as they themselves understand it (Hayek 1973; 2002; Mises 1998 [1949], ch. I, XV). In other words, the market-based economy is a tool for cooperation, which enables people to meet each other's needs. As Mises 1998 [1949, 258] puts it, "Everybody is both a means and an end in himself; an ultimate end for himself and a means to other people in their endeavors to attain their own ends (...) The market is a process, actuated by the interplay of the actions of the various individuals cooperating under the division of labor.[23]

The economic growth is the result – a kind of positive externality – of activities of households and companies in the free market. If anything, this is probably the only thing we should expect from the economic system – i.e., the improvement of objective living standards (Mises 1985).

Governments measure the GDP and support the economic growth because this is probably the least controversial possible goal common for most people. The immense majority of them "aim first of all at an improvement of the material conditions of well-being. They want more and better food, better homes and clothes, and a thousand other amenities. They strive after abundance and health" (Mises 1998 [1949], 96).

There are three important points here. First, measuring GDP and supporting the economic growth does not necessarily imply the affirmation of materialism, as income can be used to achieve various aims. Wilkinson (2007, 34) even argues that measuring income and wealth embodies "liberal neutrality by measuring something that is valuable in varying degrees to all of us."

Second, economic growth not only raises people's standard of living in terms of consumer goods, but it also positively correlates with many nonsubjective aspects of well-being, such as health, longevity, education, etc. (Wilkinson 2007). It is worth pointing out here that, given the improving health and extending life expectancy, the economic growth increases the lifetime total of happiness (or the number of healthy and happy life) of people (Johns and Ormerod 2007, 31; Wilkinson 2007).

Additionally, Friedman (2005, 14) notices that economic growth "bears social and political consequences that are morally beneficial," as it fosters tolerance, openness, and "social mobility, commitment to fairness, and dedication to democracy" (Friedman 2005, 4). Moreover, Inglehart and Welzel (2005,

---

23 See also Wicksteed (1914, 2): "[T]he economic organism, then, of an industrial society represents the instrumentality whereby every man, by doing what he can for some of his fellows, gets what he wants from other."

130) point out that "increasingly favorable existential conditions nourish a sense of human autonomy, which promotes a sense of subjective well-being."

Third, the goal of economic progress does not involve a quantitative target. Historically, GDP has not been measurable in real time for most of the time, and governments have not tried to maximized it (Johns and Ormerod 2007). Even today, with the exception of China and perhaps a few other countries, no government targets a specific rate of GDP growth.

Happiness would be a much more problematic social goal. This is because happiness is something subjective, and it is unclear how to achieve it, and whether it is possible at all during earthly existence.[24] This is probably why the U.S. Declaration of Independence (1776) is about people's right to the pursuit of happiness, not about their right to happiness. There is also no consensus on what happiness is, exactly (Bok 2010, ch. III), and how to measure it, if it can be measured at all. The problem is that happiness is an open term that no one knows exactly how to achieve and "that assumes different meanings and is attained in a variety of ways" (Kagan 2012, 87). Gilbert (2007, 70, emphasis in original) points out that even if "we say with moderate precision what we mean by words such as *happiness*, we still can't be sure that two people who claim to be happy are *having* the same experience, or that our current experience of happiness is really different from our past experience of happiness, or that we are having an experience of happiness at all."[25]

There are of course self-reports on happiness and measures of life satisfaction, but they suffer from many problems (Campbell 1981; Bertrand and Mullainathan 2001; Hamermesh 2004; Wilkinson 2007; Krueger 2008; Nussbaum 2008; Bok 2010, ch. V; Kagan 2012; McCloskey 2012; Deaton 2013, 31; Fleurbaey and Blanchet 2013, ch. 5; Ravallion 2014; White 2014, 2015).[26]

---

[24] From the religious perspective, the true happiness can only be found in Heaven (McCloskey 2012).

[25] Similarly, Kagan (2012, 79) notices that "individuals who report the same level of well-being could have behaved in different ways, achieved different goals, held different values, and experienced different feelings over their lifetimes." See also McCloskey (2012), who points out that even when researchers can survey people about happiness, they cannot assume that the same scores mean the same, and that they can have a scientifically valid objective measure of society's happiness: "We cannot ever know whether your experience of the color red is the same as mine, no matter how many brain scans we take. (The new hedonism is allied, incidentally, with the new brain science, which merrily takes the brain for the mind.) Nor can we know what red or happiness 1-2-3 is in the mind of God, the 'objective happiness' that Kahneman speaks of as though he knew it."

[26] On the more general problem of using subjective data in economic research, see: Bertrand and Mullainathan (2001); Hamermesh (2004). The former paper

I limit myself here to point out that experiences of many different kinds have to be aggregated into a single whole (Nussbaum 2008), and that satisfaction or happiness scores are bounded by construction (Johns and Ormerod 2007; Wilkinson 2007; Fleurbaey and Blanchet 2013, 183).[27] There is also a scaling problem, i.e., "the problem of converting what must be some continuous ordinal measure into a measure described by a few categories" (Hamermesh 2004, 2). And the reliability of happiness data is debatable, given a disturbingly high variability (Ravallion 2014, 152–153).

However, the fundamental issue is that utility, or happiness, is subjective. Thus, it is ordinal, not cardinal (Robbins 1932; Hicks and Allen 1934; Mises 1998 [1949]; Rothbard 2009), and it cannot be objectively measured.[28] As Rothbard (2009, 18–19, emphasis in original) points out,

> It is important to realize that there is never any possibility of *measuring* increases or decreases in happiness or satisfaction. Not only is it impossible to measure or compare changes in the satisfaction of different people; it is not possible to measure changes in the happiness of any given person. In order for any measurement to be possible, there must be an eternally fixed and objectively given unit with which other units may be compared. There is no such objective unit in the field of human valuation. The individual must determine subjectively for himself whether he is better or worse off as a result of any change. His preference can only be expressed in terms of simple choice, or *rank*. Thus, he can say, "I am better off" or "I am happier" because he went to a concert instead of playing bridge [...], but it would be completely meaningless for him to try to assign units to his preference and say, "I am two and a half times happier because of this choice than I would have been playing bridge." Two and a half times *what*?

Hence, researchers on happiness have to rely on verbal statements declaring that the subjects are happy (Kagan 2012, 80). However, for most of them it is not enough; they assign numbers to the answers or put them into a numerical

---

argues that "subjective variables cannot reasonably be used as dependent variables" (Bertrand and Mullainathan 2001, 70).

27 The obvious problem of the bounded and discrete nature of self-reported happiness scores is that beyond a certain point the measured happiness would not show any further increase. Another issue is that "noticeable changes in average happiness can come about only through substantial numbers of people changing their categories" (Johns and Ormerod 2007, 13), which is not reasonable to expect over relatively short periods.

28 However, some researchers on happiness seem to try to resurrect the idea of cardinal utility. For example, Frey and Stutzer (2002, 43) wrote: "Utility can and should be cardinally measured in the form of subjective well-being." See also: Ng 1997; Kahneman 1999; Layard 2005; Van Praag and Ferrer-i-Carbonell 2004.

scale, calculate the average, and plot it on a graph against the GDP, as if *utils* exist after all (McCloskey 2012).

The problem with subjective responses, as Hamermesh (2004, 3) notes, is that there is no apparent link from them "to any underlying measure of utility, at least measures that maintain the properties that we desire for utility functions."[29] Similarly, Kagan (2012, 80–85) notices that mere declarations of people that they are happy cannot be relied on as an authoritative source, because there is only a minimal or modest relation between people's self-descriptions and "direct observations of behaviors or biological processes that should correspond with the verbal replies" (Kagan 2012, 95). Moreover, happiness does not have an unambiguous meaning and people have different beliefs that are not always scientifically valid (e.g., scientists do not assume the existence of paranormal phenomena based on the fact that some people report believing in them) (Kagan 2012, 80-85).

And it is worth pointing out here the problem with verbal statements compared with the observed actions. As Saint-Paul (2011, 51, emphasis in original) notes,

> [T]he point of revealed preferences [...] is to allow us to make statements about the utility from a decision that has been made over a decision that has *not* been made. Direct measures of happiness tell us nothing about how happy people would feel if instead they were earning less, consuming a different basket of goods, or not be[ing] married to the same person. At best, they allow us to compare self-reported happiness between today and last year, but since moving backward in time is not an option, that does not allow us to infer that there is any self-harm in the course of action taken by the individual.

For all these reasons, happiness statements given by people constitute the explanandum rather than the explanans. As Kagan (2012, 116) notes, researchers "should use the objective conditions in a community to understand the meanings of well-being judgments rather than use the judgments to evaluate a community or society and explain its vitality."

However, even if we agree for the sake of discussion that happiness could be measured in a reliable manner, the issue remains as to why the government should care about the happiness of the citizens at all. It would entail a move away from a definition of welfare based on objective factors towards a definition based on subjective feelings. The problem is that such a society would be more paternalistic and further from liberal neutrality (White 2014). As Saint-Paul (2011, 71) points out, "[W]hen revealed preferences are tossed out the

[29] Cf. Kagan (2012, 85), who writes that happiness does not refer "to a single psychological state that can be observed in phenomena other than a verbal answer to a question" (Kagan, 2012, 85).

window, Big Brother enters through the back door. Any individual action can be scrutinized and penalized on the grounds that it exerts some unwelcome externality on somebody else's feelings."

Another issue, if we agree on happiness as an important social goal, would be to determine the 'optimal' level and distribution of happiness (Oishi et al. 2007), and how to implement ethical policy based on happiness (White 2015). After all, utility or happiness scores cannot be compared among people (McCloskey 2012; White 2015),[30] and different things bring happiness to different people (Lo and Gilmour 2004; Wierzbicka 2004; Kagan 2012), and even to the same people at different times. Should happiness policy disregard distinct sources of happiness (even the immoral ones) and focus simply on the outcome (Nussbaum 2008)? Which determinants of happiness should be prioritized, given that they are not same for all people (Beck et al. 2025)?[31]

On this basis, Dworkin (2000, 329, emphasis in original) argues against the policy of maximizing happiness (or utility differently specified) as unfair:

> [W]hatever appeal utilitarianism has depends on *not* specifying what utility means, since once any more detailed specification such as "happiness" or "success in one's aims" is chosen, it becomes plain that the goal of maximizing utility so defined, even when feasible, is unfair, because at least some people would not take utility so characterized as of dominant importance for their lives. Utilitarianism, once utility is specified, violates the second principle of ethical individualism.

The aim of an economic system, if it has any aim, is to organize how people produce, exchange, and consume. The market-based economy simply enables

---

[30] See Fleurbaey and Blanchet (2013, 193): "It appears heroic to hope that spontaneous answers to subjective well-being questionnaires could directly deliver data for ethically reasonable interpersonal comparisons."

[31] For example, Cantril (1965, 206, 222) provides us with two accounts of the imagined best life, if one is to be happy. First person, from India: "I want a son and a piece of land since I am now working on land owned by other people. I would like to construct a house of my own and have a cow for milk and ghee. I would also like to buy some better clothing for my wife. If I could do this then I would be happy." Second person, from the United States: "I would like a reasonable income to maintain a house, have a new car, have a boat, and send my four children to private schools." Assuming these people would live in one country, should the happiness policy subsidies cows for people? Or maybe boats? This example also illustrates the problem with measures of happiness or subjective well-being. The standards of answers change with people's actual conditions of life, which can explain the flatness of scores that constitute the Easterlin's paradox (Fleurbaey and Blanchet 2013, 173, 186).

people to interact freely and to realize their individual goals, i.e., pursue happiness as they define it.[32] As Mises (2008 [1956], 3) noted,

> Under capitalism the common man enjoys amenities which in ages gone by were unknown and therefore inaccessible even to the richest people. But, of course, these motorcars, television sets and refrigerators do not make a man happy. In the instant in which he acquires them, he may feel happier than he did before. But as soon as some of his wishes are satisfied, new wishes spring up. Such is human nature.

In other words, human wants are insatiable, which means that people will always feel some uneasiness or discomfort, and the state of permanent full happiness is beyond the reach of mankind, at least through social policy. Røysamb and others (2018) note that happiness or life satisfaction are influenced not only by economy and social relations, but also by life events, health and personality traits, and that genetic factors influence both personality and happiness or life satisfaction. Thus, as Diener and Lucas (1999, 227) point out, "the influence of genetics and personality suggests a limit on the degree to which policy can increase subjective well-being." More philosophically, Mises (1985, 4) notes,

> Social policy, with the means that are at its disposal, can make men rich or poor, but it can never succeed in making them happy or in satisfying their inmost yearnings. Here all external expedients fail. All that social policy can do is to remove the outer causes of pain and suffering; it can further a system that feeds the hungry, clothes the naked, and houses the homeless. Happiness and contentment do not depend on food, clothing, and shelter, but, above all, on what a man cherishes within himself. It is not from a disdain of spiritual goods that liberalism concerns itself exclusively with man's material well-being, but from a conviction that what is highest and deepest in man cannot be touched by any outward regulation. It seeks to produce only outer well-being because it knows that inner, spiritual riches cannot come to man from without, but only from within his own heart.

The above considerations might sound pessimistic, but it is not clear whether people want to really have a *happy* life (especially when happiness would be understood in a hedonistic manner) rather than a *good* life, which is multidimensional and encompasses more than happiness understood as self-reported mood or satisfaction (Nussbaum 2008; McCloskey 2012).

---

32 Please note that economists, when writing about utility, or sometimes even about happiness, apply these terms in a purely formal sense. As Mises (1998 [1949], 15) notes, "In the praxeological terminology the proposition: man's unique aim is to attain happiness, is tautological. It does not imply any statement about the state of affairs from which man expects happiness."

From the evolutionary perspective, humans did not evolve to be happy, but to survive and reproduce. Thus, happiness can be seen not as the ultimate goal, but rather as an instrument used by our genes towards that goal (Pinker 1998; Becker and Rayo 2008).[33] Actually, it is argued that people have evolved "an array of psychological mechanisms that are 'designed' to cause subjective distress under some circumstances" (Buss 2000, 17) and also ability "to adapt quickly to their circumstances, putting us on a 'hedonic treadmill'" Buss (2000, 19). Thus, it can be concluded that a "perpetual states of happiness would almost certainly have been maladaptive" (Buss 2000, 22).

In other words, it is far from obvious why the richness of human life should be reduced to single index, and why happiness should be people's ultimate goal or the most important value rather than others, such as survival and reproduction, justice and other cardinal virtues, meaningfulness, or psychological richness (McCloskey 2012; Baumeister et al. 2013; Oishi and Westgate 2022). For example, if members of a given society have such preferences that they would feel great happiness coming from torturing minorities or invading other countries, one would not praise such a society because of other moral values (Rothbard 1998, ch. 26; 2006, 30–32; Nussbaum 2008; Kagan 2012).

Similarly, one would rather oppose the idea of giving drugs to the poor people or plugging them into the pleasure machine to make them happy as a *solution* of poverty (Nozick 1974).[34] One would rather try to alleviate the *sources* of poverty, not to try to make people happy *despite* their poverty.[35] Of

[33] Pinker (1998, 37) writes that happiness evolved because "happy people are pleasant to be around, so they attracted more allies." The evolutionary perspective can also shed light on the postulated U-shaped happiness over the life cycle. It is suggested that the so-called midlife crisis may be a period that adapts us to the later part of life (Thams and Brassen 2023).

[34] See Dworkin (2000, 44) on a similar thought experiment in which there is a choice "between a life in which you in fact achieved some goal important to you, though you did not realize that you had, and a different life in which you falsely believed that you had achieved that goal and therefore had the enjoyment or satisfaction flowing from that belief." See also McCloskey (2012) and Annas (2004, 50), who points out that happiness is an achievement – i.e., "happiness comes from living in some ways and not others, that it is not something that others can give you, either by giving you stuff or by getting you into a particular state."

[35] A fictional society in which its members take a drug called 'soma' to produce feeling of happiness was described by Huxley (2006 [1932]). See Dworkin (2006) on a realistic description of negative consequences of prescribing psychotropic drugs for unhappiness in modern American society, such as being 'happy' independent of miserable lives and without motivation to improve its life. After all, the bad feelings may be cues one gets from the environment to improve her situation (Saint-Paul 2011, 56).

course, it is generally something positive when poor (as well as rich) people are happy. But their level of happiness is not completely determined by their objective well-being, with their abilities to buy food, equipment, health, education, leisure, etc. As Sen (1985, ch. 3) points out, happiness (or desire-fulfillment) is too malleable to serve as a good proxy of people's well-being. After all, given the happiness set point and hedonic adaptation (Seligman 2002), some people can be relatively happy, but disadvantaged (Sen 1985; Fleurbaey and Blanchet 2013, 168).[36] Importantly, the fact that people can adapt and be happy in different circumstances does not imply that these distinct conditions are equally desirable.

Meanwhile, economic growth enables people to increase their standard of living. Even if people are not ultimately happier,[37] they have more resources at their disposal to achieve their aims, so their capabilities are greater (Sen 1985; Wilkinson 2007; Nussbaum 2008). For example, having a real daily income of $38 instead of $15 gives the opportunities to do much more, including achieving 'happiness' in a more dignified human sense (living in a better-equipped flat, seeing private health practitioners, going on holidays abroad, visiting the cinema or theater on weekends, etc.).[38]

What is important here is to remember that people actually do *not* care about utility, but about goods and services. As Fleurbaey and Blanchet (2013, 202) put it,

---

[36] Sen (1985, 14) calls this shortcoming a "physical-condition neglect." And he writes about it as follows: "A person who is ill-fed, undernourished, unsheltered and ill can still be high up in the scale of happiness or desire-fulfilment if he or she has learned to have realistic desires and to take pleasure in small mercies. The physical conditions of a person do not enter the view of well-being seen entirely in terms of happiness or desire-fulfilment, except insofar as they are *indirectly* covered by the mental attitudes of happiness or desire" (Sen 1985, 14, emphasis in original). See also McCloskey (2012) and Graham (2009) on the paradox of the happy peasant and frustrated achievers." Kagan (2012) notices that replacing GDP with a happiness index could remove political pressure from the governments to improve the living conditions of the citizens.

[37] However, even if we acknowledge hedonic adaptation, the economic growth would make people happier during transitional periods, which could be prolonged, so to speak, by continuous growth. In other words, it is not clear what the hedonic adaptation suggests for public policy and 'optimal' pace of GDP growth (Johns and Ormerod 2007).

[38] This is the increase in median income (expressed in 2021 international dollars) that Poland has experienced in the period of 1985–2022 (World Bank Poverty and Inequality Platform and Our World in Data 2025).

> It is apparently easy for economists to forget that when the economic model makes the individual maximize u(x), this means that the individual cares about x, not u(x). If individuals cared about u(x), they would spend their time working on their mind-set rather than changing the world around them.[39]

People care about a variety of achievements, not just about their own mental states (satisfaction or happiness). They are preoccupied with obtaining what they want rather than being simply satisfied (through, e.g., lowering their aspirations and living like monks). The life satisfaction people feel and report is the *summary* of all other valuable things rather than a *source* of value itself, or the *outcome* of evaluation rather than *object* of the evaluation (Fleurbaey and Blanchet 2013, 169–174). Hence, people are not concerned about their satisfaction but,

> about the *object* of their satisfaction [...]. In a sense, their satisfaction is what they care the least about! It is not satisfaction that makes a good life, but a good life that gives satisfaction. Satisfaction is the consequence of having a life full of valuable things, but is not a source of value by itself. (Fleurbaey and Blanchet (2013, 171, emphasis in original)

In other words, from the fact that utility is a central concept in economics, researchers who study happiness economics conclude that utility (defined as subjective well-being or happiness) should also be the social goal. However, they fail to understand that 'utility' used as an economic term does *not* mean the same as happiness or 'utility' used as a psychological term. When economists talk about utility, they do not have in mind any mental state; for them it is a technical term used for theoretical representation of the process of choice. When they say that the utility of *x* exceeds the utility of *y* for person A, they do not mean that the consumption of *x* delivers more happiness (or any other positive psychological feeling) than *y*, but simply that person A chose *x* over *y*. As Saint-Paul (2011, 56–57, emphasis in original) puts it, "Utility is a useful abstract concept that summarizes our goals, and therefore what we *want*. Happiness is just a mental state: how we *feel*."

Hence, just like some behavioral economists, researchers who argue that happiness should be the society's ultimate goal commit the 'causal utility fallacy,' I wrote about in sub-chapter 2.5 (Binmore 2009). They do not consider utility as a methodological notion used to describe people's choices, but seem to believe that utility exists independently from real action, perhaps is embedded somehow in goods, and thus can be calculated before making choice.

---

[39] Thus, Oswald (1997, 1815) could not have been further from the truth when he wrote, "[E]conomic things matter only in so far as they make people happier." See also Fleurbaey and Blanchet (2013, 172–173).

In such a mistaken view, utility becomes the ultimate goal, while goods and services matter only because of their utility. People consume them in order to increase their level of utility.[40] On these grounds, some researchers on happiness economics suggest that it would be better to focus directly on utility (or happiness), especially if, according to Easterlin's paradox, income growth above a certain level does not translate into greater happiness (Scitovsky 1976; Oswald 1997; Diener 2000; Jansen et al. 2004; Easterlin 2005; Layard 2005; Lee and Goh 2023; Agrawal et al. 2025). In such an erroneous perspective, in which utility exists separately from real actions, there might be a gap between people's choices and their 'true' utility (or happiness), which provides the justification for a social policy directly aimed at happiness.

In standard welfare economics, there is no such gap, as welfare is inextricably linked to choice and preference satisfaction, and it can be improved by some change only if the individual would choose to make that change (Gul and Pesendorfer 2008; MacKerron 2012). If people did not consider a certain course of action to be the best option for them, taking into account all the constraints, they would not have behaved in such a way. However, this does not mean that individuals could not have made a better choice (if constraints are relaxed and, for example, they have better information), nor that their decision would maximize their happiness. Economics is not a theory of happiness or good life. It does not try to assess or improve people's objectives; it treats them as given, no matter whether they arise from the pursuit of happiness or not, and whether they could be considered (by whom?) conducive to happiness or not (Rothbard 1956; Gul and Pesendorfer 2008). As Gul and Pesendorfer (2008, 8) points out,

> Standard economics has no therapeutic ambition; that is, it does not try to evaluate or improve the individual's objectives. Economics cannot distinguish between choices that maximize happiness, choices that reflect a sense of duty, or choices that are the response to some impulse. Moreover, standard economics takes no position on the question of which of those objectives the agent should pursue. The purpose of economics is to analyze institutions, such as trading mechanisms and organization structures, and to ask how those institutions mediate the interests of different

---

40 I see an analogy with computer games, where the character has health, mana, and stamina bars that deplete over time but can be regenerated through items. In happiness economics, people are often modeled to function as if they have utility bars they care about, as if they can measure and calculate utility. However, as Mises (1998 [1949], 120–122) notes, "Action does not deal with physical or metaphysical units which it values in an abstract academic way [...]. To prefer and to set aside and the choices and decisions in which they result are not acts of measurement. Action does not measure utility or value; it chooses between alternatives."

> economic agents. This analysis is useful irrespective of the causes of individuals' preferences.

What is important is that aspirations and feelings can enter the utility function affecting what people want. They can, for example, rationally decide that safety, comfort, or status is more important than feelings, and purchase a big house *knowing* that it will not bring them happiness. Thus, as Saint-Paul (2011, 57) notices, "[T]hey did not make a mistake; they just care less about their own happiness than the expert who is studying their behavior."

Given the discussion above, it should already be clear why it is false that goods and services matter only because of their utility. It is in fact vice versa: economists ascribe utility to goods and services only because people take care about them. Utility is not a psychological quality that operates in the mental world behind the real objects or the qualities that are embedded in them. It is a scientific term that is used in economic theory and teaching, or – as MacKerron (2012, 707) puts it – "an analytically instrumental quantity, which individuals need not be assumed to experience or understand." Thus, when economists talk about people maximizing utility, they basically have in mind that people act the way they do, because they have some reason for it, and choose their most preferred option. What I mean here is that utility – contrary to happiness in eudaimonism (Bruni 2008) – is not the 'highest good,' the final, ultimate psychological goal; it is a technical term used for a description of the fact that people strive to achieve their various subjectively perceived goals, or to satisfy their preferences, whatever they may be (sensual pleasure, peace of mind, a harmonious family life, a sense of meaning, intellectual satisfaction, spiritual bliss, joy of the consumer spree, contentment with a job well done, etc.).

In other words, some researchers on happiness economics equate happiness with utility or treat it as its proxy (Ferrer-i-Carbonell 2013; Kapteyn 2020), although utility in modern economics has been stripped of any psychological connotations and became a technical, contentless term. As Becker and Rayo (2008, 90) note, "[H]appiness may be an important determinant of utility, but that does not mean that both coincide." For example, some people take unpleasant jobs, because they pay well. According to the theory of revealed preference, they raise their utility, even though their happiness may decrease (Becker and Rayo 2008).[41] Similarly, it is possible that some people become more miserable because of the extra working hours and related stress. However, people often work hard and sacrifice their leisure or present satisfaction, because, for example, they want to achieve something or buy something

---

41 In a survey conducted by Tversky and Griffin (2000), most respondents said that they would choose the job with the higher absolute salary and lower relative position, although they anticipated that they would be less happy in this job.

important for themselves and their kids. Thus, they believe that it is worth it, that their level of pleasure is less valuable than the satisfaction from working extra hours to buy something for their children.[42] Hence, equating utility with happiness, "researchers are making their own paternalistic statement that individuals should care more about feeling well, relative to other goals, than they actually do" (Saint-Paul 2011, 57).

Indeed, researchers who suggest that happiness should be society's ultimate goal express their normative position, which boils down to condemning consumerism and paternalism.[43] They have the right to dislike consumerism, but economists should refrain from moral judgements and accept human goals as given. When they suggest that economic growth does not make people happier, they effectively express the opinion that the actions of people, which were undertaken voluntarily and led to this economic growth, should be replaced by other actions, probably more 'noble' or with greater potential to generate 'happiness' – in the opinion of those expressing such views. As I mentioned in sub-chapter 1.5, evaluating the goals of other people and imposing our own values on others, instead of relying on the revealed preference of individuals, contradicts the principle of methodological subjectivism and value-free positive economic analysis (Hayek 1948b; Mises 1998 [1949]; Gul and Pesendorfer 2008).

---

[42] Of course, it might turn ex post that people's speculation was wrong. It is possible that, for example, their child would prefer to spend a few hours longer each week with their more relaxed parent than to get a new educational toy. However, what is important here is that market-based economy provides the opportunity to work, but does not force anyone to participate in the system. People can freely allocate their time towards work and other activities. Anyone can drop out and live outside the society (Mises 1998 [1949]).

[43] As McCloskey (2012) puts it: "There is a surprisingly puritanical edge to the new hedonics, especially about the pleasurable income other people have. Easterlin argues that 'economic growth is a carrier of a material culture of its own that ensures that humankind is forever ensnared in the pursuit of more and more economic goods.' The hedonicists see modern levels of consumption as vulgar, an arms race for status that the tax system should be arranged to stop. Hedonics has become a branch of the century-old campaign by the American clerisy against 'consumerism'—that is, the getting of the silly stuff to which the non-clerisy are so enslaved, unlike our own refined consumption of opera tickets and adventure holidays." The happiness economics could also be influenced by a version of egalitarianism that calls for the equality of enjoyment or happiness (Dworkin 2000, 42–45). Kagan (2012, 87–88) points out that Americans are especially receptive to the importance of happiness because of the nation's egalitarian ethos.

## 7. CONCLUSIONS

Capitalism was once criticized for its anarchy of production and the lack of efficiency. It was believed that properly run centrally planned economy would generate more wealth than market economy (Khalil 1992). The great material success of market-based economies and the collapse of socialistic economies have showed that this line of criticism was unjustified (Boettke et al. 2024).

However, as Schumpeter (1994, 144) points out, "[C]apitalism stands its trial before judges who have the sentence of death in their pockets. They are going to pass it, whatever the defense they may hear; the only thing a successful defense can possibly produce is a change in the indictment." Thus, the critique of capitalism has shifted from materialist into the antimaterialist one. According to this view, while capitalism produce impressive wealth, it makes people unhappy.

This is why some social researchers argue for replacing GDP with happiness as the social goal. However, happiness would be a very problematic social goal, for many reasons I have discussed in this chapter. To avoid repeating myself, let me just note here that the idea that happiness – or any other single measure of well-being – can cover all the interests and values of people, is an illusion. Thus, the policy based on happiness would essentially substitute people's own interests and values with the ones of the policymakers (White 2014, 1–7).

The antimaterialist critique of capitalism is actually hardly a new argument, as Marx had already blamed capitalism for the alleged alienation of labor, as well as for exploitation (and resulting income and wealth inequality) (MECW 1975, 3: 270–282). What is new in the recent critique is the attempt to quantify and medicalize the old claims (Novak 2010). The alienation, domination, exploitation, and unequal income and wealth distribution are linked to some deteriorating aspects of mental health in some countries (Prins et al. 2015; Eisenberg-Guyot and Prins 2022).

However, as I showed in this chapter, such attempts are far from satisfactory, both on empirical and theoretical grounds. First, deaths due to despair have not risen in all developed countries. Second, the arguments about alienation or exploitation of work are highly questionable, as people work fewer hours and are more satisfied with their work. There is also no deterioration in self-reported happiness in developed countries over the recent decades. Third, complaints about capitalism are in part complaints with regard to the scarcity of goods, and the resulting need to work and the associated disutility. Fourth, there is no reliable evidence that income and wealth inequality per se – and, for example, not poverty or deprivation – cause stress and impair physical and mental health. Fifth, complaints with regard to capitalism are also in part complaints about the constraints of civilization and the hierarchical groups existing within it, although such groups are natural even for those primates who do not build civilizations based on the functioning of the markets. The lack of proper separation of life under capitalism from life in civilization, hierarchical societies, and specific culture, and attributing all the stress people encounter solely to the economic system, is an important omission of other factors. Some researchers seem to follow Marx (MECW 1975, 29: 263) and claim that the mode of production determines the mental life (Prins et al. 2015; Sell and Williams 2019; Eisenberg-Guyot and Prins 2022), but in this way they assume something that should be proved.

# 5. Psychological factors of anti-market sentiment

## 1. INTRODUCTION

Individuals' psychological propensities, or deviations from full rationality, are usually used as arguments for government interventions to improve the functioning of the markets (e.g., O'Donoghue and Rabin 2003; Thaler and Sunstein 2008). However, the economic system may remain rational even if individuals do not behave completely rationally (Hayek 1945; Alchian 1950; Gode and Sunder 1993; Smith 2008).

This chapter – which tries to contribute to psychology or sociology rather than economics – shows that psychology can be used in defending market-based economies as well, arguing that many people display anti-market sentiment.

The starting point of this part is the observation that economists – who differ, of course, in their philosophical and political views – as a group, are more free-market friendly than other scholars in the social sciences and humanities (Klein and Stern 2007), and also than random people (Washington Post et al. 1996; Blendon et al. 1997; Caplan 2001, 2002).

This negative attitude towards capitalism and markets held by many people is puzzling for economists who are generally well aware of the enormous benefits of the market-based economy.[1] After all, since the Industrial Revolution, millions of people have emerged from poverty and improved their standard of living (Hasell et al. 2022).

It would be tempting to explain this relative pro-market attitude referring simply to the economists' greater knowledge (or more accurate beliefs) about the functioning of the markets. For example, Hayek (1955) claims that people are naturally constructivists – i.e., they believe that institutions had to be

[1] It is true that, after the collapse of the Soviet Union, few people have believed that socialism is more effective than capitalism. However, markets are commonly believed to be characterized by a set of failures, which only governments are able to correct (Stiglitz 1988).

intentionally constructed to work well, and they have problems with grasping the idea of spontaneous order. Hayek (1973) mentions three reasons why so many people still treat with suspicion the idea of the invisible hand:

(1) They cannot conceive of an order that is not deliberately made – such inability can result from the intelligent people's natural tendency to over-value intelligence and, thus, deliberate design.[2] However, this deficiency can stem also from anthropomorphic bias or animism (Hayek 1988; Strongman 2007) – i.e., the propensity to interpret all regularity and order as the result of the design of a thinking, superior mind.
(2) For them, order should have a concrete purpose, which the spontaneous order cannot provide – this way of thinking is also animalistic, as animism gives personality to non-human objects (Guthrie 1993).
(3) The spontaneous order is of abstract character, so it cannot be intuitively perceived, but must be intellectually grasped. And this is not an easy task, because the spontaneous order is a very complex phenomenon, while the science that investigates it is a relatively new one. What adds here to the problem is that economics is not about physical objects, but about people's subjective valuations. The fact that value is not a physical property of things, and creation of wealth is not simply a physical process, implies that trade and finance can increase wealth, although for untrained people commercial and financial activity seem to include merely change of hands or rearranging what already exists without any 'real production' (Hayek 1988). Also, how the pursuit of profits, instead of altruistic service to others, can bring long-term benefits to all, is not sufficiently grasped by most people.

The issue of knowledge (and accurate beliefs) is an important factor, but definitely not the only one – given that anti-market sentiment seems to be relatively strong among academics (Hayek 1949; Nozick 1997; François et al. 2019). Thus, different sets of moral values could also explain partially anti-market sentiment. Hayek (1949) wrote that the ideal of material equality led

2 See Hayek (1988, 53–54): "One's initial surprise at finding that intelligent people tend to be socialists diminishes when one realises that, of course, intelligent people will tend to over-value intelligence, and to suppose that we must owe all the advantages and opportunities that our civilisation offers to deliberate design rather than to following traditional rules, and likewise to suppose that we can, by exercising our reason, eliminate any remaining undesired features by still more intelligent reflection, and still more appropriate design and 'rational coordination' of our undertakings. This leads one to be favourably disposed to the central economic planning and control that lie at the heart of socialism."

intellectuals to endorse socialist views. More recently, Graham and others (2009), based on moral foundations theory, found that liberals – which seem to be less supportive of free markets – "consistently showed greater endorsement and use of the Harm/care and Fairness/reciprocity foundations compared to the other 3 foundations, whereas conservatives endorsed and used the 5 foundations more equally" (Graham et al. 2009, 1029).[3] Also based on moral foundations theory, Iyer and others (2012, 1) found that libertarians showed "1) stronger endorsement of individual liberty as their foremost guiding principle, and weaker endorsement of all other moral principles; 2) a relatively cerebral as opposed to emotional cognitive style; and 3) lower interdependence and social relatedness." Conversely, anti-market sentiment could result from the weaker endorsement of individual liberty compared with other moral values, from a relatively emotional cognitive style, and from higher interdependence and social relatedness.

However, there is a growing literature explaining anti-market sentiment by pointing out the psychological factors. Mises (2008 [1956]) writes that under capitalism, everyone is responsible for their successes or failures. But it is easier to blame the economic system than to take responsibility for one's own choices and their financial repercussions. What is related here is that posts occupied traditionally by the intellectuals are usually less paid than other activities. As Mises (2008 [1956], 13–15) puts it,

> As human nature is, everybody is prone to overrate his own worth and deserts. If a man's station in life is conditioned by factors other than his inherent excellence, those who remain at the bottom of the ladder can acquiesce in this outcome and, knowing their own worth, still preserve their dignity and self-respect. But it is different if merit alone decides. Then the unsuccessful feel themselves insulted and humiliated. Hate and enmity against all those who superseded them must result [...]. In order to console himself and to restore his self-assertion, such a man is in search of a scapegoat. He tries to persuade himself that he failed through no fault of his own. He is at least as brilliant, efficient and industrious as those who outshine him. Unfortunately this nefarious social order of ours does not accord the prizes to the most meritorious men; it crowns the dishonest unscrupulous scoundrel, the swindler, the exploiter, the "rugged individualist." [...] In such a society each member whose ambitions have not been fully satisfied resents the fortune of all those who succeeded better. The fool releases these feelings in slander and defamation. The more sophisticated do not indulge in personal calumny. They sublimate their hatred into a philosophy, the philosophy of anti-capitalism, in order to render inaudible the inner voice that tells them that their failure is entirely their own fault.

---

[3] See Haidt (2012) for a popular exposition of the moral foundations theory and its application to understanding differences in moral and political views. The word 'liberals' was used in the sense given to it by the American political discourse.

Hayek (1988) argues that trade, commerce, and finance have been an object of distrust and fear (of the unfamiliar, and even of sorcery and the unnatural). This is because of their intangible nature and dependence on confidentiality and certain superior knowledge, which makes the impression that merchants and financiers generate their incomes by little perceptible effort (and certainly not by hard physical work or any easily recognizable merit). According to Hayek (1988), traders "partook in a network wholly outside the perception and understanding of ordinary people" (p. 90) and "engaged in something like the transformation of the non-material in altering the value of goods" (p. 90), or in "activities that appear to add to available wealth, 'out of nothing'" (p. 91). Such emotions and attitude could led to the antipathy towards markets.

Caplan (2007) argues that people have systematic biases, such as (1) anti-market bias – the tendency to under-estimate the economic benefits of the market mechanism; (2) anti-foreign bias – the tendency to under-estimate the economic benefits of interaction with foreigners; (3) make-work bias – the tendency to under-estimate the economic benefits from conserving work; and (4) pessimistic bias – the tendency to over-estimate the severity of economic problems and under-estimate the (recent) past, present, and future performance of the economy.

Perhaps, most of Caplan's biases could be described as elements of folk economics. As Rubin (2003, 157–8), puts it, "[T]he world of folk economics is a zero-sum world, and the primary economic problem for each individual is to maximize his or her own wealth in this world."

In other words, people suffer from a kind of tribal bias. According to Foster (2014), the anti-market sentiment stems from the collectivist, anti-individualistic morality that was developed in primitive tribes in specific economic conditions of very limited resources and social interactions perceived as a zero-sum game. In such an environment, attempts to improve one's situation could be seen as greedy and threatening for the tribe. The anti-market sentiment and the positive view of centralized government control could be, thus, an inherited element of tribal impulse to control the behavior of individuals. As Hayek (1988, 11) puts it,

> Man's instincts [...] were not made for the kinds of surroundings, and for the numbers, in which he now lives. They were adapted to life in the small roving bands or troops in which the human race and its immediate ancestors evolved during the few million years while the biological constitution of homo sapiens was being formed.

The problem is that the rules of the extended order (e.g., several property, contract, self-interest, cosmopolitanism) are in conflict with instincts that enabled the tribes to function and survive (e.g., solidarity, in-group altruism, inter-group aggressiveness). In other words, people try to apply their natural instincts of caring interventions to do visible 'good,' which were shaped by living in small groups (families, tribes), to the extended order of cooperation through markets, although it is a different kind of order regulated by distinct rules (Hayek 1988).

Bagus and Bañuelos (2018) argue that the modern welfare state is justified based on a cognitive error – namely, people systematically under-estimate the tendency of others to help those in need. If people do not believe that others would support the poor to a similar extent to themselves, then they are more likely to agree that the government safety net is needed.

Huemer (2013) suggests that the main reason why people favor governments is that they have strong pro-authority psychological bias or that they even suffer from Stockholm syndrome. Thus, if Huemer (2013) is right, not only the modern welfare state, as Bagus and Bañuelos (2018) claim, but the political authority of the state in general, results from cognitive biases.

However, the government is considered to be not only the executive authority, but also the representation of one's country. Thus, it can fulfill people's sense of identity and personal significance (by feeling part of something bigger), as well as the sense of belonging to a group or a community (Nisbet 1962; Fromm 1965; Tajfel 1974; Graham et al. 2009).

Another source of anti-market sentiment, particularly strong among anthropologists, is a 'romantic syndrome,' i.e., a tendency to adopt "a utopian model of primitive society which minimizes the role of conflict, coupled with a model of man which emphasizes innate altruistic and cooperative propensities while playing down self-interest, aggressiveness, and competitiveness" (Cook 1966, 327). In such a view, of Rousseauian tradition, the motive of self-interest is not 'natural' to humans, but is the result of the rise of the market economy. Meanwhile, the primitive societies are thought to be based on reciprocity motivated by generosity and altruism (Polanyi 1944; Cook 1966).[4]

Some people can also have anti-market sentiment, because they do not accept the scarcity as an inherent feature of the reality. They believe that scarcity is only created by the artificial checks on money supply, workers' wages, and government spending enforced by bankers and capitalist (Mises 1998 [1949], 236). In other words, anti-market sentiment can be partially explained by the belief that market economy is the economic system that benefits only the rich at the expense of the exploited working class (Marx 1976 [1867]).

Last but not least, people's anti-market sentiment can be just a status quo bias (Samuelson and Zeckhauser 1988). According to the system justification theory, people tend to defend and justify the status quo and the legitimacy of the existing social order. It does not mean that they actively endorse it, but

---

4 For a more sophisticated view of morality, see Curry and others (2019).

rather that people can adapt to and often even rationalize the existing social order (Jost et al. 2004) – which is right now the welfare state.

## 2. ENVY

One of the most important psychological factors behind the anti-market sentiment is envy. According to Mises (1998 [1949], 90),

> Envy is a widespread frailty. It is certain that many intellectuals envy the higher income of prosperous businessmen and that these feelings drive them toward socialism. They believe that the authorities of a socialist commonwealth would pay them higher salaries than those that they earn under capitalism.

Contrary to feudalism, under capitalism, people's incomes are much more the results of their merits than birth or belonging to the particular social class or cast. This can increase envy, because capitalism enables, at least theoretically, everyone to succeed and compare themselves with others on this path. As Bacon observes, "Where there is no comparison, no envy; and therefore kings are not envied but by kings" (cited in Ben-Ze'ev 1992, 556). However, not only success, but also failure depends much more on personal merit, which is psychologically challenging, and can lead to the status anxiety (De Botton 2004). As Mises (2008 [1956], 11–12, emphasis in original),

> In a society based on caste and status, the individual can ascribe adverse fate to conditions beyond his own control [...]. It is quite another thing under capitalism. Here everybody's station in life depends on his own doing. Everybody whose ambitions have not been fully gratified knows very well that he has missed chances, that he has been tried and found wanting by his fellow man [...]. The much talked about sternness of capitalism consists in the fact that it handles everybody according to his contribution to the well-being of his fellow men. The sway of the principle, *to each according to his accomplishments*, does not allow of any excuse for personal shortcomings. Everybody knows very well that there are people like himself who succeeded where he himself failed. Everybody knows that many of those whom he envies are self-made men who started from the same point from which he himself started. And, much worse, he knows that all other people know it too [...]. What makes many feel unhappy under capitalism is the fact that capitalism grants to each the opportunity to attain the most desirable positions which, of course, can only be attained by a few. Whatever a man may have gained for himself, it is mostly a mere fraction of what his ambition has impelled him to win.[5]

---

[5] See also Schoeck (1987, 77): "Overwhelming and astounding inequality, especially when it has an element of the unattainable, arouses far less envy than minimal inequality, which inevitably causes the envious to think: I might have been in his place."

Envy is probably one of the major factors behind the debates about income and wealth inequality.[6] According to many people, one of the biggest problems of capitalist economies is (excessive) income and wealth inequality. At first glance, this is a bit surprising – after all, income inequality is merely a statistical relationship between the incomes of different people. Should not poverty be a more important social issue? Objectively, the problem is not that some people earn less than others, but that some people earn below the level that allows them to meet their basic needs (Frankfurt 2015). However, as I mentioned in Chapter 4, according to Wilkinson and Pickett (2009), inequality has a real impact on people's well-being. The greater the inequality in society, the more people worry about their social position, which leads to chronic stress and related negative impacts on their physical and mental health.

Hence, in this line of reasoning, the problem is not really inequality per se, but how people interpret it and respond to it. Income inequality may signal unfairness or systemic disadvantages, but also the possibility of opportunities and gains that can be achieved in the future (Graham 2008).[7] For example, Alesina and others (2004) found that inequality in the United States, contrary to Europe, has no effect on the self-reported happiness of the poor because of Americans' perception that they live in a mobile society.[8] Thus, the issue is not that some earn more than others, but that the latter are stressed about it, which is supposed to generate a lot of social problems. The true problem is, in a sense, how people deal with comparison with others – i.e., how envious of or tolerant towards inequality people are, or how strong 'a social comparison orientation'[9] or 'a sense of fairness' they have.

---

[6] See Mui (1995) for more literature about the role of envy in economics.

[7] Saint-Paul (2011, 55–56) argues that the higher status of other people from the reference group can reveal useful information about the unnoticed opportunities in one's life.

[8] See also Ravallion (2014, 150–152), who points out the research that found little evidence of *negative* external effects of rising income of social comparators on subjective welfare of the subjects. Instead, the rise in incomes of peers were found to have *positive* impact due to the mutual support or risk-sharing arrangements and positive externalities of rising community's income. More generally, studies of the relative income hypothesis find both positive and negative effects of relative income, depending on the methods used and the choice of the reference group (Brown et al. 2015).

[9] People differ in terms of the social comparison orientation, which means that only part of the population are highly interested in others and use them as the basis to evaluate their own situation. As Buunk and others (2001, 453) note, "[I]ndividuals high in social comparison orientation are relatively low in intellectual autonomy (one of the Big Five dimensions) and tend to have a strong interest in how others are doing in order to evaluate their own characteristics."

Indeed, the focus on inequality becomes less surprising when one realizes that people have a 'sense of fairness' (Schmidt and Sommerville 2011; McAuliffe 2017), and that fairness has been widely regarded as important component of morality (Rawls 1958).

However, equating fairness with income and wealth equality would be far fetched. This is because of two reasons. First, equality (sameness) is only one possible notion of fairness – but merit and need can influence fairness appraisal (Kirkland et al. 2019). Hence, not material inequality, but inequity or inequality of opportunity could actually be more problematic. According to Starmans and others (2017), "[W]hen fairness and equality clash, people prefer fair inequality over unfair equality" – i.e., they can be content with inequal outcomes if they perceive them as fair.

Second, what is seen as 'sense of fairness,' or the pursuit of equality, could actually be envy, "the most odious and antisocial of sentiments" (J. S. Mill 1859, ch. IV), resentment, or even *schadenfreude*. Some philosophers and researchers argue that egalitarianism is motivated by envy or that it is a rationalization of feelings of envy (Hayek 1960; Nietzsche 1967; Nozick 1974; Buchanan and Hartley 2000). The proper channeling of envy is crucial for economic development – according to Schoeck (1987), it became possible only when bourgeois morality guaranteed the people achieving economic success a clear conscience and an excuse from envious people. He argues, "[T]he utopian desire for an egalitarian society cannot [...] have sprung from any other motive than that of an inability to come to terms with one's own envy, and/or with the supposed envy of one's less well-off fellow men" (Schoeck (1987, 127).[10] Redistributive mechanisms that exist in societies can be, thus, seen as institutional forms that serve to reduce envy (Foster 1972).[11]

There is some empirical support for such claims. In one study, envy (as well as compassion and self-interest, but not fairness) predicted support for redistribution. A significant minority (14–18 percent) of American, Indian, and British participants of this study preferred a higher tax rate for the wealthy even if this meant less money for the poor (Sznycer et al. 2017). Another research reveals not only that "both resentment and compassion predict support for socialism," but also that "hostility toward capitalism likely has more to do with resentment of high achievers than compassion for the needy" and that "resentment

[10] Taubman and Taubman (1989, 143) observe that to many Soviet people, socialism "seems to amount to social envy."

[11] See Nozick (1974, 245) for the critique of redistribution: "It would be objectionable to intervene to reduce someone's situation in order to lessen the envy and unhappiness others feel in knowing of his situation. Such a policy is comparable to one that forbids some act (for example, racially mixed couples walking holding hands) because the mere knowledge that it is being done makes others unhappy."

of high achievers has about twice the impact as compassion for the needy in predicting hostility toward capitalism and support for raising taxes on the rich" (Ekins 2019).

The results of experiments with the ultimatum game are also indicative, as offers of less than 30 percent for the responders are often rejected, despite the fact that accepting it would make both players better off (Henrich et al. 2004).[12] According to Kirchsteiger (1994, 388), the results of the ultimatum game, i.e., the proposing players' demanding less than the whole or virtually the whole stake for themselves, "are not driven by fairness motivation on the side of the proposers but by proposers' fear of a rejection of their offers by envious responders."[13] Similarly, in the dictator game, Fehr and Schmidt (2006, 59) found that "the clear majority of non-economists is willing to sacrifice substantial amounts of the group payoff in order to ensure more equality within the group."

## 3. ILLUSION OF CONTROL

Hayek (1949, 1955) focuses on erroneous belief (fallacy) in constructivist rationalism, but I would like to expand his ideas into the emotional realm. My point is that the idea of spontaneous order is not only intellectually, but also emotionally challenging. This is because the future is inherently unknown, as is the evolution of the market – because of its decentralized character – and how it will deal with possible challenges (Mises 1998 [1949]). Although people often complain about politicians and public services, having some individuals in charge gives them a (false) sense of security and control.

Of course, both cases require faith – either in the invisible hand of the market or in the visible hand of the state. However, having faith in people forming government may be easier for people than in 'impersonal market forces.' This is because the behavior of people within government could be easier to understand (one can empathize with, e.g., the prime minister or president),[14]

---

[12] However, Binmore (1999, F19–F23) points out that when players repeat the game, they move in the optimising direction.

[13] And in the dictator game, provisions are lower than in the ultimatum game. The ultimatum game is a game in which two players interact to decide how to divide a certain sum of money. The first player proposes a division with the second player, who can accept it or reject it. In the first scenario, the money is split with the players according to the division. If there is rejection, players receive nothing. In the dictator game, the second player has no options at all, as the first player decides about the division of money (Kirchsteiger 1994).

[14] It might be so because their behavior seems to be more personal for the public (in part thanks to the media coverage) than the actions of myriad economic

and people could be evolutionarily adapted to live in hierarchical groups led by the leader (Curry et al. 2019). As Hayek (1988, 90) puts it, "[T]o become aware that we depend heavily on human efforts that we cannot know about or control is indeed unnerving – to those who engage in them as well as those who would refrain."

This feeling of being dependent on some impersonal market forces – that are not fully understandable – could be not just psychologically challenging, but, especially for intellectuals, "almost a personal humiliation" (Hayek 1988, 82). In the marketplace, the success of the products, and incomes, are not determined from the point of view of eternal, absolute, inherent (or academic, aesthetic) standards of value, but from the point of view of consumers' preferences, which are not always sublime (Mises 2008 [1956], 9).

Meanwhile, adopting a pro-market sentiment requires giving up the illusion of control (Langer 1975) and exposing oneself to the situation of anarchy and uncertainty (there is no single person who controls the marketplace). The problem here is that people do not like uncertainty and ambiguity (Fox and Tversky 1995), and the control of the environment in which people live is a natural human need that reduces anxiety (Hogarth and Makridakis 1981; Perlmuter and Monty 1977).

Hence, the search for control can lead to negative sentiments towards the free market and to positive sentiments towards government interventionism. This tendency could be strengthened by a few factors. One, the political process provides an illusion that 'someone is in charge.' It is of great importance, because our modern economy is very complex, which makes the impression that it "has outgrown our capacity to survey or control the sequence of events on which we depend" (Hayek 1988, 103). What is related here is that, for many people, the government's control over the economy is the only alternative to the control of capitalists and businessmen. After all, people tend to assume that complex structures – such as economies – are designed and controlled by somebody, and that businessmen cannot be trusted (Hayek 1988).[15]

Democracy also creates the illusion that citizens control the whole process through voting in elections. In this way, people can get the sense of secondary control (Rothbaum et al. 1982; Weisz et al. 1984). It is, however, in a sense, an

---

agents operating in the markets, but also because the government embodies the archetype of the king/queen (Moore and Gillette 1990). It is also worth citing here Foster (2014, Conclusions), who points out, "[W]e are designed to feel and express gratitude to individuals, not systemic abstractions."

15 See McNeill (1981, 35; quoted in Hayek 1988, 90) who noted that throughout history "merchants were objects of very general disdain and moral opprobrium[;] a man who bought cheap and sold dear was fundamentally dishonest[;] merchant behaviour violated patterns of mutuality that prevailed within primary groupings."

illusion, because (1) the probability that a single vote will change the outcome of a national election is nearly zero (Gelman et al. 2012); (2) citizens have only limited options to choose from, as the political leaders exert a strong impact on the electoral lists; and (3) citizens vote only once in a few years and they do not have direct control on the specific actions of already elected politicians; in other words, the assumed representation of voters by politicians is questionable (Casey 2012).

Second, the laissez-faire policy is seen as a passive approach, a 'do-nothing' stance. Although the laissez-faire does not mean leaving things just as they are (Hayek 1944), such a perception could explain a support for government interventions, especially that psychologically action is often preferred to inaction (Sunderrajan and Albarracín 2021), at least following a bad outcome when action is seen as the norm (Bar-Eli et al. 2007; Zeelenberg et al. 2002). This 'action bias' explains why regulators, lawmakers, and authorities are likely to intervene in the economy, especially after a crisis, even though inaction or the removal of a previous regulation could be the better response (Tasic 2009).[16]

Third, the interventionist stance could be a result of the availability bias (Tversky and Kahneman 1973), or neglecting the unseen effects of government policies (Bastiat 2007 [1850]; Hazlitt 1946). When people see the important and urgent social problem, they focus on solving it, ignoring possible unintended consequences. If what is easy to call to mind will influence judgments, the seen benefits of the government policies will be taken into account, while unseen costs will be likely omitted. In one experiment, participants used computer simulation models to undertake land-use planning. It turned out that they focused on the immediate, visible problems, ignoring the unseen effects (Dorner 1997).

Rozenblit and Keil (2002) call the systematic over-estimation of the understanding of complex phenomena *the illusion of explanatory depth*. It is a variant of over-confidence, but people over-estimate not only their own but also others' understanding, which suggests that people over-simplify the nature of the complex problems, and, e.g., believe that visible effects are the only ones that matter. Although it was not considered in the original study, it is possible that the interventionist stance could be a result of the illusion of explanatory depth applied to economics – i.e., the over-estimation of the understanding of how the economy works and how the government policies would affect it (Tasic 2009).

---

16 Additionally, government interventions give hope for a big and relatively quick social change, compared with leaving the fixing of this problem to the markets or civil society (Hayek 1949).

Expanding on the search for control even more, I would like to propose the hypothesis that this constructivist stance is connected with secularism – i.e., people tend to reject all the orders that are larger than their egos. The idea is that people do not want to give up the sense of control and admit that not everything depends on them.[17] In other words, they do not accept the idea of spontaneous order (*cosmos*) or equate order with *taxis* (Hayek 1973).[18]

Hence, the opposition towards the idea of the invisible hand in the market context could be similar to the opposition to the idea of the invisible hand of God in general, as both God and market *cosmos* can be seen as transcendent.[19] And in both cases the opposition seems to stem from the hubris, or the fatal conceit of constructivism – i.e., the idea that "man is able to shape the world around him according to his wishes" (Hayek, 1988, 27).

Constructivism, which is the basis of communism and socialism, sees man as the most rational being on the planet, who controls everything fully. As Chambers (1952, foreword) puts it, communism is man's second oldest faith, whose promise

> was whispered in the first days of the Creation under the Tree of the Knowledge of Good and Evil: 'Ye shall be as gods.' It is the vision of man as the central figure of the Creation, not because God made man in His image, but because man's mind makes him the most intelligent of the animals. Communism restores man to his sovereignty by denying God.

The presented hypothesis is supported by the research pointing out that religiosity is positively correlated with the support for free markets. Using data from the World Values Survey, Guiso and others (2003, 250) demonstrate that "religious people tend to be more supportive of markets."[20] Jones and others (2019,

---

17 Of course, governments (and other entities) can affect the markets, but there are always some unintended consequences, which can make the final state worse than before the intervention (Merton 1936; Hayek 1988).

18 The *taxis* is a made, exogenous order that can be described as construction or organization. The *cosmos* is a grown, endogenous, self-generating, or spontaneous order. The market is the latter (Hayek 1973).

19 Of course, the market is not transcendent in the same, metaphysical way as God. However, it is an extended order that can be seen as epistemologically transcendent (Hayek 1988).

20 However, Czeglédi (2023) points out that countries with a larger proportion of more religious people do not have more market-friendly institutions, which suggests that a positive relationship between religiosity and market friendliness is a uniquely Western feature due to Christianity and the ideology of conservative liberalism. Siedentop (2014) claims that liberalism is the offspring of the Church – i.e., Christianity was necessary for liberalism.

409) find that in the U.S., "Christianity is strongly associated with greater pro-market views relative to those who are not religious." One can also note that – compared with older generations – Millennials are less religious and at the same time more accepting of socialism (Pew Research Center 2015; Rampell 2016).

However, another hypothesis can also be presented. The anti-market sentiment and support for the strong role of government in the economy can be a substitute for faith in the controlling God. After all, people have a fundamental need to believe in a predictable, structured world, and to control the events in their environment (Burger and Cooper, 1979). This is why the feeling of personal control, which implies an orderly reality, is positively related with psychological well-being and physical health (Whitson and Galinsky 2008). However, a feeling of diminished personal control is linked with negative mental results (Abramson et al. 1978; Pennebaker and Stone 2004; Stotland and Blumenthal 1964).

In other words, people live in a world whose nature they do not fully understand or control. The vision of a random, arbitrary, or haphazard world is uncomfortable, especially that human minds instinctively seek meaning and patterns (Hayek 2017 [1952]; Mattson 2014). Thus, people create a perception of personal control to protect themselves from such a vision (Kay et al. 2008; Kay et al. 2009).

If the perception of personal control is subdued, people can endorse external sources of compensatory control to maintain the vision of the orderly, stable, and manageable world. Externally imposed sources of order can ensure people that things are under control, even though they personally may not have a sense of full control over their course of life (Antonovsky, 1979; Weisz et al. 1984).

Two major external sources of order in contemporary developed societies are God and government (Kay et al. 2009; McGregor et al. 2008). The order provided by God is common for virtually all religions (Atran and Norenzayan, 2004). As James (1902, 46) puts it, "were one asked to characterize the life of religion in the broadest and most general terms possible, one might say that it consists of the belief that there is an unseen order." Also, research supports the Polish proverb that can be translated as, "When in fear, God is dear" (orig. *jak trwoga, to do Boga*) – i.e., people turn to God in times of crises, uncertainty, and low personal control (Pargament 1997; Park 2005; Norris and Inglehart 2004).

Although the reach of the government is necessarily smaller than the God, it can also fulfill the psychological need of viewing the world as orderly and under control (Jost et al. 2004; Kay et al. 2008; Norris and Inglehart, 2004; Sullivan et al. 2010). This is supported, for example, by the studies showing that people with lower levels of personal control are more supportive of governmental control and that under systemic threat, people's belief in the legitimacy of the government increases (Jost and Hunyady 2002; Jost et al. 2004; Kay et al. 2008; Kay et al. 2009; Kay et al. 2010). Fromm (1965) sees the individual as attempting to escape from powerlessness by submission to the authority and the attempt to become a part of a bigger and more powerful whole – e.g., the government or the state. This feature of the government, that it can serve as a compensatory system of control and order, can possibly explain why so many people tend to defend the legitimacy of their governments and to support their big role in the economy, despite all the ineffectiveness and unfairness associated with it (Kay et al. 2008).

Not only the internal (personal) and external sources of control are substitutable, but both God and government are capable of helping people deal with the perception of lack in order in the world. Kay and others (2010) demonstrate that belief in God and support for governmental system exhibit a hydraulic relationship with one another – i.e., lower faith in one of these external systems increases the faith in the other. Norris and Inglehart (2004) show that government stability is negatively correlated with religious commitment. Similarly, Gruber and Hungerman (2007) find the substitutability of private and government charity – i.e., New Deal government welfare spending crowded out church charitable activity. Zuckerman and others (2018, 1202) show that better government services were related to lower religiosity, and suggested that "regarding control and predictability, the power and order emanating from God can be outsourced to the government."

These two presented hypotheses seem to be contradictory. The first assumes that anti-market sentiment stems from opposition to the idea of the order (divine or spontaneous) not designed by human's ego. Meanwhile, the second hypothesis sees the anti-market sentiment as the other side of the coin of elevated support for the government, which occurs as compensatory control in case of diminished perception of personal control or faith in God's control over the world.

However, these two hypotheses can be reduced to one statement that the support for the government and anti-market sentiment is stronger, the weaker the faith in controlling God. In other words, people have anti-market sentiment because they want to see themselves as having more control than they really have.

## 4. CONCLUSIONS

This chapter tried to answer the question why – despite all the benefits of the market-based economies – so many people display anti-market sentiment. This issue is of great importance, as only sufficiently strong support for the market-based economy will enable it to be maintained, which is a necessary guarantee of continued economic growth and prosperity (Heckelman 2000; McCloskey 2016).

In other words, this chapter shows that psychology can be used not only to argue against free markets and support government intervention, as some behavioral economists do (e.g., O'Donoghue and Rabin 2003; Thaler and Sunstein 2008), but also to defend free markets. In this part, I presented arguments that people display anti-market sentiment, which may result from a tribal bias – i.e., the fact that people could be evolutionary adapted to function in small groups rather than in today's global economy (Hayek 1973, 1988).

However, as with many complex issues, there could be several factors at work here. The anti-market sentiment may also be the result of insufficient economic education, moral beliefs centered among equality, or the psychological benefits related to the pro-government sentiment. In particular, I wanted to point out the importance of envy and the illusion of control. The idea of the spontaneous free market order is not only intellectually but also psychologically challenging, as the strong role of the government in the economy gives people (illusory) perception of control.

To be clear, this chapter is not an exercise in economics, but in psychology or sociology. And its conclusions are speculative and require further, empirical research. In particular, studies directly examining the relationship between sentiment towards free market and sense of control or envy (and measuring their relative importance) would be appreciated.[21]

---

[21] Another caveat is that in this chapter I have discussed only psychological foundations of anti-market sentiment, ignoring the pro-market sentiment. Given the popularity of the former, such an approach is probably justified. However, I agree that there are people who show strong support of free market and blame the government on almost everything. But I would say that they show *anti-government sentiment* rather than *pro-market sentiment* (after all, one *should* expect appreciation for the functioning of markets). Although suspicion of the government is perhaps understandable – given that government is the most powerful social institution and thus the greatest threat to individual freedom (Hayek 1944, 1960; Casey 2012; Huemer 2013) – it may be a part of the unsubstantiated conspiracy theories. There are some valid reasons behind beliefs in government conspiracy theories – after all, genuine government over-reach and secrecy occurred during history (Olmsted 2009). However, the research supports the psychological nature of belief in conspiracy theories. In particular, studies point out projection, anxiety, uncertainty, the feeling of lack of control, or the search for meaningful and causal relationship between events, and intentional agency behind them, as factors relevant in believing in such theories (Sullivan et al. 2010; Douglas and Sutton 2011; van Prooijen and Douglas 2018). But the available research does not reveal that libertarians are most likely to believe in conspiracy theories. Rather, conspiracy beliefs have been associated with authoritarian worldviews, or – in more recent

# 6. Synopsis and final conclusions to *Rationality, Psychology and Capitalism*

The contents of this book can be summarized as follows:

- There are several different concepts of rationality, which makes the rational discussion about rationality in economics quite challenging.
- The four general notions distinguished in this book are: (1) rationality as a description of the mental processes or reasoning of individuals; (2) rationality as a methodological tool, or framework for economical inquiry; (3) rationality as a metaphysical statement about human nature; (4) rationality as the empirical proposition that people *tend to* choose the suitable means to achieve their goals. The methodological and empirical are most important for economics.
- Behavioral economists oppose the concept of rationality implied in the *Homo economicus* (HE) model, but they refer to rationality as a description of people's behavior, even though economists use the rationality principle not as a psychological description of individuals, but as a methodological device. Thus, behavioral economics conflates rationality referring to human behavior in the real world, and rationality as the scientific basis for the social sciences in general and economics in particular. They commit a straw man fallacy and do not invalidate the rationality principle as a foundational tool for economic inquiry.
- Economics and psychology are distinct disciplines of social science and should remain separate fields that respect each other methodology.
- Psychology studies the content of people's actions. It tries to explain internal events that can result in particular action, or why people choose certain ends. Economics, however, is contentless – i.e., it is a science that treats goals simply as given, or which deals with only the formal implications of the fact that people act, in that they have some goals and use certain means to achieve these goals.
- Thanks to this means–ends grammar, economists represent human behavior ina structured way, often called as 'the economic way of thinking.' This

distinct approach, or a rational perspective, and not its subject matter, is what most distinguishes economics from psychology.

- Thus, economics is a teleological science, while psychology (or at least some of its fields) is relatively more behavioristic. Insofar as economics also studies behavior, it does this in a very specific context of economizing – i.e., under the means–ends framework.
- However, it can be argued that economics is not about conscious human behavior, but about the coordination or lack of coordination of individual behaviors between many people or about the spontaneous order – i.e., undesigned results of actions of many people. What is important here is that explaining psychologically why people chose to do what they did is of no help in explaining social orders that no one chose.
- Economics should not become more psychological. After all, economics wants to formulate general theories, which is possible only when it abstracts from psychological factors. This way, economists explain human action regardless of people's motivation – by making economics more psychological, one would reduce the generality of its theories.
- Moreover, economics is more interested in studying the effects of human actions rather than their motives, and on aggregate outcomes rather than individual behavior. Economists focus on the behavior of markets, not individuals, as they are interested in directional changes on the margin in response to changes in the environment, rather than how particular individuals react.
- The criticism of economics for not being psychological enough or psychologically accurate stems from several reasons. First of all, there is a lack of understanding of the methodological differences between psychology and economics and of the nature of the latter. The rationality principle provides a universal grammar of economic explanations, while economics is, to a large extent, a logical rather than an empirical science. The fact that it examines the realm of subjective meaning does not mean that it involves mental-state psychology.
- Some social scientists hold the mistaken view that one needs to understand human nature to conduct proper economic research. They also consider the economics point of view as too limited and seem not to fully understand the issues of subjectivity and utility in economics, treating the latter as if it existed separately from real action and was its determinant or cause rather than reflection or summary. In this way, they commit causal utility fallacy.
- However, in some areas, there is potential for fruitful cross-fertilization between economics and psychology. In particular, the role of expectations seems to be an important psychological factor that could be helpful in explaining certain economics phenomena.

- For economists, psychological theories are not satisfactory theories of business cycles.
- This is because: (1) they violate the proper methodology of economics; (2) they ignore important economic factors; (3) instead, they appeal to psychological phenomena, but do not adequately explain their genesis, course, and why they should result in business cycles; (4) they assume a causal relationship from mental states to objective market reality, introducing changes in mental states as *diabolus ex machina*; (5) they do not adequately explain all features of business cycles; (6) they ignore the concept of the invisible hand and systemic (ecological) rationality; (7) they constitute ex post narratives about particular business cycles rather than general theories that allow for predictions; and (8) they assume a dubious view of human nature.
- The content of the analysis does not determine its form – the fact that the subject of economics seems to be similar to that of psychology does not mean that economics should adopt a similar research methodology.
- Economics is not empty without psychology; it is not a mere generalization of psychological tendencies in the context of the economizing of scarce resources; and it does not have to be grounded in psychology to be fully scientific.
- It is not true that rational behavior can occur only under conditions of risk, while under conditions of uncertainty individuals are left relying solely on 'animal spirits.'
- Economic factors affect the subjective well-being of people. However, this does not mean that capitalism should be blamed for people's mental health problems. The claims that capitalism is responsible for inequalities and for alienation, exploitation, and domination, which leads to the deterioration of mental health, do not stand up to careful examination and are not supported by empirical data.
- The fact that some negative psychological and social problems exist in modern capitalist economies does not mean that they are caused by capitalism or are inherent to this economic system. They can result from living in civilization, hierarchical societies, and specific culture, or some societal changes. Blaming capitalism for almost all social ills is a causal over-simplification fallacy.
- Status-seeking lies in human nature. The market-based economy makes it a positive-sum game.
- Economics systems should not be assessed from a psychological perspective. The fact that some people feel depressed or stressed under capitalism does not necessarily say anything meaningful about capitalism.
- The GDP should not be replaced by some happiness index. This is because it is far from obvious as to why happiness should be people's ultimate goal,

and whether it would be possible to implement ethical policy based on happiness.

- Happiness would be a very problematic social goal also because it is not clear what it is, how to achieve it, and how to measure it, if it can be defined, achieved, and measured at all. After all, as economics teaches, utility (or happiness in this case) is subjective and ordinal, and it cannot be objectively measured (as there are no *utils*).
- The aim of the economics system, if it has any aim, is to organize how people produce, exchange, and consume. Capitalism, or the market-based economy, simply enables people to interact freely and effectively, and to realize their individual goals. If there is something more one should expect from the economic system, it is rather economic growth – as it enables people to improve their standard of living. Even if people are not happier then, they have more resources at their disposal to achieve their aims, so their opportunities are greater.
- The idea that happiness – or any other single measure of well-being – can cover all the interests and values of people, is an illusion. Thus, the policy based on happiness would substitute people's own values with the ones of the policymakers.
- Researchers who argue that happiness should be society's ultimate goal erroneously equate happiness with utility and commit the causal utility fallacy.
- Psychological factors can be used to argue that people hold anti-market sentiment.
- This negative sentiment towards the market may result from the fact that market logic conflicts with humans' tribal instincts shaped by evolution.
- The anti-market sentiment may also be the result of moral beliefs centered among equality, envy, and the psychological benefits related to the pro-government sentiment, in particular the (illusory) perception of control.

The above points do not, of course, constitute the entirety of my contributions for the methodology of economics. However, they clearly show that my analysis enriches the debate on rationality in economics and on the role of psychology in economics research. My analysis reveals the shortcomings of the naïve view that orthodox economics either abstracts too much from psychology or adopts evidently an inadequate psychologically model of human behavior. This book advances our understanding of the nature of economics and its foundation – i.e., the rationality principle. My work also points out the shortcomings of blaming capitalism for negative mental health outcomes, and of evaluating economics systems in terms of happiness or from the psychological perspective.

What are the policy implications of this book? First of all, it presents arguments that undermine the critique of orthodox economics expressed by behavioral economics. Thus, it weakens the political implications of the latter – i.e., that certain government policies could nudge people to overcome their psychological flaws and act more rationally (Thaler and Sunstein 2008). However, the fact that individuals are not perfectly rational is not a real argument against the laissez-faire, as markets can be efficient even if individuals are imperfect, political leaders are prone to the same biases as private citizens, and political processes lack self-equilibrating properties of the markets (in other words, incentives to fight bias are stronger in private than in political actions; one vote does not matter, while economic mistakes directly impact agents' welfare). As Glaeser (2004, 412) puts it,

> [T]he case for laissez-faire is based more on the fallibility of the state than on the perfection of markets. Adam Smith's support for laissez-faire was grounded on the knowledge that governments often impoverish and slaughter their own citizenry. Human beings constantly err, but the welfare losses created by private errors are surely second-order relative to the welfare losses created by governments. Individuals may procrastinate and foolishly invest, but they do not voluntarily enroll in concentration camps.

Second, the book actually reverses the line of argumentation used by the behavioral economists, showing that negative sentiment towards the free market can be a kind of tribal bias towards sets of rules and behaviors typical for small groups rather than for the Great Society (Hayek 1973). In other words, psychological factors, such as instinct for equality, envy, or (illusory) perception of control, can explain distrust in the markets.

Third, the monograph responds to claims that capitalism negatively affects people's subjective well-being. Fourth, it argues that happiness should not become the goal of economic policy, and that the happiness index should not replace the GDP. Thus, this publication could be seen as a thorough defense of the traditional economics framework and market-based economies against behavioral imperialism and psychological reductionism.

The book does not examine all views on rationality in economics and on methodology of economics, nor does it exhaust all the issues at the intersection of economics and psychology, because those topics are extremely extensive and nuanced fields of economics, psychology, and methodology of science. For a more complete picture, a study of how psychology and economics could enrich each other would be particularly fruitful. Also, the discussion of the extended mind (Dekker and Remic 2024), the role of psychological factors in finance (Kahneman and Riepe 1998), and of risk in economics and psychology (Arrow 1982), seems to me to be of great importance.

# References


Abdukadirov S. (ed.), 2016, *Nudge Theory in Action*, Palgrave Advances in Behavioral Economics, Cham: Palgrave Macmillan, https://doi.org/10.1007/978-3-319-31319-1.

Abramson L. Y., Seligman M. E. P., Teasdale J. D., 1978, "Learned helplessness in humans: Critique and reformulation," *Journal of Abnormal Psychology*, 87, 49–74, https://doi.org/10.1037/0021-843X.87.1.49.

Agassi J., Jarvie I. C., 1980, "The rationality of irrationalism," *Metaphilosophy*, 11(2), 127–133.

Agrawal S., Sharma N., Agrawal R., Iazzolino G., Bruni M. E., 2025, "Beyond GDP: A triple helix framework for a happiness economy," *Social Indicators Research*, 179, 67–94, https://doi.org/10.1007/s11205-025-03604-y.

Akerlof, G. A., Dickens, W. T., 1982, "The economic consequences of cognitive dissonance," *The American Economic Review*, 72(3), 307–319.

Akerlof G. A., Shiller R. J., 2009, *Animal Spirits: How Human Psychology Drives the Economy, and Why It Matters for Global Capitalism*, Princeton, NJ and Oxford: Princeton University Press.

Alchian A. A., 1950, "Uncertainty, evolution, and economic theory," *Journal of Political Economy*, 58(3), 211–221.

Alesina A., Tella R. D., MacCulloch R., 2004, "Inequality and happiness: Are Europeans and Americans different?" *Journal of Public Economics*, 88, 2009–2042.

Allais M., 1953, "Le comportement de l'homme rationnel devant le risque: critique des postulats et axiomes de l'école Américaine," *Econometrica*, 21(4), 503–546.

Allport G. W., 1955, *Becoming*, New Haven, CT: Yale University Press.

Alter M., 1982, "Carl Menger and 'Homo Oeconomicus': Some thoughts on Austrian theory and methodology," *Journal of Economic Issues*, 16(1), 149–160.

American Psychological Association, 2016, *Glossary of Psychological Terms*, http://www.apa.org/research/action/glossary.aspx, accessed March 1, 2017.

American Psychological Association, 2018, "Stress in America: Generation Z," *Stress in America™ Survey*, https://www.apa.org/news/press/releases/stress/2018/stress-gen-z.pdf, accessed September 14, 2023.

Andersen F. B., Djugum M. E. T., Sjåstad V. S., Pallesen S., 2023, "The prevalence of workaholism: A systematic review and meta-analysis," *Frontiers in Psychology*, 14, 1252373, https://doi.org/10.3389/fpsyg.2023.1252373.

Andreoni J., Miller J. H., 2002, "Giving according to GARP: An experimental test of the consistency of preferences for altruism," *Econometrica*, 70(2), 737–753.

Annas J., 2004, "Happiness as achievement," *Daedalus*, 133(2), 44–51.

Antonovsky A., 1979, Health, Stress, and Coping, San Francisco: Jossey-Bass.

Ariely D., 2009, *Predictably Irrational*, New York, NY: HarperCollins.

Arrow K. J., 1982, "Risk perception in psychology and economics," *Economic Inquiry*, 20, 1–9, https://doi.org/10.1111/j.1465-7295.1982.tb01138.x.

Atran S., Norenzayan A., 2004, "Religion's evolutionary landscape: counterintuition, commitment, compassion, communion," *The Behavioral and Brain Sciences*, 27(6), 713–770. https://doi.org/10.1017/s0140525x04000172.

Azariadis C., 1981, "Self-fulfilling prophecies," *Journal of Economic Theory*, 25(3), 380–396, https://doi.org/10.1016/0022-0531(81)90038-7.

Bagus P., María Carrasco Bañuelos, E. 2018. "The Welfare Bias," Working Paper, 2nd Annual Madrid Conference on Austrian Economics, November 15–16, Madrid, Spain.

Balasubramanian S., Cashin P., 2019, "Gross national happiness and macroeconomic indicators in the Kingdom of Bhutan," IMF Working Papers, No. 2019/015, International Monetary Fund.

Balcerowicz L., 1994, "Transition to the market economy: Poland, 1989–93 in comparative perspective," *Economic Policy*, 9(19), 71–97, https://doi.org/10.2307/1344601.

Balcerowicz L., 1995, *Socialism, Capitalism, Transformation*, Budapest, London, New York, NY: Central European University Press.

Bar-Eli M., Azar O. H., Ritov I., Keidar-Levin Y., Schein G., 2007, "Action bias among elite soccer goalkeepers: The case of penalty kicks," *Journal of Economic Psychology*, 28(5), 606–621.

Barberis N., 2009, *The Psychology of the Financial Crisis*, Lecture at the Association of Yale Alumni Reunion Weekend, June 5, 2009, https://www.youtube.com/watch?v=gh_EbIPcnSk, accessed July 3, 2023.

Barberis N., 2013, "Psychology and the financial crisis of 2007–2008," in: Haliassos M. (ed)., *Financial Innovation: Too Much or Too Little?*, MIT Press Cambridge, MA, 15-28.

Barens I., 2011, "'Animal spirits' in John Maynard Keynes's general theory of employment, interest and money: Some short and sceptical remarks," Darmstadt Discussion Papers in Economics, No. 201, Technische Universität Darmstadt, Department of Law and Economics, Darmstadt.

Barrett L. F., 2009, "The future of psychology: Connecting mind to brain," *Perspectives on Psychological Science: A Journal of the Association for Psychological Science*, 4(4), 326–339, https://doi.org/10.1111/j.1745-6924.2009.01134.x.

Bassie V. L., 1955, "Recent developments in short-term forecasting," in: *Short-Term Economic Forecasting*, Princeton, NJ: Princeton University Press, 7–52, http://www.nber.org/chapters/c2900.

Bastiat F., [1850] 1996, *Economic Harmonies*, trans. W. Hayden Boyers, Irvington-on-Hudson, NY: Foundation for Economic Education.

Bastiat F., [1850] 2007, "That which is seen, and that which is not seen," in: *The Bastiat Collection*, 2nd edn, Auburn, AL: Ludwig von Mises Institute, 1–48.

Baumeister R. F., Vohs K. D., Aaker J. L., Garbinsky E. N., 2013, "Some key differences between a happy life and a meaningful life," *The Journal of Positive Psychology*, 8(6), 505–516, https://doi.org/10.1080/17439760.2013.830764.

Beck E. D., Cheung F., Thapa S., Jackson J. J., 2025, "Towards a personalized happiness approach to capturing change in satisfaction," *Natural Human Behavior*, 9, 1391–1404, https://doi.org/10.1038/s41562-025-02171-z.

Becker G. S., 1962, "Irrational behavior and economic theory," *Journal of Political Economy*, 70(1), 1–13.

Becker G. S., 1976, *The Economic Approach to Human Behavior*, Chicago, IL: The University of Chicago Press.

Becker G. S., 1993, "The Economic Way of Looking at Life," Coase-Sandor Institute for Law & Economics, Working Paper, No. 12.
Becker G. S., Murphy K. M., 2000, *Social Economics: Market Behavior in a Social Environment*, Cambridge, MA: Harvard University Press.
Becker G. S., Rayo L., 2008, "Comment on 'Economic Growth and Subjective Well-Being: Reassessing the Easterlin Paradox' by Stevenson and Wolfers," *Brookings Papers on Economic Activity*, vol. 2008, Spring, 88–95.
Ben-Ze'ev A., 1992, "Envy and inequality," *The Journal of Philosophy*, 9, 551–581.
Bentham J., 1823 [1780], *An Introduction to the Principles of Morals and Legislation*, Oxford: Clarendon Press.
Berg E. L., Besharov D. J., 2016, "Patterns of global migration," in: Besharov D. J., Lopez M. H. (eds), *Adjusting to a World in Motion: Trends in Global Migration and Migration Policy*, International Policy Exchange Series, New York, NY: Oxford University Press, 58–78, https://doi.org/10.1093/acprof:oso/9780190211394.003.0003.
Berger P. L., 1966, "Identity as a problem in the sociology of knowledge," *European Journal of Sociology*, 7, 105–115.
Berggren N., 2011, "Time for behavioral political economy? An analysis of articles in behavioral economics," *The Review of Austrian Economics*, 25(3), 1–23, https://doi.org/10.1007/s11138-011-0159-z.
Bernanke B., Blanchard O., 2025, "What caused the US pandemic-era inflation?" *American Economic Journal: Macroeconomics*, American Economic Association, 17(3), 1–35.
Bertrand M., Mullainathan S., 2001, "Do people mean what they say? Implications for subjective survey data," *American Economic Review*, 91(2), 67–72.
Binmore K., 1999, "Why experiment in economics?" *The Economic Journal*, 109(453), February, F16–F24.
Binmore K., 2009, *Rational Decisions*, Princeton, NJ: Princeton University Press.
Blendon R. J., et al. (1997), "Bridging the gap between the public's and economists' views of the economy," *Journal of Economic Perspectives*, 11(3), 105–118.
Boettke P., Candela R. A., Truitt T. L., 2024, *The Socialist Calculation Debate: Theory, History, and Contemporary Relevance*, Elements in Austrian Economics, Cambridge: Cambridge University Press.
Böhm-Bawerk E., 1898, *Karl Marx and the Close of His System: A Criticism*, trans. A. M. Macdonald, London: T. Fisher Unwin.
Böhm-Bawerk E., 1930, *The Positive Theory of Capital*, trans. W. Smart, New York, NY: G. E. Stechert & Co.
Bok S., 2010, *Exploring Happiness: From Aristotle to Brain Science*, New Haven, CT: Yale University Press.
Boland L. A., 1981, "On the futility of criticizing the neoclassical maximization hypothesis," *The American Economic Review*, 71(5), December, 1031–1036.
Bondo H. K., Presskorn-Thygesen T., 2022, "On some antecedents of behavioural economics," *History of the Human Sciences*, 35(3/4), 58–83, https://doi.org/10.1177/09526951211000950.
Borjas G., 2010, *Labour Economics*, 5th international edn, New York, NY: McGraw-Hill.
Braghieri L., Ro'ee L., Makarin A., 2022, "Social media and mental health," *American Economic Review*, 112(11), 3660–3693, https://doi.org/10.1257/aer.20211218.
Brennan G., 2007, "The grammar of rationality," in: Peter F., Schmid H. B. (eds.), *Rationality and Commitment*, Oxford: Oxford University Press, 105–123.

Britannica, 2023, "Stress," Encyclopedia Britannica, https://www.britannica.com/science/stress-psychology-and-biology, accessed September 13, 2023.

Brown S., Gray D., Roberts J., 2015, "The relative income hypothesis: A comparison of methods," *Economic Letters*, 130, 47–50.

Bruni L., 2008, "Back to Aristotle? Happiness, *eudaemonia*, and relational goods," in: Bruni L., Comim F., Pugno M. (eds), *Capabilities and Happiness*, Oxford: Oxford University Press, 114–139.

Bruni L., Sugden R., 2007, "The road not taken: How psychology was removed from economics, and how it might be brought back," *The Economic Journal*, 117(516), 146–173, https://doi.org/10.1111/j.1468-0297.2007.02005.x.

Brynjolfsson E., Oh J. H., 2012, "The attention economy: Measuring the value of free digital services on the internet," ICIS 2012 Proceedings. 9, https://aisel.aisnet.org/icis2012/proceedings/EconomicsValue/9, accessed February 5, 2026.

Brzezinski M., 2019, "Diagnosing unhappiness dynamics: Evidence from Poland and Russia," *Journal of Happiness Studies*, 20, 2291–2327, https://doi.org/10.1007/s10902-018-0044-6.

Buchanan C., Hartley P., 2000, *Equity as a Social Goal*, Wellington, New Zealand: New Zealand Business Round Table.

Buchanan J. M., 1982, "Order defined in the process of its emergence," *Literature of Liberty*, 5(4), Winter, 12–13.

Burger J. M., Cooper H. M., 1979, "The desirability of control," *Motivation and Emotion*, 3(4), 381–93, https://doi.org/10.1007/BF00994052.

Buss D. M., 2000, "The evolution of happiness," *American Psychologist*, 55(1), 15–23, https://doi.org/10.1037//0003-066X.55.1.15.

Buunk B. P., Oldersma F. L., de Dreu C. K. W., 2001, "Enhancing satisfaction through downward comparison: The role of relational discontent and individual differences in social comparison orientation," *Journal of Experimental Social Psychology*, 37, 452–467.

Bylund P., 2011, "The 'mystery' of the endowment effect," *Mises Daily*, November 28, https://mises.org/mises-daily/mystery-endowment-effect, accessed September 6, 2025.

Bylund P., 2023, "The objective science of subjective value," *Mises Wire*, October 16, https://mises.org/mises-wire/objective-science-subjective-value, accessed September 6, 2025.

Camerer C., 2008, "The case for mindful economics," in Caplin A., Schotter A. (eds), *The Foundations of Positive and Normative Economics: A Handbook*, Oxford: Oxford University Press, 43–69.

Camerer C., Loewenstein G., 2004, "Behavioral economics: past, present, future," in: Camerer C., Loewenstein G., Rabin M. (eds), *Advances in Behavioral Economics*, Princeton, NJ: Princeton University Press, 3–51.

Camerer C., Loewenstein G., Prelec D., 2005, "Neuroeconomics: How neuroscience can inform economics," *Journal of Economic Literature*, 43(1), 9–64.

Campbell A., 1981, *The Sense of Well-Being in America*, New York, NY: McGraw-Hill.

Cantril H., 1965, *The Pattern of Human Concern*, New Brunswick, NJ: Rutgers University Press.

Caplan B., 2001, "What makes people think like economists? Evidence on economic cognition from the 'Survey of Americans and Economists on the Economy'," *Journal of Law and Economics*, 44(October), 395–426.

Caplan B., 2002, "Systematically biased beliefs about economics: Robust evidence of judgmental anomalies from the Survey of Americans and Economists on the Economy," *Economic Journal,* 112(April), 1–26.

Caplan B., 2007, *The Myth of the Rational Voter: Why Democracies Choose Bad Policies*, Princeton, NJ: Princeton University Press.

Carver T. N., 1918, "The behavioristic man," *Quarterly Journal of Economics*, 33(1), November, 195–199.

Case A., Deaton A., 2020, *Deaths of Despair and the Future of Capitalism*, Princeton, NJ: Princeton University Press.

Casey G., 2012, *Libertarian Anarchy: Against the State*, London and New York, NY: Continuum.

Cass D., Shell K., 1983, "Do sunspots matter?" *Journal of Political Economy*, 91(2), April, 193–227, https://doi.org/10.1086/261139.

Chambers W., 1952, *Witness*, New York, NY: Random House.

Chicago Booth Review, 2016, "Are markets efficient?" *The Big Question*, June 30, https://review.chicagobooth.edu/economics/2016/video/are-markets-efficient, accessed November 9, 2021.

Clark A., 2018, "Four decades of the economics of happiness: Where next?" *Review of Income and Wealth*, 64(2), 245–269, https://doi.org/10.1111/roiw.12369.

Clark A., Frijters P., Shields M., 2008, "Relative income, happiness and utility: An explanation for the Easterlin paradox and other puzzles," *Journal of Economic Literature*, 46, 95–124.

Clark A., Oswald A., 1996, "Satisfaction and comparison income," *Journal of Public Economics*, 61, 359–381.

Clark J. M., 1918a, "Economics and Modern Psychology: I," *Journal of Political Economy*, 26(1), 1–30.

Clark J. M., 1918b, "Economics and Modern Psychology: II," *Journal of Political Economy*, 26(2), 136–166.

Clouet B., Lai A., 2022, "Global study reveals most workers enjoy what they do," Gallup Blog, November 3, https://news.gallup.com/opinion/gallup/404495/global-study-reveals-workers-enjoy.aspx, accessed February 20, 2024.

Coats A. W., 1976, "Economics and psychology: The death and resurrection of a research programme," in: Latsis S. J. (ed.), *Method and Appraisal in Economics*, Cambridge: Cambridge University Press, 43–64.

Cohen J. L., 1979, "On the psychology of prediction: Whose is the fallacy?" *Cognition*, 7, 385–407.

Colander D., 2014, "The wrong type of pluralism: Toward a transdisciplinary social science," *Review of Political Economy*, 26, 516–525.

Cook S., 1966, "The obsolete 'anti-market' mentality: A critique of the substantive approach to economic anthropology," *American Anthropologist*, 68(2), 323–345.

Courtois S., Werth N., Panné J.-L., Paczkowski A., Bartošek K., Margolin J.-L., 1999, *The Black Book of Communism: Crimes, Terror, Repression*, trans. Murphy J., Kramer M., Cambridge, MA and London: Harvard University Press.

Cowen T., 2000, *What Price Fame?*, Cambridge, MA: Harvard University Press.

Coyle D., 2018, "Homo Economicus, AIs, humans and rats: Decision-making and economic welfare," *Journal of Economic Methodology*, 1–11, https://doi.org/10.1080/1350178X.2018.1527135.

Crespo R. F., 2017, *Economics and Other Disciplines: Assessing New Economic Currents*. New York, NY: Routledge.

Cruz-e-Silva V., Cavalieri M. A. R., 2022, "Patterns of interdisciplinary citations and asymmetry between economics and the neighboring social sciences from 1959 to 2018," *Nova Economia*, 32(01), Jan–Apr, 261–291, https://doi.org/10.1590/0103-6351/6591.

Curry O. S., Jones Chesters M., Van Lissa C. J., 2019, "Mapping morality with a compass: Testing the theory of 'morality-as-cooperation' with a new questionnaire," *Journal of Research in Personality*, 78, 106–124, https://doi.org/10.1016/j.jrp.2018.10.008.

Czapiński J., Panek T. (eds), 2015, *Diagnoza społeczna 2015*, www.diagnoza.com, accessed October 31, 2023.

Czeglédi P., 2023, "Why is the West unique in linking religiosity to market friendliness?" *Economic Affairs*, 43(1), 73–88, https://doi.org/10.1111/ecaf.12557.

Damásio A., 1994, *Descartes' Error: Emotion, Reason, and the Human Brain*, New York, NY: Putnam Publishing.

Dattani S., Rodés-Guirao L., Ritchie H., Roser M., 2023, "Mental Health," https://ourworldindata.org/mental-health, accessed February 5, 2026.

Davis J. B., 2018, "Behavioral economics and the positive–normative distinction: Sunstein's *Choosing Not to Choose* and behavioral economics imperialism," *Ethics and Economics*, 15(1), 1–15.

De Botton A., 2004, *Status Anxiety*, New York, NY: Pantheon Books.

De Grauwe P., 2013, *Lectures on Behavioral Macroeconomics*, Princeton, NJ and Oxford: Princeton University Press.

Deaton A., 2013, *The Great Escape: Health, Wealth, and the Origins of Inequality*, Princeton, NJ: Princeton University Press.

Dekker E., Remic B., 2019, "Two types of ecological rationality: Or how to best combine psychology and economics," *Journal of Economic Methodology*, 26(4), 291–306, https://doi.org/10.1080/1350178X.2018.1560486.

Dekker E., Remic B., 2024, "Hayek's extended mind: On the (im)possibility of Austrian behavioural economics," *Journal of Institutional Economics*, 20(e19), 1–19, https://doi.org/10.1017/S1744137424000055.

Denzau A. T., North D. C., 1994, "Shared mental models: Ideologies and institutions," *Kyklos*, 47, 3–31, https://doi.org/10.1111/j.1467-6435.1994.tb02246.x.

Diamond D. W., Dybvig P. H., 1983, "Bank runs, deposit insurance, and liquidity," *Journal of Political Economy*, 91(3), 401–419.

Dickinson Z. C., 1919, "The relations of recent psychological developments to economic theory," *The Quarterly Journal of Economics*, 33(3), May, 377–421.

Diener E., 2000, "Subjective well-being: The science of happiness and a proposal for a national index," *American Psychologist*, 55, 34–43.

Diener E., Lucas R. E., 1999, "Personality and subjective well-being," in Kahneman D., Diener E., Schwarz N. (eds), *Well-being: The Foundations of Hedonic Psychology*, New York, NY: Russell Sage Foundation, 213–229.

Dorner D., 1997, *The Logic of Failure: Recognizing and Avoiding Error in Complex Situations*, Cambridge, MA: Perseus Press.

Douglas K. M., Sutton R. M., 2011, "Does it take one to know one? Endorsement of conspiracy theories is influenced by personal willingness to conspire," *The British Journal of Social Psychology*, 50(3), 544–552, https://doi.org/10.1111/j.2044-8309.2010.02018.x.

Downs A., 1957, *An Economic Theory of Democracy,* New York, NY: Harper & Brothers.

Drakopoulos S., Katselidis I., 2024, *Economics and Psychology*, London and New York: Routledge.

Driver J., 2022, "The history of utilitarianism", in: Zalta E. N., Nodelman U. (eds.), *The Stanford Encyclopedia of Philosophy*, Winter 2022 Edition, https://plato.stanford.edu/archives/win2022/entries/utilitarianism-history/, accessed September 23, 2024.

Duesenberry J. S., 1949, *Income, Saving and the Theory of Consumer Behaviour*, Cambridge, MA: Harvard University Press.

Dworkin R. M., 2000, *Sovereign Virtue: The Theory and Practice of Equality*, Cambridge, MA: Harvard University Press.

Dworkin R. W., 2006, *Artificial Happiness: The Dark Side of the New Happy Class*, New York, NY: Carroll & Graf.

Eagleton-Pierce M., 2016, *Neoliberalism: The Key Concepts*, London and New York, NY: Routledge.

Easterlin R., 1974, "Does economic growth improve the human lot? Some empirical evidence," in: David P., Reder M. (eds.), *Nations and Households in Economic Growth*, New York, NY: Academic Press, 89–125.

Easterlin R., 2005, "Feeding the illusion of growth and happiness: A reply to Hagerty and Veenhoven," *Social Indicators Research,* 74(3), 429–443.

Einhorn H. J., Hogarth R. M., 1981, "Behavioral decision theory: Processes of judgment and choice," *Annual Review of Psychology*, 32, 53–88, https://doi.org/10.1146/annurev.ps.32.020181.000413.

Eisenberg-Guyot J., Prins S., 2022, "The impact of capitalism on mental health: An epidemiological perspective," in: Bhugra D., Moussaoui D., Craig T. J. (ed.), *Oxford Textbook of Social Psychiatry*, (Oxford, online edn, Oxford Academic, August 1, 2022), 195–C22.P129, https://doi.org/10.1093/med/9780198861478.003.0022, accessed May 17, 2023.

Ekins E., 2019, "What Americans think about poverty, wealth, and work," Survey Report, Cato Institute, September 24, 2019, https://www.cato.org/publications/survey-reports/what-americans-think-about-poverty-wealth-work, accessed August 1, 2023.

Engelhard P., Fehl U., Geue H., 1996, "I. Austrian Methodology: Praxeology as a quasi-formal science," *Cultural Dynamics*, 8(3), 271–293. https://doi.org/10.1177/092137409600800304.

Evans J. St. B. T., Over D. E., Manktelow K. I., 1993, "Reasoning, decision making and rationality," *Cognition*, 49, 165–187.

Fama E., 1970, "Efficient capital markets: A review of theory and empirical work," *Journal of Finance*, 25(2), 383–417.

Farmer R. E. A., 2013, "Animal spirits, financial crises, and persistent unemployment," *The Economic Journal*, 123(May), 317–340. https://doi.org/10.1111/ecoj.12028.

Farmer R. E. A., Woodford M., 1997, "Self-fulfilling prophecies and the business cycle," *Macroeconomic Dynamics*, 1(4), 740–769, https://doi.org/10.1017/S1365100597005051.

Fehr E., Schmidt K. M., 2006, "The economics of fairness, reciprocity and altruism: Experimental evidence and new theories," in: Kolm S. C., Ythier J. M. (eds.), *Handbook of the Economics of Giving, Altruism and Reciprocity*, Vol. 1, Foundations, 615–691, Amsterdam: North-Holland.

Ferrer-i-Carbonell A., 2013, "Happiness economics," *SERIEs*, 4(1), 335–360.

Fetter F. A., 1915, *Economic Principles,* New York, NY: The Century Co.

Fisher I., 1926, *Mathematical Investigations in the Theory of Value and Prices*, New Haven, CT: Yale University Press.

Fleurbaey M., Blanchet D., 2013, *Beyond GDP: Measuring Welfare and Assessing Sustainability*, Oxford: Oxford University Press.

Fogel R. W., 2000, "The extension of life in developed countries and its implications for social policy in the twenty-first century," *Population and Development Review*, 26, 291–317, http://www.jstor.org/stable/3115220.

Foster G. M., 1972, "The anatomy of envy: A study in symbolic behavior," *Current Anthropology*, 13(2), 165–202.

Foster P., 2014, *Why We Bite the Invisible Hand: The Psychology of Anti-Capitalism*, Toronto, ON: Pleasaunce Press.

Foulkes L., Andrews J. L., 2023, "Are mental health awareness efforts contributing to the rise in reported mental health problems? A call to test the prevalence inflation hypothesis," *New Ideas in Psychology*, 69(April), 1–6, https://doi.org/10.1016/j.newideapsych.2023.101010.

Fourcade M., Ollion E., Algan Y., 2015. "The superiority of economists." *Journal of Economic Perspectives*, 29(1), 89–114, https://doi.org/10.1257/jep.29.1.89.

Fox, C. R., Tversky, A., 1995, "Ambiguity aversion and comparative ignorance," *The Quarterly Journal of Economics*, 110(3), 585–603. https://doi.org/10.2307/2946693.

François A., Le Gall C., Magni-Berton R., 2019, "Why do academics oppose the market economy? Sophistication and perception of market failures," *French Politics*, 17, https://doi.org/10.1057/s41253-019-00088-4.

Frank R. H., 1985, *Choosing the Right Pond: Human Behavior and the Quest for Status*, New York, NY: Oxford University Press.

Frank R. H., 1999, *Luxury Fever: Why Money Fails to Satisfy in an Era of Excess*, New York, NY: Free Press.

Frankfurt H. G., 2015, *On Inequality*, Princeton, NJ: Princeton University Press.

Frankl V., 2004, *On the Theory and Therapy of Mental Disorders: An Introduction to Logotherapy and Existential Analysis*, New York, NY: Brunner-Routledge.

French D., 2009, *Early Speculative Bubbles and Increases in the Supply of Money*, 2nd edn, Auburn, AL: Ludwig von Mises Institute.

Freud S., 1922, *Beyond the Pleasure Principle*, London and Vienna: The International Psycho-Analytical Press.

Freud S., 2002, *Civilization and Its Discontents*, London: Penguin Books.

Frey B., Stutzer A., 2002, *Happiness and Economics: How the Economy and Institutions Affect Human Well-Being*, Princeton, NJ: Princeton University Press.

Friedman B. M., 2005, *The Moral Consequences of Economic Growth*, New York, NY: Knopf.

Friedman D., 1990, *Price Theory: An Intermediate Text*, Cincinnati, OH:: South-Western Publishing Co.

Friedman M., 1953, "The methodology of positive economics," in: *Essays in Positive Economics*, Chicago, IL: The University of Chicago Press, 3–43.

Friedman M., Savage L., 1948, "The utility analysis of choices involving risk," *The Journal of Political Economy*, 56(4), 279–304.

Frijters P., Haisken-DeNew J. P., Shields M. A., 2004, "Money does matter! Evidence from increasing real incomes and life satisfaction in East Germany following reunification," *American Economic Review*, 94(3), 730–740.

Fromm E., 1965, *Escape from Freedom*, New York: Avon Books.

Funder D., Ozer D., 1983, "Behavior as a function of the situation," *Journal of Personality and Social Psychology*, 44, 107–112, https://doi.org/10.1037/0022-3514.44.1.107.

Garber P. M., 1990, "Famous first bubbles", *The Journal of Economic Perspectives*, 4(2), 35–54, https://doi.org/10.1257/jep.4.2.35.

Gedikli C., Miraglia M., Connolly S., Bryan M., Watson D., 2023, "The relationship between unemployment and wellbeing: An updated meta-analysis of longitudinal evidence," *European Journal of Work and Organizational Psychology*, 32(1), 128–144, https://doi.org/10.1080/1359432X.2022.2106855.

Geiger N., 2016, "'Psychological' elements in business cycle theories: Old approaches and new insights," *The European Journal of the History of Economic Thought*, 23(3), 478–507, https://doi.org/10.1080/09672567.2014.951670.

Gelman A., Silver N., Edlin A., 2012, "What is the probability your vote will make a difference?" *Economic Inquiry*, 50(2), 321–326.

Giattino Ch., Ortiz-Ospina E., Roser M., 2020, "Working Hours," Our World In Data, https://ourworldindata.org/working-hours, accessed November 1, 2023.

Gigerenzer G., 2018, "The bias in behavioral economics," *Review of Behavioral Economics*, 5(3–4), 303–336, http://dx.doi.org/10.1561/105.00000092.

Gigerenzer G., 2021, "Axiomatic rationality and ecological rationality," *Synthese*, 198, April, 3547–3564, https://doi.org/10.1007/s11229-019-02296-5.

Gilbert D., 2007, *Stumbling on Happiness*, New York, NY: Vintage Books.

Gilboa I., 2015, "Rationality and the Bayesian paradigm," *Journal of Economic Methodology*, 22(3), 312–334, https://doi.org/10.1080/1350178X.2015.1071505.

Gintis H., 2004, "Towards the unity of the behavioral sciences," *Politics, Philosophy & Economics*, 3(1), 37–57.

Giocoli N., 2003, *Modeling Rational Agents: From Interwar Economics to Early Modern Game Theory*, Cheltenham, UK and Northampton, MA, USA: Edward Elgar Publishing.

Glaeser E. L., 2003, "Psychology and the market," *NBER Working Papers*, No. 10203, https://ssrn.com/abstract=483887, accessed March 4, 2024.

Glaeser E. L., 2004, "Psychology and the market," *American Economic Review*, 94(2), 408–413. https://doi.org/10.1257/0002828041302208.

Gode D., Sunder S., 1993, "Allocative efficiency of markets with zero-intelligence traders: market as a partial substitute for individual rationality", *Journal of Political Economy*, 101(1), 119–137.

Gordon D., 1991, *Resurrecting Marx: The Analytical Marxists on Freedom, Exploitation, and Justice*, Piscataway, NJ: Transaction Publishers.

Gordon M. J., 1987, "Insecurity, growth, and the rise of capitalism," *Journal of Post Keynesian Economics*, 9(4), Summer, 529–551.

Graham C., 2008, "Some insights on development from the economics on happiness," in: Bruni L., Comim F., Pugno M. (eds), *Capabilities and Happiness*, Oxford: Oxford University Press, 81–113.

Graham C., 2009, *Happiness Around the World: The Paradox of Happy Peasants and Miserable Millionaires*, Oxford: Oxford University Press.

Graham J., Haidt J., Nosek B. A., 2009, "Liberals and conservatives rely on different sets of moral foundations," *Journal of Personality and Social Psychology*, 96(5), 1029–1046, https://doi.org/10.1037/a0015141.

Graziano M., 2013, *Epistemology of Decision: Rational Choice, Neuroscience and Biological Approaches*, Dordrecht: Springer.

Gruber J., Hungerman D. M., 2007, "Faith-based charity and crowd-out during the Great Depression," *Journal of Public Economics*, 91(5-6), 1043–1069, https://doi.org/10.1016/j.jpubeco.2006.11.004.

Grüne-Yanoff T., 2012, "Paradoxes of rational choice theory," in: Roeser S., Hillerbrand R., Sandin P., Peterson M. (eds.), *Handbook of Risk Theory*, Dordrecht: Springer, https://doi.org/10.1007/978-94-007-1433-5_19.

Guiso L., Sapienza P., Zingales L., 2003, "People's opium? Religion and economic attitudes," *Journal of Monetary Economics*, 50(1), 225–282. https://doi.org/10.1016/s0304-3932(02)00202-7.

Gul F., Pesendorfer W., 2008, "The case for mindless economics," in: Caplin A., Schotter A. (eds), *The Foundations of Positive and Normative Economics: A Handbook*, Oxford: Oxford University Press, 3–39.

Guthrie S. E., 1993, *Faces in the Clouds: A New Theory of Religion*, Oxford: Oxford University Press.

Haberler G. 1946, *Prosperity and Depression: A Theoretical Analysis of Cyclical Movements*, 3rd edn, Lake Success, NY: United Nations.

Hagerty M. R., Veenhoven R., 2003, "Wealth and happiness revisited–Growing national income *does* go with greater happiness," *Social Indicators Research*, 64(1), 1–27, https://doi.org/10.1023/A:1024790530822.

Haidt J., 2012, *The Righteous Mind: Why Good People Are Divided by Politics and Religion*, New York, NY: Pantheon Books.

Hamermesh D. S., 2004, "Subjective Outcomes in Economics," *NBER Working Papers*, No. 10361, March, http://www.nber.org/papers/w10361, accessed September 26, 2025.

Hands D. W., 2010, "Economics, psychology, and the history of consumer choice theory," *Cambridge Journal of Economics*, 34(4), 633–648.

Hands D. W., 2014, "Normative ecological rationality: Normative rationality in the fast-and-frugal-heuristics research program," *Journal of Economic Methodology*, 21(4), 396–410, https://doi.org/10.1080/1350178X.2014.965907.

Hands D. W., 2015, "Normative rational choice theory: Past, present, and future," http://dx.doi.org/10.2139/ssrn.1738671, accessed August 29, 2024.

Harrison G., Ross D., 2010, "The methodologies of neuroeconomics," *Journal of Economic Methodology*, 17(2), 185–196.

Hart R., Hart D., 2025, "New frontier: Positive economic psychology," *Open Psychology*, 7(1), https://doi.org/10.1515/psych-2025-0004.

Hasell J., Roser M., Ortiz-Ospina E., Arriagada P., 2022, "Poverty," Our World In Data, https://ourworldindata.org/poverty, accessed July 11, 2023.

Haviland W. A., Prins H. E. L., McBride B., Walrath D., 2011, *Cultural Anthropology: The Human Challenge*, 13th edn, Belmont, CA: Wadsworth/Cengage Learning.

Hayek F. A., 1937, "Economics and knowledge," *Economica*, 4(13), 33–54.

Hayek F. A., 1944, *The Road to Serfdom*, Chicago, IL: The University of Chicago Press.

Hayek F. A., 1945, "The use of knowledge in society," *American Economic Review*, 35(4), 519–530.

Hayek F. A., 1948a, "Individualism: True and false," in: *Individualism and Economic Order,* Chicago, IL: The University of Chicago Press, 1–32.

Hayek F. A., 1948b, "The facts of the social sciences," in: *Individualism and Economic Order*, Chicago, IL: The University of Chicago Press, 57–76.

Hayek F. A., 1949, "The intellectuals and socialism," *University of Chicago Law Review*, 16(3), Article 7, 417–433.

Hayek F. A., 1955, *The Counter-Revolution of Science: Studies on the Abuse of Reason*, London: The Free Press of Glencoe, Collier-Macmillan Limited.
Hayek F. A., 1960, *The Constitution of Liberty*, Chicago, IL: The University of Chicago Press.
Hayek F. A., 1967, *Studies in Philosophy, Politics, and Economics*, Chicago, IL: The University of Chicago Press.
Hayek F. A., 1973, *Law, Legislation and Liberty, Vol I: Rules and Order*, Chicago, IL: The University of Chicago Press.
Hayek F. A., 1975 [1939], *Profits, Interest and Investment*, Clifton: Augustus M. Kelley Publishers.
Hayek F. A., 1988, "The fatal conceit: The errors of socialism," in: Bartley W. W. (ed.), *The Collected Works of F. A. Hayek*, Vol. 1, London: Routledge.
Hayek F. A., 2002, "Competition as a discovery procedure," *Quarterly Journal of Austrian Economics*, 5 (2002), 9–23, trans. M. S. Snow.
Hayek F. A., 2008 [1935], "Prices and production," in: Salerno J. T. (ed.), *Prices and Production and Other Works*, Auburn, AL: Ludwig von Mises Institute, 189–329.
Hayek F. A., 2017 [1949], "What is mind?," in: Vanberg V. (ed.), *The Sensory Order and Other Writings on the Foundations of Theoretical Psychology: The Collected Works of F. A. Hayek,* Vol. 14, Chicago: The University of Chicago Press, 348–360.
Hayek F. A., 2017 [1952], "The sensory order: An inquiry into the foundations of theoretical psychology," in: Vanberg V. (ed.), *The Sensory Order and Other Writings on the Foundations of Theoretical Psychology: The Collected Works of F. A. Hayek*, Vol. 14, Chicago, IL: The University of Chicago Press, 348–360.
Hazlitt H., 1946, *Economics in One Lesson*, New York, NY: Harper & Brothers.
Heckelman J. C., 2000, "Economic freedom and economic growth: A short-run causal investigation," *Journal of Applied Economics*, 3(1), 71–91, https://doi.org/10.1080/15140326.2000.12040546.
Henrich J., Boyd R., Bowles S., Camerer C., Fehr E., Gintis H., 2004, *Foundations of Human Sociality: Economic Experiments and Ethnographic Evidence from Fifteen Small-Scale Societies*, Oxford: Oxford University Press.
Henriques G. R., 2004, "Psychology defined," *Journal of Clinical Psychology*, 60, 1207–1221. https://doi.org/10.1002/jclp.20061.
Herbranson W., Schroeder J., 2010, "Are birds smarter than mathematicians? Pigeons (*Columba livia*) perform optimally on a version of the Monty Hall Dilemma," *Journal of Comparative Psychology*, 124(11), 1–13.
Herfeld C., 2021, "Understanding the rationality principle in economics as a functional a priori principle," *Synthese*, 198, 3329–3358, https://doi.org/10.1007/s11229-020-02730-z.
Hicks J., 1946, *Value and Capital*, Oxford: Clarendon Press.
Hicks J., Allen R. G. D., 1934, "A reconsideration of the theory of value," *Economica*, 1, 52–76.
Higgs K., 2021, "A brief history of consumer culture," *The MIT Press Reader*, January 11, https://thereader.mitpress.mit.edu/a-brief-history-of-consumer-culture/, accessed September 14, 2023.
Hirsch F., 1976, *Social Limits to Growth*, Cambridge, MA: Harvard University Press.
Hirshleifer D., 2008, "Psychological bias as a driver of financial regulation," *European Financial Management*, 14, 856–874, https://doi.org/10.1111/j.1468-036X.2007.00437.x.
Hirshleifer J., 1985, "The expanding domain of economics", *American Economic Review*, 75(6), 53–68.

Hodgson G. M., 2012, "On the limits of rational choice theory", *Economic Thought*, 1(1), 94–108.

Hoffmans L., 2012, "The most hated bull market ever", *Forbes*, August 17, https://www.forbes.com/sites/larahoffmans/2012/08/17/the-most-hated-bull-market-ever/?sh=6aa51aaa11a8, accessed June 21, 2023.

Hogarth, R. M., Makridakis, S., 1981, "Forecasting and planning: An evaluation," *Management Science*, 27(2), 115–138, http://www.jstor.org/stable/2631282.

Hudík M., 2011, "Why economics is not a science of behaviour," *Journal of Economic Methodology*, 18(2), 147–162, https://doi.org/10.1080/1350178X.2011.575949.

Huelsmann J. G., 2016, "Cultural consequences of monetary interventions," *Journal des Economistes et des Etudes Humaines*, 22(1), 77–98.

Huemer M., 2013, *The Problem of Political Authority: An Examination of the Right to Coerce and the Duty to Obey*, New York, NY: Palgrave Macmillan.

Huerta de Soto J., 1998, "The ongoing Methodenstreit of the Austrian School," *Journal des Economistes et des Etudes Humaines*, 8(1), 75–113.

Huerta de Soto J., 2006, *Money, Bank Credit, and Economic Cycles*, Auburn, AL: Ludwig von Mises Institute.

Hume D., 1987 [1777], "The rise and progress of the arts and sciences," in: *Essays, Moral, Political, and Literary*, Indianapolis, IN: Liberty Fund.

Hutchison T. W., 1998, "Ultra-deductivism from Nassau Senior to Lionel Robbins and Daniel Hausman," *Journal of Economic Methodology*, 5(1), 43–91, https://doi.org/10.1080/13501789800000003.

Hutto D., Ravenscroft I., 2021, "Folk psychology as a theory", in: Zalta E. N. (ed.), *The Stanford Encyclopedia of Philosophy* (Fall 2021 Edition), https://plato.stanford.edu/archives/fall2021/entries/folkpsych-theory/, accessed June 23, 2023.

Huxley A., 2006 [1932], *Brave New World*, New York, NY: HarperCollins.

Hwang S. H., Bowles S., 2012, "Is altruism bad for cooperation?," *Journal of Economic Behavior & Organization*, 83, 330–341.

IMF, with minor processing by Our World in Data, 2025, "Government spending as share of GDP," https://archive.ourworldindata.org/20250624-125417/grapher/historical-gov-spending-gdp.html, accessed August 7, 2025.

Imhoff R., Zimmer F., Klein O. et al., 2022, "Conspiracy mentality and political orientation across 26 countries," *Nature Human Behaviour*, 6, 392–403, https://doi.org/10.1038/s41562-021-01258-7.

Inglehart R., Welzel Ch., 2005, *Modernization, Cultural Change, and Democracy: The Human Development Sequence*, New York, NY: Cambridge University Press.

Iyer R., Koleva S., Graham J., Ditto P., Haidt J., 2012, "Understanding libertarian morality: The psychological dispositions of self-identified libertarians," *PloS one*, 7(8), e42366. https://doi.org/10.1371/journal.pone.0042366.

James O., 2008, *The Selfish Capitalist: Origins of Affluenza,* London: Vermilion.

James W., 1902, *The Varieties of Religious Experience: A Study in Human Nature,* New York: Longmans, Green, and Co.

Jansen A., Wang R., Behrens P., Hoekstra R., 2024, "Beyond GDP: A review and conceptual framework for measuring sustainable and inclusive wellbeing," *The Lancet Planetary Health*, 8(9), e695–e705, https://doi.org/10.1016/S2542-5196(24)00147-5.

Jarvis M. J., 2004, "Why people smoke," *British Medical Journal*, January 31, 328(7434), 277–279, https://doi.org/10.1136/bmj.328.7434.277.

Jason G. J., 2017, "'Debunking neosocialism,' Review of *Selfishness, Greed, and Capitalism: Debunking Myths about the Free Market*, by Christopher Snowdon,"

*The Journal of Ayn Rand Studies*, 17(1), 84–103, https://doi.org/10.5325/jaynrandstud.17.1.0084.

Jennings R., 1855, *Natural Elements of Political Economy*, London: Longman, Brown, Green and Longmans.

Jensen M. C., Meckling, W. H., 1994, "The nature of man," *Journal of Applied Corporate Finance*, 7(2), 4–19, http://dx.doi.org/10.2139/ssrn.5471.

Jevons W. S., 1878, "The periodicity of commercial crises, and its physical explanation," *Journal of the Statistical and Social Inquiry Society of Ireland*, vol. 7, part 54, 334–342.

Johns H., Ormerod P., 2007, "Happiness, economics and public policy," London: Institute of Economic Affairs.

Jolls Ch., Sunstein C. R., Thaler R., 1998, "Behavioral approach to law and economics," *Stanford Law Review*, 50(5), 1471–1550.

Jones A. T., Hadsell L., Burrus R. T., 2019, "Capitalist views and religion," *Eastern Economic Journal*, 45(3), 384–414, https://www.jstor.org/stable/48702884.

Jost J. T., Banaji M. R., Nosek B. A., 2004, "A decade of system justification theory: Accumulated evidence of conscious and unconscious bolstering of the status quo," *Political Psychology*, 25(6), 881–919, https://doi.org/10.1111/j.1467-9221.2004.00402.x.

Jost J. T., Hunyady O., 2002, "The psychology of system justification and the palliative function of ideology," *European Review of Social Psychology*, 13(1), 111–153, https://doi.org/10.1080/10463280240000046.

Kagan J., 2012, *Psychology's Ghosts: The Crisis in the Profession and the Way Back*, New Haven, CT: Yale University Press.

Kahneman D., 1999, "Objective happiness," in: Kahneman D., Diener E., Schwarz N. (eds), *Well-being: The Foundations of Hedonic Psychology*, New York, NY: Russell Sage Foundation, 3–25.

Kahneman D., 2011, *Thinking, Fast and Slow*, New York, NY: Farrar, Straus and Giroux.

Kahneman D., Deaton A., 2010, "High income improves evaluation of life but not emotional well-being," *The Proceedings of the National Academy of Sciences*, Vol. 107, No. 38, 16489–16493, https://doi.org/10.1073/pnas.1011492107.

Kahneman D., Knetsch J. L., Thaler R. H., 1990, "Experimental tests of the endowment effect and the coase theorem," *Journal of Political Economy*, 98(6), 1325–1348, http://www.jstor.org/stable/2937761.

Kahneman, D., Riepe, M. W., 1998, "Aspects of investor psychology," *The Journal of Portfolio Management Summer*, 24(4), 52–65.

Kahneman D., Tversky A., 1979, "Prospect theory: An analysis of decision under risk," *Econometrica*, 47(2), 263–291, https://doi.org/10.2307/1914185.

Kahneman D., Tversky A. (eds.), 2000, *Choices, Values, and Frames*, Cambridge: Cambridge University Press.

Kapteyn A., 2020, "Income growth is unlikely to help, but we can learn from international comparisons," *Behavioural Public Policy*, 4(2), 188–197, https://doi.org/10.1017/bpp.2019.42.

Kay A. C., Gaucher D., Napier J. L., Callan M. J., Laurin K., 2008, "God and the government: Testing a compensatory control mechanism for the support of external systems," *Journal of Personality and Social Psychology*, 95(1), 18–35, https://doi.org/10.1037/0022-3514.95.1.18.

Kay A. C., Shepherd S., Blatz C. W., Chua S. N., Galinsk A. D., 2010, "For God (or) country: The hydraulic relation between government instability and belief in religious sources of control," *Journal of Personality and Social Psychology*, 99(5), 725–739, https://doi.org/10.1037/a0021140.

Kay A. C., Whitson J. A., Gaucher D., Galinsky A. D., 2009, "Compensatory control: Achieving order through the mind, our institutions, and the heavens," *Current Directions in Psychological Science*, 18(5), 264–268, http://www.jstor.org/stable/20696046.

Keynes J. M., 2018 [1936], *The General Theory of Employment, Interest, and Money*, London: Palgrave Macmillan.

Khalil E. L., 1992, "Marx's understanding of the essence of capitalism," *History of Economics Review*, 17(1), 19–32, https://doi.org/10.1080/10370196.1992.11733102.

Kindleberger Ch., Aliber R., 2005, *Manias, Panics and Crashes: A History of Financial Crises*, 5th edn, New York, NY: John Wiley & Sons.

Kirchgässner G., 2013, "The weak rationality principle in economics," *Swiss Journal of Economics and Statistics*, 149 (1), 1–26.

Kirchsteiger G., 1994, "The role of envy in ultimatum games," *Journal of Economic Behavior & Organization*, 25(3), 373–389, https://doi.org/10.1016/0167-2681(94)90106-6.

Kirkland K., Jetten J., Nielsen M., 2019, "But that's not fair! The experience of economic inequality from a child's perspective," in: Jetten J., Peters K. (eds), *The Social Psychology of Inequality*, Springer, 209–222, https://doi.org/10.1007/978-3-030-28856-3.

Kirzner I. M., 1976, *The Economic Point of View*, Menlo Park, CA: Institute for Human Studies.

Kirzner I. M., 2001, *Ludwig von Mises: The Man and His Economics*, Wilmington, DE: ISI Books.

Klein D. B., Stern Ch., 2007, "Is there a free-market economist in the house? The policy views of American Economic Association members," *The American Journal of Economics and Sociology*, April, 662, 309–334.

Knight F. H., 1969, *The Ethics of Competition and Other Essays*, Freeport, NY: Books for Libraries Press.

Koenig H. G., 2012, "Religion, spirituality, and health: The research and clinical implications," *ISRN Psychiatry*, 2012(278730), https://doi.org/10.5402/2012/278730.

Kokorikou D. S., Sarigiannidis I., Fiore V. G., Parkin B., Hopkins A., El-Deredy W., Dilley L., Moutoussis M., 2023, "Testing hypotheses about the harm that capitalism causes to the mind and brain: A theoretical framework for neuroscience research," *Frontiers in Sociology*, 8, 1030115, https://doi.org/10.3389/fsoc.2023.1030115.

Kolodny N., Brunero J., 2023, "Instrumental rationality," in: Zalta E. N., Nodelman U. (eds.), *The Stanford Encyclopedia of Philosophy*, Summer 2023 Edition, https://plato.stanford.edu/archives/sum2023/entries/rationality-instrumental/, accessed February 5, 2026.

Koppl R., 1991, "Retrospectives: Animal spirits." *Journal of Economic Perspectives*, 5(3), 203–210, https://doi.org/10.1257/jep.5.3.203.

Koski J. E., Xie H., Olson I. R., 2015, "Understanding social hierarchies: The neural and psychological foundations of status perception," *Social Neuroscience*, 10(5), 527–550, https://doi.org/10.1080/17470919.2015.1013223.

Krueger A. B., 2008, "Comment on '*Economic Growth and Subjective Well-Being: Reassessing the Easterlin Paradox*' by Stevenson and Wolfers," *Brookings Papers on Economic Activity*, Spring, 95–100.

Kurrild-Klitgaard P., 2001, "On rationality, ideal types and economics: Alfred Schüutz and the Austrian School," *The Review of Austrian Economics*, 14(2/3), 119–143, https://doi.org/10.1023/A:1011199831428.
Kyburg H. E., 1983, "Rational belief," *Behavioral and Brain Sciences*, 6(2), 231–273, https://doi.org/10.1017/S0140525X00015661.
Lachmann L. M., 1977, "Economics as a social science," in: Lachmann L. M., *Capital, Expectations, and the Market Process: Essays on the Theory of the Market Economy*, Kansas City, KS: Sheed Andrews & McMeel, 166–180.
Lagueux M., 2010, "The forgotten role of the rationality principle in economics," *Journal of Economic Methodology*, 11(1), 31–51, https://doi.org/10.1080/1350178042000177996.
Lane R. E., 2000, *The Loss of Happiness in Market Democracies*, New Haven & London: Yale University Press
Langer E. J., 1975, "The illusion of control," *Journal of Personality and Social Psychology*, 32(2), 311–328.
Langlois R. N., 1998, "Rule-following, expertise, and rationality: A new behavioral economics?," in: Dennis K. (eds), *Rationality in Economics: Alternative Perspectives*, Recent Economic Thought Series, vol. 62, Dordrecht: Springer, 55–78.
Latsis S. J., 1976, "A research programme in economics," in: Latsis S. J. (ed.), *Method and Appraisal in Economics*, Cambridge: Cambridge University Press, 1–41.
Lavington F., 1922, *The Trade Cycle: An Account of the Causes Producing Rhythmical Changes in the Activity of Business*, London: P.S. King & Son.
Layard R., 2005, *Happiness: Lessons from a New Science*, New York, NY: The Penguin Press.
Lea S. E., Tarpy R. M., Webley P., 1987, *The Individual in the Economy: A Survey of Economic Psychology*, Cambridge: Cambridge University Press.
Lecouteux G., 2016, "From *Homo Economicus* to *Homo Psychologicus*: The Paretian foundations of behavioural paternalism," *Oeconomia – History/Methodology/ Philosophy*, 6(2), 175–200, https://doi.org/10.4000/oeconomia.2324.
Lee Y.-Y., Goh K.-L., 2023, "The happiness–economic well-being nexus: New insights from global panel data," *SAGE Open*, 13(4), https://doi.org/10.1177/21582440231199659.
Leibenstein H., 1976, *Beyond Economic Man: A New Foundation for Microeconomics*, Cambridge, MA: Harvard University Press.
Levine D., 2012, *Is Behavioral Economics Doomed? The Ordinary versus the Extraordinary*, Cambridge: Open Book Publishers.
Levitt S. D., List J. A., 2008, "Homo economicus evolves," *Science*, 319(5865), 909–910, https://doi.org/10.1126/science.1153640.
Lewin S. B., 1996, "Economics and psychology: Lessons for our own day from the early twentieth century," *Journal of Economic Literature*, 34(3), 1293–1323.
Li Ch., 2020, "The rationality principle as a universal grammar of economic explanations," *Journal of Philosophical Economics*, XIII, 2(2), 58–80, https://doi.org/10.46298/jpe.10735.
Lo L., Gilmour R., 2004, "Culture and conceptions of happiness: Individual oriented and social oriented SWB," *Journal of Happiness Studies*, 5, 269–291.
Long R. T., 2004, "Anti-psychologism in economics: Wittgenstein and Mises," *The Review of Austrian Economics*, 17(4), 345–369.
Long R. T., 2006, "Realism and abstraction in economics: Aristotle and Mises versus Friedman," *The Quarterly Journal of Austrian Economics*, 93, 3–23.

Lopes L. L., 1982, "Doing the impossible: A note on induction and the experience of randomness," *Journal of Experimental Psychology: Learning, Memory, and Cognition*, 8(6), 626–636, https://doi.org/10.1037/0278-7393.8.6.626.
Lopes L. L., 1983, "Some thoughts on the psychological concept of risk," *Journal of Experimental Psychology: Human Perception and Performance*, 9(1), 137–144.
Lopes L. L., 1991, "The rhetoric of irrationality," *Theory & Psychology*, 1(1), 65–82, https://doi.org/10.1177/0959354391011005.
Lucas R. E. Jr., 1972, "Expectations and the neutrality of money," *Journal of Economic Theory*, 4(2), 103–124.
Lucas R. E. Jr., 2002, *Lectures on Economic Growth*, Cambridge, MA: Harvard University Press.
Luce R. D., Raiffa H., 1957, *Games and Decisions: Introduction and Critical Survey*, New York, NY: Wiley.
Lynch J., Davey-Smith G, Hillemeier M., Shaw M., Raghunathan T., Kaplan G., 2001, "Income inequality, the psycho-social environment and health: Comparisons of wealthy nations," *Lancet*, 358(9277), 194–200, July 21, https://doi.org/10.1016/S0140-6736(01)05407-1.
Machaj M., 2024, *Monetary Policy and Inflation: Quantity Theory of Money*, Abingdon and New York, NY: Routledge.
Machlup F., 1936, "Why bother with methodology?" *Economica*, 3(9), February, 39–45.
Machlup F., 1946, "Marginal analysis and empirical research," *The American Economic Review*, 36(4), 519–554.
Machlup F., 1978, *Methodology of Economics and Other Social Sciences*, New York, NY: Academic Press, 267–281.
Mackay Ch., 1852, *Extraordinary Popular Delusions and the Madness of Crowds*, 2nd edn, London: Office of the National Illustrated Library, http://www.econlib.org/library/Mackay/macEx.html, accessed June 23, 2023.
Mackenbach J. P., 2002, "Income inequality and population health," *The British Medical Journal*, Editorial, January 5, 324(7328), 1–2, https://doi.org/10.1136/bmj.324.7328.1.
MacKerron G., 2012, "Happiness economics from 35,000 feet," *Journal of Economic Surveys*, 26(4), 705–735, https://doi.org/10.1111/j.1467-6419.2010.00672.x.
Malkiel B. G., 2003, "The efficient market hypothesis and its critics," *Journal of Economic Perspectives*, 17(1), Winter, 59–82.
Markowitz H. M., 1952, "Portfolio selection," *The Journal of Finance*, 7(1), 77–91, https://doi.org/10.2307/2975974.
Marshall A., 1923, *Money, Credit and Commerce*, London: Macmillan.
Marx K., 1976 [1867], *Capital*, Vol. I, London: Penguin Classics.
Mas-Collel A., Whinston M., Green J., 1995, *Microeconomic Theory*, New York, NY: Oxford University Press.
Mattson M. P., 2014, "Superior pattern processing is the essence of the evolved human brain," *Frontiers in Neuroscience*, 8, 265. https://doi.org/10.3389/fnins.2014.00265.
McAuliffe K., Blake P., Steinbeis N. et al., 2017, "The developmental foundations of human fairness," *Nature Human Behaviour*, 1, 0042, https://doi.org/10.1038/s41562-016-0042.
McAuliffe M., Triandafyllidou A. (eds.), 2021, *World Migration Report 2022*, International Organization for Migration, Geneva.
McChesney F. S., 2013, "Behavioral economics: Old wine in irrelevant new bottles?," *Supreme Court Economic Review*, 21(1), 43–76.

McCloskey D., 2012, "Happyism," *New Republic*, June 8, http://www.newrepublic.com/article/politics/magazine/103952/happyism-deirdre-mccloskey-economics-happiness, accessed September 11, 2025.
McCloskey D., 2016, *Bourgeois Equality: How Ideas, Not Capital or Institutions, Enriched the World*, vol. 3 of *The Bourgeois Era*, Chicago, IL: University of Chicago Press.
McGregor I., Haji R., Nash K. A., Teper R., 2008, "Religious zeal and the uncertain self," Basic and Applied Social Psychology, 30(2), 183–188. https://doi.org/10.1080/01973530802209251.
McKenzie R. B., 2010, *Predictably Rational? In Search of Defenses for Rational Behavior in Economics*, Heidelberg: Springer-Verlag, https://doi.org/10.1007/978-3-642-01586-1.
McKenzie R. B., Tullock G., 2012, *The New World of Economics: A Remake of a Classic for New Generations of Economics Students*, 6th edn, Berlin: Springer-Verlag.
McNeill W. H., 1981, *A Defence of World History*, Royal Society Lecture.
MECW, 1975, *Marx and Engels Collected Works*, New York, NY, and London: International Publishers.
Melberg H. O., 1998, "Psychology and economic fluctuations: Pigou, Mill and Keynes," https://web.archive.org/web/20091027111028/http://geocities.com/hmelberg/papers/981101.htm, accessed June 29, 2023.
Merton R. K., 1936, "The unanticipated consequences of purposive social action," *American Sociological Review*, 1(6), 894–904.
Milani F., 2011, "Expectation shocks and learning as drivers of the business cycle," *The Economic Journal*, 121, 379–401, https://doi.org/10.1111/j.1468-0297.2011.02422.x.
Mill J. S., 1844, "On the definition of political economy; and on the method of investigation proper to it," in: *Essays on Some Unsettled Questions of Political Economy*, Project Gutenberg, http://www.gutenberg.org/files/12004/12004-h/12004-h.htm#ESSAY_V, accessed March 5, 2024.
Mill J. S., 1859, *On Liberty*, London: J. W. Parker and Son.
Mills J., 1867, "On credit cycles and the origin of commercial panics." *Transactions of the Manchester Statistical Society*, 1867-1868, 11–40.
Minsky H. P., 1992, "The Financial Instability Hypothesis," Working Paper No. 74, Levy Economics Institute of Bard College, May.
Minsky H. P., 2008, *Stabilizing An Unstable Economy*, New York, NY: McGraw-Hill.
Minsky H. P., 2015, *Can It Happen Again? Essays on Instability and Finance*, New York, NY: Routledge.
Mischel W., Shoda Y., Rodriguez M. I., 1989, "Delay of gratification in children," *Science*, 244(4907), 933–938, https://doi.org/10.1126/science.2658056.
Mises L., 1985, *Liberalism in the Classical Tradition*, trans. Raico R., The Foundation for Economic Education, Irvington-on-Hudson, NY, and Cobden Press, San Francisco, CA.
Mises L., 1990, *Money, Method, and the Market Process*, Norwell, MA: Kluwer Academic Publishers.
Mises L., 1998 [1949], *Human Action: A Treatise on Economics*, The Scholar's Edition, Auburn, AL, Ludwig von Mises Institute.
Mises L., 2006 [1928], "Monetary stabilization and cyclical policy," in: Mises L., *The Causes of the Economic Crisis and Other Essays Before and After the Great Depression*, Greaves P. Jr. (ed.), Auburn, AL: Ludwig von Mises Institute, 53–153.
Mises L., 2007 [1957], *Theory and History: An Interpretation of Social and Economic Evolution*, Auburn, AL: Ludwig von Mises Institute.

Mises L., 2008 [1956] *The Anti-Capitalistic Mentality*, Auburn, AL: Ludwig von Mises Institute.
Mitchell W. C., 1914, "Human behavior and economics: A survey of recent literature," *The Quarterly Journal of Economics*, Nov., 29(1), 1–47.
Moffitt T. E, et al., 2011, "A gradient of childhood self-control predicts health, wealth, and public safety," *Proceedings of the National Academy of Sciences of the United States of America*, 108(7), 2693–2698, http://www.jstor.org/stable/41002200.
Molière J. B., 1926, *The Plays of Moliere*, trans. Waller A. R., Edinburgh: John Grant.
Montesano A., 1993, "On the twofold meaning of rationality in economics," *International Studies in the Philosophy of Science*, 7(1), 65–67, http://dx.doi.org/10.1080/02698599308573450.
Moore R. L., Gillette D., 1990, *King, Warrior, Magician, Lover: Rediscovering the Archetypes of the Mature Masculine*, San Francisco, CA: Harper San Francisco.
Mueller A. P., 2001, "Financial cycles, business activity, and the stock market," *The Quarterly Journal of Austrian Economics*, 4(1), 3–21, https://doi.org/10.1007/s12113-001-1000-5.
Mui, V.-L., 1995, "The economics of envy," *Journal of Economic Behavior & Organization*, 26(3), 311–336.
Mullainathan S., Thaler R. H., 2000, "Behavioral economics," *NBER Working Papers*, No. 7948.
Muramatsu R., 2009, "The death and resurrection of economics with psychology: Remarks from a methodological standpoint," *Brazilian Journal of Political Economy* (Center of Political Economy), 29(1), 62–81.
Muth J. F., 1961, "Rational expectations and the theory of price movements," *Econometrica*, 29(3), 315–335.
Natanson M. (ed.), 1962, "Introduction," in: Schuetz A., *Collected Papers: Vol. 1, The Problem of Social Reality*, The Hague: Martinus Nijhoff, xxv–xlvii.
Newman J., 2021, "Sunspots and animal spirits: The origin of Keynes's cycle theory," https://ssrn.com/abstract=3810069, accessed June 29, 2023.
Ng Y. K., 1997, "A case for happiness, cardinalism, and interpersonal comparability," *The Economic Journal*, 107(445), 1848–1858.
Nietzsche F., 1967, *On the Genealogy of Morals*, trans. W. Kaufmann, New York, NY: Random House.
Nisbet R. A., 1962, *Community and Power*, New York, NY: Oxford University Press.
Norris P., Inglehart R., 2004, *Sacred and Secular: Religion and Politics Worldwide*, Cambridge: Cambridge University Press.
Novak J., 2010, "Does more equal really mean all better?" Book Review, *Institute of Public Affairs Review*, 62(3), 54–55, https://ipa.org.au/wp-content/uploads/archive/1282197028_document_novak.pdf, accessed August 27, 2025.
Nozick R., 1974, *Anarchy, State, and Utopia*, Oxford: Basil Blackwell.
Nozick R., 1997, "Why do academics oppose capitalism?" in: Nozick R. (ed.), *Socratic Puzzles*, Cambridge, MA: Harvard University Press.
Nussbaum M. C. 2008, "Who is the happy warrior? Philosophy poses questions to psychology," *Journal of Legal Studies*, 37, S81–S113.
O'Connell M. F., 2010, "Affluence versus Equality? A Critique of Wilkinson and Pickett's Book '*The Spirit Level*'," Working Paper 2010–09, School of Psychology, University College Dublin, Dublin, Ireland.
O'Donoghue T., Rabin M., 2003, "Studying optimal paternalism, illustrated by a model of sin taxes," *American Economic Review*, 93(2), 186–191.

O'Driscoll G. P., Jr., 1977, *Economics as a Coordination Problem: The Contributions of Friedrich A. Hayek*, Kansas City, KS: Sheed Andrews and McMeel.
O'Driscoll G. P. Jr., 2008, "Asset bubbles and their consequences," *Cato Institute Briefing Papers*, 103, 1–10.
O'Driscoll G. P. Jr., Rizzo M. J., 1996, *The Economics of Time and Ignorance*, New York, NY: Routledge.
OECD, 2020, *How's Life? 2020: Measuring Well-being*, OECD Publishing, Paris, https://doi.org/10.1787/9870c393-en, accessed October 31, 2023.
OECD Better Life Index, 2023, Life Satisfaction, https://www.oecdbetterlifeindex.org/topics/life-satisfaction/, accessed October 31, 2023.
Oishi S., Diener E., Lucas R., 2007, "The optimum level of well-being: Can people be too happy?" *Perspectives in Psychological Science*, 2(4), 346–360.
Oishi S., Westgate E. C., 2022, "A psychologically rich life: Beyond happiness and meaning," *Psychological Review*, 129(4), 790–811, http://dx.doi.org/10.1037/rev0000317.
Olmsted K. S., 2009, *Real Enemies: Conspiracy Theories and American Democracy, World War I to 9/11*, Oxford: Oxford University Press.
Oppenheimer F., 1926, *The State*, New York, NY: Vanguard Press.
Ortiz-Ospina E., Roser M., 2013, "Happiness and life satisfaction," Our World In Data, https://ourworldindata.org/happiness-and-life-satisfaction, accessed October 31, 2023.
Oswald A. J., 1997, "Happiness and economic performance," *Economic Journal*, 107, 1815–1831.
Pareto V., 2014 [1906], *Manual of Political Economy: A Critical and Variorum Translation Edition*, reprint edited by Montesano A., Zanni A., Bruni L., Chipman J. S., and McLure M., Oxford: Oxford University Press.
Pargament K. I., 1997, *The Psychology of Religion and Coping*, New York–London: Guilford Press.
Park C. L., 2005, "Religion as a meaning-making framework in coping with life stress," *Journal of Social Issues*, 61(4), 707–729. https://doi.org/10.1111/j.1540-4560.2005.00428.x.
Pennebaker J. W., Stone L. D., 2004, "Translating traumatic experiences into language: Implications for child abuse and long-term health," in Koenig L. J., Doll, L. S., O'Leary A., Pequegnat W. (eds.), From Child Sexual Abuse to Adult Sexual Risk: Trauma, Revictimization, and Intervention, Washington, DC: American Psychological Association, 201–216.
Pérez-Álvarez M., 2018, "Psychology as a science of subject and comportment, beyond the mind and behavior," *Integrative Psychological and Behavioral Science*, March, 52(1), 25–51, https://doi.org/10.1007/s12124-017-9408-4.
Perlmuter L. C., Monty R. A., 1977, "The importance of perceived control: Fact or fantasy? Experiments with both humans and animals indicate that the mere illusion of control significantly improves performance in a variety of situations," *American Scientist*, 65(6), 759–765, http://www.jstor.org/stable/27848177.
Pesendorfer W., 2006, "Behavioral economics comes of age: A review essay on 'Advances in Behavioral Economics'," *Journal of Economic Literature*, 44, 712–721.
Petrea I, Haggenburg M., 2014, "Mental health care," in: Rechel B., Richardson E., McKee M. (eds), *Trends in Health Systems in the Former Soviet Countries*, Copenhagen: European Observatory on Health Systems and Policies, Observatory Studies Series, https://www.ncbi.nlm.nih.gov/books/NBK458299/, accessed February 5, 2026.

Pew Research Center, 2015, "America's changing religious landscape: Christians decline sharply as share of population, unaffiliated and other faiths continue to grow," http://www.pewforum.org/2015/05/12/americas-changing-religious-landscape/, accessed January 3, 2016.
Pigou A., 1926, *Industrial Fluctuations*, London: Macmillan.
Pinker S., 1998, *How the Mind Works*, London: Penguin Books.
Pinker S., 2018, *Enlightenment Now: The Case for Reason, Science, Humanism and Progress*, New York, NY: Viking Press.
Pinker S., 2021, *Rationality: What Is It, Why It Seems Scarce, Why It Matters*, New York, NY: Viking Press.
Plott Ch. R., Zeiler K., 2005, "The willingness to pay-willingness to accept gap, the endowment effect and subject misconceptions," *American Economic Review*, 95, 530–545.
Polanyi K., 1944, *The Great Transformation*, New York, NY: Farrar & Rinehart.
Popper K., 1964, *The Poverty of Historicism*, New York: Harper & Row.
Popper K., 1985, "The rationality principle," in: Miller D. (ed.), *Popper Selections*, Princeton, NJ: Princeton University Press, 357–365.
Prins S. J., Bates L. M., Keyes K. M., Muntaner C., 2015, "Anxious? Depressed? You might be suffering from capitalism: Contradictory class locations and the prevalence of depression and anxiety in the USA," *Sociology of Health and Illness*, 37(8), 1352–1372, https://doi.org/10.1111/1467-9566.12315.
Rabin M., 2002, "A perspective on psychology and economics," *European Economic Review*, 46, 657–685.
Rampell C., 2016, "Millennials have a higher opinion of socialism than of capitalism," *The Washington Post*, February 2, https://www.washingtonpost.com/news/rampage/wp/2016/02/05/millennials-have-a-higher-opinion-of-socialism-than-of-capitalism/, accessed November 11, 2016.
Ravallion M., 2014, "Poor, or just feeling poor? On using subjective data in measuring poverty," in: Clark A. E., Senik C. (eds), *Happiness and Economic Growth: Lessons from Developing Countries*, Oxford: Oxford University Press, 140–174.
Rawls J., 1958, "Justice as fairness," *The Philosophical Review*, 67(2), 164–194.
Rego, S., Arantes, J., Magalhães, P., 2018, "Is there a sunk cost effect in committed relationships?" *Current Psychology*, 37, 508–519, https://doi.org/10.1007/s12144-016-9529-9.
Reiss B., 2017, *Wild Nights: How Taming Sleep Created our Restless World*, New York, NY: Basic Books.
Rich P., 2016, "Axiomatic and ecological rationality: Choosing costs and benefits," *Erasmus Journal for Philosophy and Economics*, 9(2), 90–122.
Ridley M., Rao G., Schilbach F., Patel V., 2020, "Poverty, depression, and anxiety: Causal evidence and mechanisms," *Science*, 370(6522), eaay0214, https://doi.org/10.1126/science.aay0214.
Rizzo M., 1982, "Mises and Lakatos: A reformulation of Austrian methodology," in: Kirzner I. (ed.), *Method, Process, and Austrian Economics: Essays in Honor of Ludwig von Mises*, Lexington, MA and Toronto, ON: Lexington Books, 53–73.
Rizzo M., 2015, "The problem of rationality: Austrian economics between classical behaviorism and behavioral economics," in: Boettke P., Coyne C. (eds), *The Oxford Handbook of Austrian Economics*, Oxford: Oxford University Press, 364–392.
Rizzo M., 2017, "Rationality—What? Misconceptions of neoclassical and behavioral economics," https://ssrn.com/abstract=2927443, May 15, 2023.

Rizzo M., Whitman G., 2020, *Escaping Paternalism: Rationality, Behavioral Economics, and Public Policy*, New York, NY: Cambridge University Press, e-book version, https://doi.org/10.1017/9781139061810.
Robbins L., 1932, *An Essay on The Nature and Significance of Economic Science*, London: Macmillan.
Rosen S., 1986, "The theory of equalizing differences," in: Ashenfelter O. C., Layard R. (eds.), *Handbook of Labor Economics*, Vol. 1, Amsterdam: North Holland, 641–692.
Roser M., Arriagada P., Hasell J., Ritchie H., Ortiz-Ospina E., 2023, "Economic Growth", https://ourworldindata.org/economic-growth, accessed February 5, 2026.
Ross D., 2014, *Philosophy of Economics*, New York, NY: Palgrave Macmillan.
Ross D., 2023, "Economics is converging with sociology but not with psychology," *Journal of Economic Methodology*, https://doi.org/10.1080/1350178X.2022.2049854.
Rothbard M. N., 1956, "Toward a reconstruction of utility and welfare economics," in: Sennholz M. (ed.), *On Freedom and Free Enterprise: Essays in Honor of Ludwig von Mises*, Princeton, NJ: D. Van Nostrand, 224–262.
Rothbard M. N., 1985, "Preface," in: Mises L., *Theory and History: An Interpretation of Social and Economic Evolution*, Washington, D.C.: Ludwig von Mises Institute.
Rothbard M. N., 1998, *The Ethics of Liberty*, New York, NY and London: New York University Press.
Rothbard M. N., 2000, *America's Great Depression*, 5th edn, Auburn, AL: Ludwig von Mises Institute.
Rothbard M. N., 2006, *For a New Liberty: The Libertarian Manifesto*, Auburn, AL: Ludwig von Mises Institute.
Rothbard M. N., 2009, *Man, Economy, and State with Power and Market*, scholar's edn, 2nd edn, Auburn, AL: Ludwig von Mises Institute.
Rothbard M. N., 2011, "Praxeology as the method of the social sciences," in: *Economic Controversies*, Auburn, AL: Ludwig von Mises Institute, 29–58.
Rothbaum F., Weisz J. R., Snyder S. S., 1982, "Changing the world and changing the self: A two-process model of perceived control," *Journal of Personality and Social Psychology*, 42(1), 5–37, https://doi.org/10.1037/0022-3514.42.1.5.
Rötheli T. F., 2021, "The business cycle and the cycles of behavioral economics," https://ssrn.com/abstract=3818967, accessed August 5, 2025.
Røysamb E., Nes R. B., Czajkowski N. O., Vassend O., 2018, "Genetics, personality and wellbeing: A twin study of traits, facets and life satisfaction," *Scientific Reports*, 8, 12298, https://doi.org/10.1038/s41598-018-29881-x.
Rozenblit L., Keil F., 2002, "The misunderstood limits of folk science: An illusion of explanatory depth," *Cognitive Science*, 26: 521–562.
Rubin P. H., 2003, "Folk economics," *Southern Economic Journal*, 70(1), 157–171. https://doi.org/10.2307/1061637.
Ryu S., Fan L., 2023, "The relationship between financial worries and psychological distress among U.S. adults," *Journal of Family and Economic Issues*, 44(1), 16–33, https://doi.org/10.1007/s10834-022-09820-9.
Saint-Paul G., 2011, *The Tyranny of Utility*, Princeton, NJ: Princeton University Press.
Salerno, J. T., 1991, "The concept of coordination in Austrian macroeconomics." *Champions of Freedom: Austrian Economics: Perspectives on the Past and Prospects for the Future*, 325–343.
Salerno J. T., 2012, "A reformulation of Austrian business cycle theory in light of the financial crisis," *The Quarterly Journal of Austrian Economics*, 15(1), 3–44.

Samuelson P., 1938, "A note on the pure theory of consumer's behavior," *Economica*, 5, 61–71.
Samuelson P., 1948, "Consumption theory in terms of revealed preference," *Economica*, 15, 243–253.
Samuelson W., Zeckhauser R., 1988, "Status quo bias in decision making," *Journal of Risk Uncertainty*, 1, 7–59, https://doi.org/10.1007/BF00055564.
Schmidt M. F. H., Sommerville J. A., 2011, "Fairness expectations and altruistic sharing in 15-month-old human infants," *Plos One* 6(10), e23223, https://doi.org/10.1371/journal.pone.0023223.
Schoeck H., 1987, *Envy: A Theory of Social Behaviour*, Indianapolis, IN: Liberty Fund.
Schuetz A., 1943, "The problem of rationality in the social world," *Economica*, New Series, 10(38), 130–149.
Schuetz A., 1967, *The Phenomenology of the Social World*, Evanston, IL: Northwestern University Press.
Schumpeter J. A., 1939, *Business Cycles: A Theoretical, Historical, and Statistical Analysis of the Capitalist Process*, New York, NY: McGraw-Hill.
Schumpeter J. A., 1984, "The meaning of rationality in the social sciences," *Zeitschrift für die gesamte Staatswissenschaft / Journal of Institutional and Theoretical Economics*, 140(4), 577–593.
Schumpeter J. A., 1994, *Capitalism, Socialism, and Democracy*, London and New York, NY: Routledge.
Schumpeter J. A., 2006 [1954], *History of Economic Analysis*, Routledge, Taylor & Francis e-Library.
Scitovsky T., 1976, *The Joyless Economy: An Inquiry into Human Satisfaction and Consumer Dissatisfaction*, Oxford: Oxford University Press.
Seligman M., 2002, *Authentic Happiness: Using the New Positive Psychology to Realize Your Potential for Lasting Fulfillment*, New York, NY: Simon & Schuster.
Sell S. K., Williams O. D., 2019, "Health under capitalism: A global political economy of structural pathogenesis," *Review of International Political Economy*, 27(1), 1–25, https://doi.org/10.1080/09692290.2019.1659842.
Sen A. K., 1985, *Commodities and Capabilities*, Amsterdam: North-Holland.
Shearmur J., 1992, "Subjectivism, explanation and the Austrian tradition," in: Caldwell B. J., Boehm S. (eds), *Austrian Economics: Tensions and New Directions*, Recent Economic Thought Series, vol. 30, Dordrecht: Springer, 103–128, https://doi.org/10.1007/978-94-011-2186-6_4, accessed January 29, 2024.
Shiller R. J., 2015, *Irrational Exuberance*, revised and expanded third edition, Princeton, NJ and Oxford: Princeton University Press.
Shostak F., 1997, "In defense of fundamental analysis: A critique of the efficient market hypothesis," *Review of Austrian Economics*, 10(2), 27–45.
Shostak F., 2022, "Stop trying to turn economics into a branch of psychology," *Mises Wire*, January 20, https://mises.org/wire/stop-trying-turn-economics-branch-psychology, accessed May 15, 2023.
Siedentop L., 2014, *Inventing the Individual: The Origins of Western Liberalism*, Cambridge, MA: Belknap Press.
Sieroń A. 2019, *Money, Inflation and Business Cycles: The Cantillon Effect and the Economy*, Abingdon and New York, NY: Routledge.
Sieroń A., 2020, "Some problems of behavioral economics," *European Research Studies Journal*, XXIII(4), 336–362.
Sieroń A., 2024, "Krytyka psychologicznych teorii cyklu koniunkturalnego," *Optimum: Economic Studies*, 117(3), 38–59.

Simon H. A., 1957, *Models of Man, Social and Rational: Mathematical Essays on Rational Human Behavior in a Social Setting*, New York, NY: Wiley.
Simon H. A., 1978, "Rationality as process and as product of thought," *The American Economic Review*, 68(2), Papers and Proceedings of the Ninetieth Annual Meeting of the American Economic Association, 1–16.
Skidelsky R., 2020, *What's Wrong with Economics: A Primer for the Perplexed*, New Haven, CT and London: Yale University Press.
Slutsky E. E., 1915, "Sulla teoria del bilancio del consumatore," *Giornale Degli Economisti,* 51: 1–26 [translated as "On the theory of the budget of the consumer," in: Stigler G. L., Boulding K. (eds), 1952, *Readings in Price Theory*, Homewood, IL: Richard D. Irwin, 27–56.
Smith A., 1976 [1759], *The Theory of Moral Sentiments*, Oxford: Clarendon Press.
Smith A., 2008 [1776], *An Inquiry into the Nature and Causes of the Wealth of Nations*, Oxford: Oxford University Press.
Smith V. L., 1999, "Reflections on human action after 50 years," *Cato Journal,* 19(2) (Fall), 195–214.
Smith V. L., 2003, "Constructivist and ecological rationality in economics," *American Economic Review*, 93(3), 465–508.
Smith V. L., 2005, "Behavioral economics research and the foundations of economics," *Journal of Socio-Economics*, 32(2), 135–150.
Smith V. L., 2008, *Rationality in Economics: Constructivist and Ecological Forms*, Cambridge, UK: Cambridge University Press.
Snowdon B., Vane H., Wynarczyk P., 1994, "An interview with Roger W. Garrison," in: *A Modern Guide to Macroeconomics: An Introduction to Competing Schools of Thought*, Aldershot: Edward Elgar Publishing, 383–397.
Speakman J. R., 2013, "Evolutionary perspectives on the obesity epidemic: Adaptive, maladaptive, and neutral viewpoints," *Annual Review of Nutrition*, 33, 289–317, https://doi.org/10.1146/annurev-nutr-071811-150711.
Spohn W., 2002, "The many facets of the theory of rationality," *Croatian Journal of Philosophy*, 2(6), 249–264.
Stangor Ch., 2010, *Introduction to Psychology*, Saylor Academy, https://saylordotorg.github.io/text_introduction-to-psychology/index.html, accessed February 5, 2026.
Starmans C., Sheskin M., Bloom P., 2017, "Why people prefer unequal societies," *Nature Human Behaviour*, 1, 0082, https://doi.org/10.1038/s41562-017-0082.
Stevenson B., Wolfers J., 2008, "Economic growth and subjective well-being: Reassessing the Easterlin Paradox," *Brookings Papers on Economic Activity*, Spring, 1–87.
Stewart-Brown S. L., Schrader-Mcmillan A., 2011, "Parenting for mental health: What does the evidence say we need to do? Report of Work package 2 of the DataPrev project," *Health Promotion International*, 26(S1), December, i10–i28, https://doi.org/10.1093/heapro/dar056.
Stigler G. J., 1961, "The economics of information," *The Journal of Political Economy*, 69(3), June, 213–225.
Stigler G. J., Becker G. S., 1977, "De gustibus non est disputandum," *The American Economic Review*, 67(2), 76–90.
Stiglitz J. E., 1988, *Economics of the Public Sector*, New York, NY: W. W. Norton.
Stotland E., Blumenthal A. L., 1964, "The reduction of anxiety as a result of the expectation of making a choice," Canadian Journal of Psychology / Revue canadienne de psychologie, 18(2), 139–145. https://doi.org/10.1037/h0083492.

Strongman L., 2007, "The anthropomorphic bias: How human thinking is prone to be self-referential," Working Papers, No. 4-07, Lower Hutt, New Zealand: The Open Polytechnic of New Zealand.

Sturm T., 2012, "The 'rationality wars' in psychology: Where they are and where they could go," *Inquiry*, 55(1), 66–81.

Sullivan D., Landau M. J., Rothschild Z., 2010, "An existential function of enemyship: Evidence that people attribute influence to personal and political enemies to compensate for threats to control," *Journal of Personality and Social Psychology*, 98, 434–449.

Sunderrajan A., Albarracín D., 2021, "Are actions better than inactions? Positivity, outcome, and intentionality biases in judgments of action and inaction," *Journal of Experimental Social Psychology*, 94(104105), https://doi.org/10.1016/j.jesp.2021.104105.

Sunstein C. R., Rizzo M., 2021, "Is Hayekian behavioral economics an oxymoron?" *Cato Policy Report*, July/August.

Sznycer D., Seal M. F. L., Sell A., Lim J., Porat R., Shalvi S., Halperin E., Cosmides L., Tooby J., 2017, "Support for redistribution is shaped by compassion, envy, and self-interest, but not a taste for fairness," *PNAS Proceedings of the National Academy of Sciences of the United States of America*, 114(31), 8420–8425, https://doi.org/10.1073/pnas.1703801114.

Tajfel H., 1974, "Social identity and intergroup behaviour," *Social Science Information*, 13(2), 65–93, https://doi.org/10.1177/053901847401300204.

Tasic S., 2009, "The illusion of regulatory competence," *Critical Review*, 21(4), 423–436, https://doi.org/0.1080/08913810903441369.

Taubman W., Taubman J., 1989, *Moscow Spring*, New York, NY: Summit Books.

Taussig F., 1911, *Principles of Economics*, London: Macmillan.

Thaler R., 1985, "Mental accounting and consumer choice," *Marketing Science*, 4(3), 199–214.

Thaler R., Sunstein C. R., 2008, *Nudge: Improving Decisions about Health, Wealth, and Happiness*, New Haven, CT: Yale University Press.

Thaler R. H., 2000, "From Homo Economicus to Homo Sapiens," *The Journal of Economic Perspectives*, 14(1), Winter, 133–141.

Thaler R. H., 2015, *Misbehaving: The Making of Behavioral Economics*, New York, NY: W.W. Norton and Company.

Thaler R. H., 2016, "Behavioral economics: Past, present, and future." *American Economic Review*, 106(7), 1577–1600, http://dx.doi.org/10.1257/aer.106.7.1577.

Thams F., Brassen S., 2023, "The need to change: Is there a critical role of midlife adaptation in mental health later in life?" *eLife*, 12, e82390, https://doi.org/10.7554/eLife.82390.

The Conference Board, 2023, "Job Satisfaction 2023," https://www.conference-board.org/research/job-satisfaction, accessed October 31, 2023.

The U.S. Declaration of Independence, 1776, https://www.archives.gov/founding-docs/declaration-transcript, accessed February 21, 2024.

Tolkien J. R. R., 1955, *Lord of the Rings: The Return of the King*, London: George Allen & Unwin.

Truc A., Santerre O., Gingras Y., Claveau F., 2020, "The Interdisciplinarity of Economics," http://dx.doi.org/10.2139/ssrn.3669335, accessed April 11, 2023.

Tversky A., Griffin, D. 2000, "Endowments and contrast in judgments of well-being," in: Kahneman D., Tversky A. (eds), *Choices, Values, and Frames*, Cambridge: Cambridge University Press, 709–725.

Tversky A., Kahneman D., 1973, "Availability: A heuristic for judging frequency and probability," *Cognitive Psychology*, 5(2), 207–232. https://doi.org/10.1016/0010-0285(73)90033-9.

Tversky A., Kahneman D., 1981, "The framing of decisions and the psychology of choice," *Science*, 211(4481), 453–458, https://doi.org/10.1126/science.7455683.

U.S. Bureau of Labor Statistics, 2025, Unemployment Rate [UNRATE], Federal Reserve Bank of St. Louis; https://fred.stlouisfed.org/series/UNRATE, accessed August 27, 2025.

van Praag B., Ferrer-i-Carbonell A., 2004, *Happiness Quantified: A Satisfaction Calculus Approach*, New York, NY: Oxford University Press.

van Prooijen J. W., Douglas K. M., 2018, "Belief in conspiracy theories: Basic principles of an emerging research domain," *European Journal of Social Psychology*, 48(7), 897–908, https://doi.org/10.1002/ejsp.2530.

Vanberg V. J., 2004, "The rationality postulate in economics: Its ambiguity, its deficiency and its evolutionary alternative," *Journal of Economic Methodology*, 11(1), 1–29, https://doi.org/10.1080/1350178042000177987.

Veblen T., 1898, "Why is economics not an evolutionary science?" *The Quarterly Journal of Economics*, 12(4), 373–397.

Veblen T., 1918, *The Theory of the Leisure Class: An Economic Study of Institutions*, New York, NY: B. W. Huebsch.

Veenhoven R., Hagerty M., 2006, "Rising happiness in nations 1946–2004: A reply to Easterlin," *Social Indicators Research*, 79(3), 421–436.

Von Neumann J., Morgenstern O., 1944, *Theory of Games and Economic Behavior*, Princeton, NJ: Princeton University Press.

Walsh V., 1996, *Rationality, Allocation and Reproduction*, Oxford: Clarendon Press.

Ward L. F., 1893, "The psychologic basis of social economics," *Annals of the American Academy of Political and Social Science*, 3, 72–90.

Washington Post, Kaiser Family Foundation, Harvard University Economics Polls. (1996). *Survey of Americans and Economists on the Economy*. Stores, CT: Roper Center for Public Opinion Research.

Weber M., 1978, *Economy and Society: An Outline of Interpretive Sociology*, Guenther R., Wittich C. (eds.), Berkeley and Los Angeles, CA: University of California Press.

Weber M., 2012 [1908], "The theory of marginal utility and the 'fundamental law of psychophysics'," in: Bruun H. H. and Whimster S. (eds), *Max Weber: Collected Methodological Writings*, London: Routledge, 242–251.

Weisz J. R., Rothbaum F. M., Blackburn T. C., 1984, "Standing out and standing in: The psychology of control in America and Japan," *American Psychologist*, 39(9), 955–969, https://doi.org/10.1037/0003-066X.39.9.955.

White E. N., 2009, "Lessons from the Great American Real Estate Boom and Bust of the 1920s," NBER Working Paper Series, 15573.

White M. D., 2013, *The Manipulation of Choice: Ethics and Libertarian Paternalism*, New York, NY: Palgrave Macmillan.

White M. D., 2014, *The Illusion of Well-Being: Economic Policymaking Based on Respect and Responsiveness*, New York, NY: Palgrave Macmillan.

White M. D., 2015, "The problems with measuring and using happiness for policy purposes," Mercatus Research, *Mercatus Center at George Mason University*, Arlington, VA, July.

Whitson J. A., Galinsky A. D., 2008, "Lacking control increases illusory pattern perception," *Science*, 322(5898), 115–117, https://doi.org/10.1126/science.1159845.

WHO, 2023, "Stress," February 21, https://www.who.int/news-room/questions-and-answers/item/stress, accessed September 13, 2023.

Wicksteed P. H., 1914, "The scope and method of political economy in the light of the 'marginal' theory of value and of distribution," *The Economic Journal*, 24(93), 1–23.

Wierzbicka A., 2004, "'Happiness' in cross-linguistic and cross-cultural perspective," *Daedalus*, 133(2), 34–43.

Wilkinson R. D., Pickett K., 2009, *The Spirit Level: Why More Equal Societies Almost Always Do Better*, London: Allen Lane/Penguin Group UK; Bloomsbury Publishing.

Wilkinson W., 2007, "In pursuit of happiness research," *Policy Analysis*, No. 590, April 11, Washington, DC: Cato Institute.

Wiśniewski J. B., 2019, "Wpływ teorii makroekonomicznych na etyczną jakość praktyki finansowej," *Annales. Etyka W Życiu Gospodarczym*, 22(4), 7–20, https://doi.org/10.18778/1899-2226.22.4.01, accessed June 23, 2023.

World Bank Poverty and Inequality Platform, with major processing by Our World in Data, 2025, "Median income or consumption per day – World Bank," https://archive.ourworldindata.org/20250808-181753/grapher/daily-median-income.html, accessed September 20, 2025.

Zak P. J., Knack S., 2001, "Trust and growth," *The Economic Journal*, 470(111), April, 295–321.

Zeelenberg M., van den Bos K., van Dijk E., Pieters R., 2002, "The inaction effect in the psychology of regret," *Journal of Personality and Social Psychology*, 82, 314–327.

Zeira A., 2022, "Mental health challenges related to neoliberal capitalism in the United States," *Community Mental Health Journal*, 58(2), 205–212, https://doi.org/10.1007/s10597-021-00840-7.

Zou X., 2018, "Can the greater fool theory explain bubbles? Evidence from China," Working Paper, no. 2018-04, Rutgers University, Department of Economics, New Brunswick, NJ.

Zouboulakis M., 2014, *The Varieties of Economic Rationality*, London: Routledge.

Zuckerman M., Li C., Diener E., 2018, "Religion as an exchange system: The interchangeability of god and government in a provider role," *Personality and Social Psychology Bulletin*, 44(8), 1201–1213, https://doi.org/10.1177/0146167218764656.

# Index

Printed and bound by CPI Group (UK) Ltd, Croydon, CR0 4YY
17/06/2026
14902652-0005